D0316381

From the Library of
(Ms) C. L. PLUMMER

A CENTURY OF SOUTH AFRICAN POETRY

Introduced and
Edited by Michael Chapman

AD. DONKER/PUBLISHER

AD. DONKER (PTY) LTD
Hyde Park Corner
Jan Smuts Avenue
Hyde Park
2196 Johannesburg

AD. DONKER LTD
1 Prince of Wales Passage
117 Hampstead Road
London NW1 3EE

First published 1981

ISBN 0 949937 85 1 (hardback)
ISBN 0 949937 86 X (paperback)

Typesetting by Jean Mc Callum
Printed and bound by National Book Printers, Goodwood, Cape

Contents

Introduction

i

A Century of South African Poetry contains close on 300 poems by 137 South African English poets and the criteria for selection have been primarily 'literary' rather than 'sociological'. It seems necessary to emphasise this at the start as there is a school of thought which believes that literature written in politically turbulent situations is of value simply for what it says, not for how it is said. While I have not ignored the often far-from-reductive relationship between poetry and historical pressures, I have chosen poems in the first instance for their imaginative qualities: their linguistic inventiveness, their forceful expressiveness.

I have for instance excluded pages of bombast by nineteenth-century settler rhymesters on the subject of the so-called Kaffir Wars – the longest poem being 'The Kaffir War – A Satire' (1846) – over twenty pages of tedious couplets – which, while of undoubted interest to the cultural historian, is of strictly limited interest to the literary critic, or to the reader of poetry today. Similarly, by including a more comprehensive range of contemporary South African political poetry than has hitherto appeared in anthologies, my main consideration has continued to be poetic, rather than political, strategies. Of course, the two are not really separable, but their most fundamental connection will be found in matters of structure, image-making, myth-making and sentence-shaping – matters intrinsically literary.

This anthology takes into account 150 years of South African English poetry, from Thomas Pringle in the 1820s to the Soweto poets of the 1970s. The first fifty years of settler poetry is covered briefly yet representatively. The emphasis, however, falls after 1870 when, under the impetus of the mining revolution, a consequent urbanisation, and a renewed British Imperial interest in things

'African', South African imaginative literature began to find a wider readership and greater publishing opportunities. Furthermore, it began to find a voice concerned not only with the African exoticism and vindications of Empire expected both by a late nineteenth-century overseas public and by 'British' South Africans, but also with dilemmas recognisably modern.

A modern voice – for which matters both of 'local colour' and exile from the British cultural continuum have ceased to be issues – has firmly established itself since the 'wind of change' and Sharpeville (1960), and half the anthology is devoted to poetry of the last twenty years. These years have seen the appearance of local publishers willing to concentrate on South African English literature and on the expectations not of London or New York, but of Johannesburg and Soweto. There are very real signs at present of a South African literature, and particularly poetry, boom. It is the aim of *A Century of South African Poetry* to convey this contemporary poetic vitality and to see today's poets in relation to the most memorable poetry of the past.

Presumably this is the task of any anthology which at all seeks to be representative. Yet, despite the valuable contribution of previous anthologists – notably Stapleton, Wilmot, Crouch, Slater, Macnab, Butler, Cope and most recently Butler and Mann – South African poetry is still regarded by many as boring, academic in the worst sense of the term ('an educated man's affair . . . We have no popular songs' – Butler), the preserve of stuffy nineteenth-century school-masters and clerics and their counterparts today, and most recently of hectoring political polemicists. Roy Campbell is usually regarded as something apart, either favourably as a tornado sweeping over a genteel colonial tea party or negatively as a bullying and overgrown schoolboy, while the rest of the terrain is popularly thought to be barren – the leading poet since Campbell, Douglas Livingstone, is still too often confused with his namesake, David!

Ironically, the 'educated man's affair' presented by most previous anthologies has, until recently, also been dismissed out of hand by the majority of South African educational institutions – as 'verse' and therefore not worthy of academic consideration. (The quaint Oxford Dictionary distinction between 'verse' and 'poetry – as elevated expression' is evidently still tremendously important in the 'colonies'!) Whatever their individual merits, earlier South African anthologies would seem to have failed to stimulate the interest either of that mythical 'general reader' or of the literati.

Yet South African English poetry does make fascinating reading; and, no doubt partly because of the more personalised nature of poetic utterance, has displayed a considerably greater stylistic versatility than the fiction, which is too often constricted by the demands of social realism. The poetry, on the other hand, has successfully adopted both public and private voices, the familiar and the surreal, the traditional and the avant-garde. It has at different times absorbed the spirit of English Romanticism and the Victorian music-hall, the Great Tradition and modernist experimentation, Afro-American militancy and post-1945 European anti-poetry. It has unselfconsciously assumed an international recognisability while its peculiar strength continues to be drawn from its own backyard – from the veld, white suburbia and the black township streets.

Unfortunately, the full extent of this healthy diversity is not markedly apparent in existing anthologies. Stapleton in *Poetry of the Cape of Good Hope* (1828) made promising forays into 'popular' periodical poetry (or should I say verse?) and was subsequently condemned for having printed doggerel. And by the time of Wilmot's *The Poetry of South Africa* (1887) a perceptible trend began to emerge. Wilmot concentrated on work dealing patriotically with the landing of the 1820 Settlers as well as with other stirring episodes in South African history. Poetry was narrowly assumed to be a publicly responsible act with its language and tones taken from the prevailing British Culture. And Slater in *The Centenary Book of South African Verse* (1925), although he found little of value in Wilmot, continued – paradoxically in a most colourfully expressed Introduction – to promote a literary traditionalism as the 'right' style for South Africa:

> The new form – or formlessness – of much modern poetry is scarcely a sign of healthy development and strength. It betokens, rather, a weakness and a lack of true originality. It is as though a man, in order to appear peculiar, walked upon his hands instead of his feet. This eccentric mode of progression might possibly enable him to make a minute study of the pavements and pillar-boxes, but it eliminates the mountains and the stars.

As late as his *New Centenary Book of South African Verse* (1945) Slater was still favouring the 'mountains and the stars': elevated utterance, a Victorian romanticism – this despite the impressively unremitting realism of his own major poem, 'Drought'.

It was the 'educated' public voice, too, which set the tone of Butler's important *A Book of South African Verse* (1959). In his Introduction he summed up the character of South African English poetry thus:

> South African poetry is, then, an educated man's affair. I cannot detect a peculiar style, or verse form, or intonation. At most one might remark on the frequency of an attribute which Professor G.H. Durrant finds in the work of David Wright (*Standpunte* XI,3): a simple openness which could not be learned in England. Many of the best recent poems have a confessional quality about them.

And:

> Social pressures in South Africa are such that we are forced to examine big words like Liberty, Love, Justice, Truth and Civilisation (particularly when coupled with the epithet White). What was a platitude a generation ago, and may still be in England, suddenly becomes startling and immediate here, where it can no longer be taken for granted.
> ...
> Our awareness of what we are up to, that we are reading things into the world, makes us self-conscious and cautious in our imagery.

What Butler described here, and what his 1959 anthology following Slater virtually enshrined as *the* South African English tradition, is a line of liberal humanist poetic activity. This begins with Pringle, is taken up significantly by the poet Slater (albeit at times uncomfortably) and culminates, in the 1940s and fifties, in those poets of World War II and its immediate aftermath: Butler himself, Currey, Delius, Eglington, Wright – all of whom were first given prominence by the 1959 anthology.

This is a poetry which, in keeping with those conciliatory ideals traditionally associated with English intellectual life, broadly characterises a humane and reasonable speaking voice which dominates over image-making. The tones are 'familiar', community-inspired; and, while there is a willingness to criticise social authority (for example, Pringle's sustained campaign against repressive colonial rule), the poetry's syntax, which is usually logically arranged, implies an underlying confidence in given moral and literary values.

It is a poetry which can yield its own music once the ear is attuned: the deeply felt religious conviction of Cripps's 'The Black Christ's Crusade', for instance; or the peculiar tension between the stark facts of war and a calmly reporting voice such as we find in the war poetry of Clothier, Butler, Currey and Eglington; or Paton's compassion reinforcing by contrast the hurt of racial injustices; or Butler's almost imperceptible shifts from the discursive to the illustrative in order to examine a central concern of the post-Second World War years – the dilemma of the English-speaking South African, indebted to a Western European heritage, yet seeking for himself a home in South Africa.

In short, the liberal humanist voice is richer and more varied than Butler's own remarks ('I cannot detect a peculiar style, or verse form, or intonation') might seem to imply. Goodwin writing in the 1950s, for example, is capable of making serious business of outrageous word-play ('Glorious?'), Sowden powerfully incorporates biblical material into a modern context ('Hosea'), while Brettell's 'Giraffes' inhabit a fabulous world. Moreover, the colloquial rhythms of Butler's 'Tourist Insight into Things', as well as the psychologically-orientated images and startling juxtapositions both of Macnab's 'Hippopotamus' and Swart's 'Walk on to Headland Height', anticipate the radically altered sensibility of style which, under the impetus of new socio-literary pressures, will most fully reveal itself during the 1960s – from a 'familiar' to a more 'extreme' poetry.

In addition – and this is ignored by Butler's 1959 Introduction – this period 1940-1960 significantly shows black poets (notably Peter Abrahams and H.I.E. Dhlomo) trying to establish an authentic black voice of protest. Their literary struggle in many ways parallels Pringle's earlier attempts to forge an idiom with an indigenous 'feel' – Pringle, of course, in the 1820s having initiated a South African tradition of protest poetry. Just as Pringle had to try to free himself – and never quite succeeded – from received English literary conventions (conventions better suited to a 'soft' Nature than to a harsh, alien African environment), so both Abrahams and Dhlomo, over a hundred years later, had to try to break away from an established mission-school idiom: one derived variously from the Bible and from a diet of English literary studies – particularly the Romantic poets – and one aimed to equip a relatively elite black professional class. (This mission-school idiom, incidentally, is impressively utilised in 'Santa Cruz: The Holy Cross', written in 1898 by A.K. Soga, who has been aptly described by Tim Couzens, in his doctoral study *The New African,* as the 'first really serious black South African poet writing in English.)

Both Pringle and Dhlomo, by reason of the visionary insights they display, remain centrally important figures in South African literature. Pringle, forseeing a future pattern of racial conflict, was prepared in the name of freedom and justice to challenge both the Cape government and the community at large. 'Makanna's Gathering' goes to the lengths of praising in rousing battle rhythms that great nineteenth-century warrior prophet of the AmaXhosa, a sworn enemy of the British colonial regime and probably South Africa's first political prisoner on Robben Island (the 'Isle of Makana'); while 'The Forester of the Neutral Ground' sympathetically treats a seminal South African theme: the tragedy of miscegenation. Pringle's diction, however, rarely does full credit to his subject-matter and there are curious, though understandable, lapses from an appropriately austere idiom to Augustan periphrases, from a harsh realism to idealised sketches of noble savages, from a restrained human sympathy to an evangelical fervour.

In Dhlomo's 'Valley of a Thousand Hills' (1941), too, an outmoded English idiom at times undermines the prophetic nature of a work which antipicates by almost forty years the black nationalist ideals and epic forms of such Soweto poems as Madingoane's 'black trial' (1979). Nevertheless, despite its sometimes Shelleyan 'tang', Dhlomo's poetry does pointedly alert the reader to those underlying South African political tensions of the 1940s and fifties: tensions which seldom feature in the work of white poets of the time, of rising black nationalist expectations and liberalism's inability to accommodate them. Dhlomo's embittered 'Not for Me', for example, presents an unusually perceptive view of South African involvement in World War II: the failure at home to implement those ideals of fairness and human dignity about which the war had been fought.

Such political frictions are also reflected in an increasing number of poems (for instance, ' "Civilised" Labour Policy' and 'Shantytown') written during the thirties and forties by anonymous blacks in newspapers such as *Ilanga Lase Natal* – one of the few outlets for black protest writing at the time. Also, Peter Abrahams (better known as a novelist) attempted to confront social dilemmas by turning away from British literary models to Afro-American poets such as Langton Hughes. It is here, in Dhlomo's use of a traditional African past in order to survey the present, and in Abrahams's bare Americanised utterance, that the origins of the Soweto style of the 1970s may be sought.

Apart from Abrahams however, these early black poets (as I have said) did not fully succeed in severing themselves from, or tellingly transforming, their standard literary schooling. And, as in the case of their white contemporaries, their work – in spite of its African subject-matter – still manages to insist overwhelmingly on the 'familiar'. The liberal humanist line has its own internal divisions; yet, whether Pringle is attacking Somerset's frontier policies, whether Dhlomo is urging black workers to fight for right (usually meant metaphorically in Dhlomo's case), or whether Butler is attempting to 'strike root' in South African soil, the vocabulary, the rhythms, the tones, derive fairly obviously from the Great Tradition.

ii

Literary traditionalism, then, has from the beginnings notably informed South African English poetic activity and continues to do so today, significantly in the work of a Patrick Cullinan or promisingly in a Chris Mann, where the level-headed suburban voice is often ironically undercut by an absurd context. Nevertheless, and in spite of what most anthologies might imply, humanism, 'familiar' art, is not *the* South African English tradition – but only one important aspect of it. There is another broad stylistic line of development which must be noted: one which has been treated somewhat gingerly not only by earlier anthologies, but also by the recent Butler/Mann *A New Book of South African Verse in English* (1979). This is: an exciting literary radicalism (not necessarily the same as a political radicalism) which since the 1820s has appeared, sometimes furtively, at other times boldly, alongside an 'official' South African English liberal humanism.

Besides allowing for a greater diversity within the 'traditional', *A Century of South African Poetry* aims to give greater prominence to the 'radical', to the experimental, the demythicising stance; to that poetry in which image dominates over statement, the cryptic over mellifluous syntax – to a poetry which often daringly signals its emancipation from received conventions. Despite what Guy Butler had to say as recently as 1969 (in his opening address at the Conference of the English Academy, Grahamstown),

> It is possible that for what we have to say at this stage of our development we need old-fashioned techniques which are no longer helpful in Europe.

the South African reality has always been too complex and varied to be wholly accommodated by conventional modes. Even the first fifty years of settler poetry (1820-1870) cannot be fully appreciated without placing alongside the 'educated' voice of a Pringle or a Dugmore its popular equivalent: the vernacular of the Cape periodicals (Brooks's 'The Emigrant Shoemakers', which amusingly treats a central issue of these years – the discrepancy between expectation and the reality of life in the colonies); or Bain's patois ('Kaatje Kekkelbek') as well as his 'urban' poetry appealing wittily to a relatively sophisticated town society that was willing to be entertained ('To Choose a Wife by Lighting a Candle'). The 1979 Butler/Mann anthology certainly does note some interesting experiments with patois and also some popular songs; but, as in other anthologies, Andrew Geddes Bain is under-represented while Brooks continues to be ignored – this early South African satirist no doubt being considered a writer of mere doggerel. Yet if Pringle gave initial impetus to a line of liberal humanist literary activity, it was Brooks and Bain who initiated not an 'alternative tradition', but a stimulating option to the 'educated man's affair' that has for too long been regarded as the mainstream of South African English poetry.

More than any other poet, however, it is Albert Brodrick (another figure under-represented in anthologies) who, in the 1870s, indicated the beginnings of a marked shift of sensibility in South African poetry: from a nineteenth-century world of given moral assumptions to a twentieth-century 'man-made' world governed by chicanery, wit and the unpredictability of the share market. Both his *Fifty Fugitive Fancies in Verse* (1875) – the first book of English poetry to be published north of the Vaal – and his *Wanderer's Rhymes* (1893) record the many voices of Brodrick, the merchant known at the time as the 'poet laureate of the Transvaal' – from the vivid Victorian epic 'Rorke's Drift' (the Zulu Wars were also to inspire Moodie and Selwyn) to the ironic and colloquial observations of 'Wanted a President'; from the inventive use of English-Dutch dialect in the ballad 'Jong Koekemoer' to 'The Wheel of Fortune', in which the new imagery of the diamond and gold fields serves as metaphors of life and fate. Incidentally, it is worth noting that the schism which we encounter in Brodrick between poetry as public responsibility and the demands of the individual voice is evident too in another late nineteenth-century poet, William Selwyn. If his moving 'Hymn Written during the Zulu War' has often been anthologised, his parodies have not. 'The Loss of the Six Hundred' focuses in an unusually amusing way on a new South African 'tragedy': ruination on the Rand stock exchange!

These early industrial pressures were to come to a head during the 1920s and thirties in Francis Carey Slater's poetry dealing with the impact of the mining fever on the pastoral character of South African life, and also in the work of William Plomer, who ironically employs jaunty ballad rhythms in order to convey the brashness of a Rand industrial townscape. In fact, Plomer's processes of demythicism and his use of the African locale as a metaphor of metaphysical nightmare capture an authentic note of modernity; and his poetry anticipates in important ways Douglas Livingstone's tough nature poetry and the psychologically haunting world of Ruth Miller in the 1960s.

Albert Brodrick, then, stands at the beginning of a stimulating, though neglected, period of South African English poetry: 1870-1940. First, these years saw the brief appearance of diggers' songs which, if not particularly penetrating in their social analyses, did interestingly introduce their own mythology – the beautiful and heartless Dame Fortune, a life of opportunism, of the sudden joy of discovery and the utter despair of lives wasted in search of a South African 'holy grail'.

By contrast a strong sense of realism generally informs Boer War poetry (1899-1902), often written by soldiers themselves, as for example Signaller Wore's 'A Tale of the Worcestershire Regiment South Africa, 1900': a poem which accurately describes Boer guerilla tactics. Moreover, poems exploiting 'gor blimey' diction provided a common language for the ordinary soldier, while such rhetorically eloquent assumptions of Empire as Kipling's 'Recessional' often received short shrift in parodies like F.W. Reitz's 'Gods of the Jingo'. As Malvern van Wyk Smith says in *Drummer Hodge – The Poetry of the Anglo-Boer War* (1978): 'The Boer War came to establish firmly what may be called the working class view of war.' Notwithstanding, the war also inspired such formally accomplished poems as Maquarie's starkly compressed 'Sniped', as well as Kipling's 'Bridge-guard in the Karroo' which transcends mere sentiments of Empire (the civilising British hand) to present the lone sentry as a symbol of the ordinary man's capacity for imposing some kind of order on a vast and hostile world.

A great deal of South African English poetry of the late nineteenth and early twentieth centuries has tended to be scornfully dismissed as 'veld and vlei' verse: that is, hymns to the 'mystery' of the wide outdoors. Certainly much sentimental drivel does exist and reading through many of the collections of the time can be a decidedly unrewarding experience. Nevertheless, the best of these 'veld and vlei' poems do have a precision of language and a resonant use of natural imagery, while they at least attempt to provide an unsentimental view of a recurrent nineteenth-century colonial nostalgia for the almost ethical superiority of mists and English dells (for example: Ould's 'London, August' and 'Red'; Runcie's 'The Bells of Allah'; or Walrond's 'Cosmos').

Walrond, Ould and, among others, Lefebvre and Mabel Alder were in 1908 – for about seven years – members of a Johannesburg poetry circle, *The Veldsingers Club*. The club has been condemned by Miller and Sergeant, in their rather solemn *A Critical Survey of South African Poetry in English* (1957) for having 'no direction' and for avoiding the peculiar circumstances of the South African situation. This is largely true; yet Miller and Sergeant, while they mention the fact, do not pursue what is particularly interesting about some of the Veldsinger poetry: its evident debt to the imagism of the times. This is something which may be seen not only in Walrond's 'Eve' with its psychologically modern use of the temptress motif, or in Mabel Alder's 'The Street of Peacocks', effective in its negative capability with a mysterious symbolism reaching beyond fact and reason, or in Lefebvre's prePrufrockian 'A Reminiscence', but also in other poems of these years not directly inspired by Veldsinger meetings. There is Runcie's imagist-inspired 'Three Phases' with its disturbing use of Christian symbolism, Kolbe's 'The Sparrows of Little Jesus' where a conventional piety is given added freshness by an unusual use of the childhood motif, or Sampson's 'Murder in the Hut' whose dramatic juxtapositions lend a macabre intensity to an experience common to the nineteenth-century colonial mind – the vicarious transference of adulterous temptations to torridly imagined African tribal contexts.

A more traditional use of African tribal situations is, at the turn of the century, to be found in the poetry of the first Rhodesians, Cripps, Gouldsbury and Fairbridge (who was born in South Africa), as well as in the work of the South Africans Scully and Gibbon. Fairbridge in particular, in the mythic quality of 'Magwere who Waits Wondering' and in the unadorned diction of 'Burial', anticipates both Slater's powerfully evoked Xhosa world as well as his original use (in South African English poetry) of those traditional African oral conventions of repetition, parallelism and ideophones. This brings me back to my earlier point: that the period 1870-1940 does have certain larger coherences, with many of its prior thematic and stylistic preoccupations being treated later and with far greater authority by Slater and Plomer – and also by Roy Campbell.

Campbell with considerable flair shows the possibilities, glimpsed by earlier South African poets, of utilising the advantages both of a sophisticated European imagism (late nineteenth-century French modernists particularly impressed him) and the vitality and bright colours of indigenous settings. In 'The Zulu Girl', for example, the European allusions – to Rimbaud's 'Les Chercheuses de poux' ['Women Hunting Lice'] and also obliquely to 'Mary and Child' – lend an added richness to the African scene: depicted as a manifestation of those heroic and explosive energies – the life force – that Campbell found so compelling.

It is almost a commonplace that 'Campbell and Plomer started a totally new direction in South African English poetry – their fierce criticism and rejection of established values set them on a course from which there was no turning back'. Thus Jack Cope in the Introduction to the *Penguin Book of South African Verse* (1968) which begins with Campbell. But, as I have already suggested, such a statement considerably oversimplifies matters. For if Plomer anticipates post-1960 modernity, he finds inspiration in the Imperial designs of the late nineteenth century. And if Campbell is more assured in his use of language, more technically proficient than earlier South African poets, his affinities are not simply with an avant-garde European symbolism, but in no small measure with nineteenth-century colonial hunter romances.

If Campbell could appreciate the exciting image-making capacities of the French modernists and even sense the truly revolutionary nature of Eliot's 'The Waste Land' (he reviewed the work favourably in *Voorslag* at the same time, in the mid-1920s, as Slater was complaining of the 'formlessness' of modern poetry) he did not absorb the full intellectual or literary significance of modernism, with its notions of alienation, relative and cubist world-views. Campbell's world is not one of angst, of desperate fictive re-creations of fractured systems; therefore, unlike modernists, he does not feel the necessity of inventing new structures – dislocated, fragmented – in order more forcefully to convey a modern sense of rupture from a line of philosophical and literary traditionalism. Although he aimed satiric swipes at Natal colonial philistinism and its refusal to recognise his poetic 'genius', Campbell's is not a fundamental radicalism. Behind his rebellious stances is a strongly conservative cast of mind, revealing itself in an ultimate confidence in traditional verse forms, in hierarchical religious and social orders, and in those uncomplicated colonial 'virtues' of manliness, robustness, healthy outdoor endeavour.

It is in fact Campbell's romantic conception of heroic individualism – particularly his South African new world heroes and the hunter's paradise – that Douglas Livingstone was to react against in his *Sjambok* poems of 1964. In Livingstone's poetry Campbell's solar colours – the 'scarlet flowers' and 'golden rays' – have faded to tawny yellows and greens (closer in character to Plomer's disenchanted landscapes). Moreover, the exceptional white-hunter-type of Campbell's 'To a Pet Cobra' has, in Livingstone, been transformed into an Adam-after-the-Fall: boorish, colloquial; a colonial out of his element after the 'wind of change'. The archetypal white hunter of Livingstone's title poem 'Sjambok', for example, has ironically been reduced to playing the role of a tourist-guide, vicariously reliving in his anecdotes the savage lore of a frontier society.

Of course, the fact that Livingstone should find relevant archetypes to react against in Campbell's poetry testifies to the vigour and mythic quality of the earlier poet's imagination. If Campbell looks back to a world that has not yet experienced the fragmentation of the Renaissance ideal (the change of metaphor is apt as other formative influences on his work were the Portuguese Renaissance poet Camoens, and the Elizabethan dramatists), he in many ways looks ahead, not to the liberal humanist forms of South African English poetry in the 1940s and fifties, but to the post-1960 work of Livingstone, Ruth Miller, Clouts and Nortje: to a poetry daring in its use of imagery, extreme rather than moderate, dramatic rather than discursive.

Actually Campbell, by the time of his last collection, *Talking Bronco* (1947), seems to have decided that a more flexible diction might be better suited to the mood of the times, and in the Preface to the 1950 Cape Town edition of *Adamastor* (first published in 1930) he says:

> In *Adamastor* [where, among others, appeared 'The Zebras', 'The Serf', 'The Zulu Girl', 'To a Pet Cobra', 'The Sisters', 'Rounding the Cape'] the language is still somewhat formal and 'poetic' . . . but, I think the process can be detected in some of the poems that was to lead [in *Talking Bronco*] to the blending of the everyday vernacular with classical verse forms.

In 'Dreaming Spires' – from the *Talking Bronco* collection – Campbell presents not the heroic individual of the earlier To-a-Pet-Cobra-years, but a very different 'hunter' who bounds across the bush after giraffes on a motor cycle – a 'hunter' closer in style and sensibility to the anti-heroic archetypes of Livingstone's 'Sjambok' and Clouts's 'For the Thunder'.

iii

The distinct emergence in the 1960s of a literature sharply distinguished by a sense of new alternatives is of course not unconnected with an altered apprehension of reality during these years, both in southern Africa and abroad. The 1960s saw a general disillusionment with post-War humanist ideals (resulting, particularly in the United States, in a re-emergence of artistic experimentation); while in southern Africa the failure of the ideals of gradualism (Anthony

Delius's extract *The Lament of the Liberals* is something of a swan-song), the apocalypse of Sharpeville, the post-colonial mood of Africa, South Africa's break from the Commonwealth, the creation of a new martyr in Nelson Mandela, are all symbolic of the fact that – at least, as far as the white English-speaking South African was concerned – the 1960s marked the end of an era: an era which had generally been characterised, on the part of South African English writers of the previous decade, by more or less confident assumptions about the civilising role of English culture.

Just as radical cultural shifts in Europe and the United States at the turn of the century gave impetus to apocalyptic visions, so the southern African climate of the last twenty years has increasingly favoured an 'imagination of disaster'. If we are looking for a real event symbolically marking the beginning of a phase of South African literary activity peculiarly modern, there is Sharpeville. If we are looking for a symbolic book of poems, there is Livingstone's *Sjambok, and other poems from Africa* (1964). Written in Zambia at a time of social transition, this collection captures, in its very texture, the tensions of disruption and difficult re-adjustment. Like Soweto poetry of the 1970s, the *Sjambok* collection has a fundamental modernity which asserts itself as a deeply felt awareness of beginnings and endings.

Whereas the liberal humanist mind tends to see art as the refined expression of established truth, Livingstone sees art as a desperate game: a means, in a seemingly indeterminate world, of generating new possibilities from *within* poetic language itself. In 'Stormshelter' modern man, stripped of the comfort of his 'Old saws and their ancient rhythms', bleakly concludes that life is a matter of bare survival: 'There is only one thing to do – /wheel, stamping, into that brittle rain.' Yet paradoxically the poetic artefact itself is not bleak. Even as we read of an inability to create, we participate in an act of imaginative enlargement. The meticulous craftsmanship, the vibrancy, the metaphorical richness, while they do not deny the toughness of a twentieth-century 'scientific' world, testify deviously to the value of the 'poetic' view of experience. As far as Livingstone is concerned here, the conventions favoured by a previous generation of South African English poets are suddenly felt to be inadequate. He seems to say that in an apparently fractured world things are kept *apart* by rational discourse, yet may be synthesised, with difficulty, in a fictive universe of metaphor, symbol and mythic re-imaginings.

Such modernist strategies, in which a sense of reality is seen to reside largely in artificial contracts of language, also inform the poetry of Ruth Miller, Sydney Clouts and Arthur Nortje, all writing at the same time as Livingstone. No doubt the modernist poetic revolution initiated in English by Pound and Eliot has to a certain extent influenced these poets; however, modernism's experimental use of mask, of objective correlative, of metalanguage, does not make its impact on their work superficially as an aesthetic theory, but as a necessary artistic means of coping with their own disturbing perceptions of psychological and cultural crisis.

In Ruth Miller's 'Spider', for instance, poetry is made out of the difficulty of making poetry, with the metapoem operating as a salving force in a world of chance and uncertainty (the poet herself was at the time suffering from terminal cancer). Similarly, Nortje in 'Waiting' translates his inner torment into a struggle with language. Alienated from country and self, he talks lucidly, desperately seeking order and control, even as his imagination conjures up hallucinatory townscapes: labyrinths of metaphysical exile. And Clouts, deliberately confusing image and metaphor, also uses language itself as a means of coming to terms with a world in which 'humanism', 'depth', 'significance', looking 'within', has, he believes, led to tragedy. Following on the 'new realism' of Robbe-Grillet and post-1945 European poets such as Zbigniew Herbert, Clouts – discovering the 'tyranny' of analogy and metaphor – learns to look to the 'pebble outside': a true mystery simply because it is a pebble.

It is obvious that, confronted by a modernist element of game playing, traditional humanist aesthetic criteria will often be found to be inadequate means of approaching a Livingstone or a Clouts. Or for that matter a Wopko Jensma, who strips away familiar literary allusion leaving bare utterance, itself paradoxically regenerative in a 'post-cultural' world. Peter Horn, too, frequently upsets traditional humanist expectations. His poetry deliberately denies the validity of imaginative richness and insists instead on a Brechtian use of plain language as the only effective means of confronting social injustices. Metaphor and mask are felt to be bourgeois-inspired evasions of the true economic and political realities of South Africa.

Apart from Horn, the above-mentioned poets are all represented in the 1979 Butler/Mann anthology – but mostly by 'safe' examples. As Ian Glenn has said:

> There is, whether admitted or not, an editorial bias against certain themes or styles . . . a dislike of modernism and post-modernism; a distrust of the political and the public [this however applies more in the case of the contemporary than the nineteenth century] ; a suspicion of political statement or ideology; a preference for reasonable moderation (whatever or wherever that may be); a dislike of the bloody, the ugly, the vulgar, the sordid, the apocalyptic, the frightening.
>
> [Review, *English in Africa*, 6(2) September, 1979]

It is perhaps partly as a result of this apparent bias against literary radicalism that Livingstone's much-anthologised 'Gentling a Wildcat', for instance, does not in Butler/Mann find its natural and important corollary in either 'The Zoo Affair' or 'Under Capricorn'. Yet the surrealistic quality of both these poems (from *The Anvil's Undertone,* 1978) is a valuable indication not only of Livingstone's own poetic development – an imagination which, over twenty years, has kept touch with the temper of the southern African region – but also of the increasingly urgent images and techniques found necessary by many poets to accommodate an increasingly urgent South African situation.

'Under Capricorn', for example – by means of unanalysed juxtaposition, the cinematic device of montage – evokes a deliberately ambiguous relationship between a motorist (probably a white man), a symbolic figure of an old African and an hallucinatory landscape in flux. At a personal level the poem, vividly displaying Livingstone's powers of defamiliarisation, dramatises a state of acute anxiety (of the alienated individual trapped in a world seemingly governed by the logic of the absurd). At a wider level we are offered a frightening picture of Albert Memmi's 'impossible historical situation': a clash of Western and African models, of the technological and the rural, of white and black, all set against a nightmarish backdrop. This created situation suggests a complex of potential meanings, with ambiguity and indeterminacy built into the poem's very structure. This in itself says something about contemporary South African social reality: here we have a white man, caught in a landscape in transition, aware of the inevitable movement of change yet fearful of an uncertain future.

By way of contrast, a Soweto poet such as Mafika Gwala, in 'Getting off the Ride' (1977), has a far less ambiguous view of both historical and artistic procedures. As far as Gwala is concerned, the purpose of art is the utilitarian one of 'conscientising' a communal black audience; the function of the artist is actively to help change a world that has pluralistic possibilities. Behind 'Getting off the Ride' lies the assumption that in a human universe man is himself the ultimate organising principle, and it is this organisation that becomes the form of the poem. Thus, in a crisis situation, contemplation is regarded as a bourgeois luxury, as is the 'perfection' of the art-object and insistence on its immutability. Gwala would tend to see the artist not in liberal humanist terms as a superior moral intelligence, nor even according to modernist criteria as primarily a craftsman, but as *homo sociologicus* – art-for-life's-sake. One perception must immediately follow another, for history is *process* and the poem must capture, forcefully, all the imperfections of an historically-conditioned (not an eternal) nature. The poem is therefore not closed form, but open form composed, breathlessly, at points along the historical road: a road which – without the devious twists of irony, subtlety or ambiguity – is seen in pre-Azania 1980 as opening up to a revolutionary future.

Soweto poetry began appearing in the mid-1960s in *The Classic* magazine (Johannesburg) and has continued to reflect an increasing post-Sharpeville racial polarisation. Taking its impetus initially from South African student (SASO) Black Consciousness responses to apartheid legislation, and subsequently from the 1976 disturbances, it is the single most important socio-literary phenomenon of the decade. Accused of having a sameness about it, this poetry has over the last ten years developed its own internal emphases: from the first graphic sketches of township existence in the poetry of Casey Motsisi and, more significantly, Oswald Mtshali (a poetry directed in protest at a predominantly white readership) to the later poetry of resistance – a mobilising rhetoric adopting epic forms and traditional African oral techniques in order to impart to a black audience a message of consciousness and race-pride.

Further, alongside the utter contemporaneity of Mothobi Mutloatse's experimental 'proemdra', 'Ngwana wa Azania' ('Prose, Poem and Drama in one . . . We will donder conventional literature: old-fashioned reader and critic alike. We are going to pee, spit and shit on literary convention before we are through'), we find poems that make a highly contemporary use of an African past, still living but in danger of being forgotten – Ndebele's 'Little Dudu', for example, whose imagery blends the human and non-human worlds in order to suggest the traditional African concept of the unity of being; or Gwala's 'Kwela Ride' which ironically alludes to tribal initiation ceremonies in the context of a *dompas* (pass book) arrest. Not belonging to the sort of pre-Verwoerdian black intellectual elites that previous generations of black South African writers had belonged to, Soweto poets have made total their rejection of Western individualism and those petit bourgeois expectations that have, in any case, been legislated further and further beyond their reach. Instead, they have attempted to re-introduce an African humanism, which has particularly made itself felt in a reverence for family and in an enunciation of the principles of communalism.

Soweto poetry has also been accused of simplifying the complex dialectics of socio-political struggle, and of thereby all too often issuing forth as mere rant – a facile revolutionary romanticism. While there is some truth in this charge, the best poetry has fully taken into account the metaphysics of action and hate. Mongane Serote, for example, both loves and hates 'City Johannesburg'; and if he is at times tempted to resort to violence (as in the bizarre 'Poem on Black and White'), he is all the time aware of the terrible price that may have to be paid in terms of his own humanity.

As I said earlier, Soweto poetry has certain thematic and stylistic affinities with the poetry, in the 1940s, of Peter Abrahams (its immediacy) and H.I.E. Dhlomo (its prophetic note and its use of a traditional past). Unlike Dhlomo, however, today's black poets do not, whether they like it or not, have the problem of shaking off a British literary influence which was often debilitating because unapt under the circumstances. Ironically, this is largely because twenty-five years of Verwoerdian Bantu Education has virtually robbed the present-day black generation of a facility with the English language and, as a result, with English literary traditions. (Nor of course has the racy Runyonesque Sophiatown prose writing of the pre-Sharpeville era been able to serve as a model for today's black authors, this literature being almost totally proscribed in South Africa.) Yet, despite the disadvantages both of operating in a literary vacuum and of an education policy of basic vernacular instruction in a modern economy, the creative imagination – as it has always done – has found ways of turning obstacles to its own advantage. In the case of Soweto poets, it has forged a stark English idiom utterly appropriate to the immediacy of township existence. While one may locate certain black American echoes in this poetry, these exist not so much as a result of the influence of Afro-American literature as such, but more as a result of a legitimate township milieu of jazz, American B films and of an international Black Power rhetoric. Moreover, the language of prophecy in today's black poetry has also inevitably had to shed reliance on obviously imported literary models (such as hampered Dhlomo) and has tailored itself to specific South African demands. Soweto poetry – which takes its larger unity from a common consciousness of being black (whether African, Indian or coloured) under a system of institutionalised discrimination – may be thought of as a 'movement' of the last decade; and it therefore seemed convenient to group this poetry at the end of the anthology.

The above survey does not of course aim to be comprehensive and, in the limited space available, has at times had to resort to somewhat schematic distinctions between the 'traditional' and the 'radical'. Nevertheless, such broad categories are useful in critical discussion, as long as we realise that they are not necessarily mutually exclusive. No poet is neatly this or that, but rather we are always talking about degrees of emphasis, about hierarchies of values. Poets such as Livingstone, Ruth Miller, Cullinan and Macnamara, for instance, have all in their own ways and in different degrees combined the bizarre and the commonplace, the romantic and the scientific. Moreover, many traditional motifs (the exile of the white South African, for example, or the clash between 'Apollonian Europe' and 'Dionysian Africa') have, in the hands of such contemporary poets as Hope, Nicol, Gray and Branford, been adroitly adapted to changing circumstances which have constantly cut across the old stereotyped divisions. Then I have said little of the satiric poetry of earlier journalist-poets such as Blackburn and Colvin, and more recently Delius. Neither have I mentioned many of the fine individual voices which have continued to find inspiration in love, religion, family relationships, academic life, art or literature itself.

But whatever the themes, and whether it has employed experimental techniques or pushed traditionalism in genuine new directions, the South African poetic imagination of the last twenty years has repeatedly registered a crisis of authority: a sense of dislocation from received values which is reflected in the central metaphors of change, transition, cultural plurality, and in often startlingly altered attitudes to poetic language and to the function of literature itself. Soweto poetry, in particular, has during the 1970s initiated lively, often heated, debate in little magazines on the appropriate critical responses to literature in a racially explosive society. And one looks forward to this spirit of questioning making itself increasingly felt in South African university English Departments which have tended to shy away from the fact that they are part of a modern South Africa with a challenging literature of its own. Once the reader is willing to extend his or her critical responses beyond an often restricting humanism, South African English poetry does yield a rich diversity to *literary,* as well as to sociological, study.

iv

Finally, a note on selection procedures in *A Century of South African Poetry*. While I have included a number of relatively unfamiliar names, some readers may be surprised at my exclusion of, for example, F.T. Prince. I feel however that Prince (like Laurence Lerner and Charles Madge) has thoroughly embraced the British tradition and should be left there. Yet I have included R.N. Currey and David Wright, voluntary exiles like Prince. In the case of such South Africans living permanently abroad, my criteria for inclusion have not simply been ones of birth or subject-matter, but of some evidence of a commitment to South African literature. Currey and Wright have continued to find poetic inspiration in their position 'between two worlds', have continued to publish in South Africa, and have also contributed critical articles on South African literature. By the same token, Campbell and Plomer remain South African figures whether living in England, Portugal or Japan, and I have not restricted myself to selections from their 'African' poems. As far as Boer War poetry is concerned, I have taken into account the international character of the conflict and have included poems, whether by South Africans or not, on the topic of the war itself. Unlike Jack Cope's *Penguin Book of South African Verse* (1968), I have confined myself to poems written originally in English and to translations undertaken only by the author himself. Until South Africans are proficiently multi-lingual, the most satisfactory arrangement would seem to be separate anthologies catering for different languages.

The question of Rhodesian/Zimbabwean representation was more difficult to resolve. Traditionally, early Rhodesians such as Cripps, Gouldsbury and Fairbridge have been included in South African anthologies partly out of colonial sentiment, partly for the valid reason that the pioneer column that headed north in the late nineteenth century had close ties with South Africa, and early Rhodesian poetry was received by a South African reading public. It seems right then to include at least a token Rhodesian/Zimbabwean representation, not only from the liberal humanist line culminating in Brettell, but also from the more recent, more radical, voices of the independence struggle – a conflict which, for various reasons, was of pointed interest to South Africans of all colours. Just as early Rhodesian poetry has unusual historical significance in a book of South African poetry, so does the contemporary Zimbabwean poetry of, among others, Borell, Zimunyu, Style, Chidyausiku, Mungoshi and Chipeya (these latter two have recently commenced publishing their work in the Johannesburg-based *Staffrider* magazine). I should emphasise, however, that Rhodesian/Zimbabwean poetry is being viewed here from a South African perspective. For a more comprehensive picture the interested reader is directed to the available anthologies from that country – for Rhodesia, now Zimbabwe, has for many years been in the process of establishing its own literary traditions.

The only omission from *A Century of South African Poetry* that I regret is the exiled Dennis Brutus's 'Letter 18' (from *Letters to Martha,* 1968). In this poem Brutus contributes an effectively restrained voice to a 'tradition' of South African prison literature. However, as Brutus is listed in terms of the Suppression of Communism Act, the inclusion of his poetry would have meant the automatic banning of this anthology in South Africa. While I think it morally indefensible and politically naive that Brutus should be silenced in South Africa, I do think it imperative that the 137 voices in *A Century of South African Poetry* be heard in their own country. For, in spite of what we might hear from American Africanists or at Commonwealth Literature Conferences, South African literature is more and more finding its own momentum within South Africa itself, not in exiled communities, whether voluntary or otherwise. This is something painfully, though eloquently, understood by Achmed Dangor's 'The Voices that are Dead', the poem which almost prophetically concludes this anthology.

It is in this country, too, that a healthy critical tradition must develop: one prepared to interpret South African literature's significance in the first instance for South Africans. As far as poetry criticism is concerned, what struck me was the failure of existing anthologies to provide the reader with any sense of literary relationship or development. Unfortunately, the 1979 Butler/Mann anthology does not take up and expand upon the important critical survey which accompanied the earlier 1959 edition. Moreover, South African anthologies have generally arranged poets either alphabetically of by chronology of birth: conventions which, while adequate in British or American contexts (where traditions have been established), seem inadequate in the largely unexplored South African literary field. In an attempt to make some overall sense of South African poetic development, I have – in addition to offering a critical Introduction – arranged poets more or less according to the dates when their important work first appeared either in magazines or collections, whichever seemed more appropriate. Those poets writing in the 1960s and seventies, however, have with significant exceptions in the sixties been arranged alphabetically, while 'movements' have been loosely grouped (for example, the Boer War, the Veldsingers, early Rhodesians, modernism in the 1960s, Zimbabwean poetry, Soweto poetry). Furthermore, as the Introduction indicates, I found it extremely illuminating placing poets in periods dictated not simply by matters of chronology, but more importantly by shifts of sensibility and style.

In conclusion I should like to thank: Professor André de Villiers, Janine Bekker and Sharon Ries of the National English Literary Museum, Grahamstown, for providing the biographical appendix; Professor Ernest Pereira of the University of South Africa, Professor Stephen Gray of the Rand Afrikaans University, Dr Tim Couzens of the African Studies Centre, University of the Witwatersrand, Dr C. Henning of the University of Durban-Westville, Marcia Leveson of the University of the Witwatersrand, Mrs M. Macey of the Kimberley Public Library and Isobel Hofmeyr of the South African Council for Higher Education, for making available to me their research, also the UNISA inter-library loan service and the photocopying staff for helping me in my manuscript preparation.

Michael Chapman
University of South Africa, 1981

1820–1870

Thomas Pringle

Afar in the Desert

Afar in the Desert I love to ride,
With the silent Bush-boy alone by my side:
When the sorrows of life the soul o'ercast,
And, sick of the Present, I cling to the Past;
When the eye is suffused with regretful tears,
From the fond recollections of former years;
And shadows of things that have long since fled
Flit over the brain, like the ghosts of the dead:
Bright visions of glory—that vanished too soon;
Day-dreams—that departed ere manhood's noon;
Attachments—by fate or by falsehood reft;
Companions of early days—lost or left;
And my Native Land—whose magical name
Thrills to the heart like electric flame;
The home of my childhood; the haunts of my prime;
All the passions and scenes of that rapturous time
When the feelings were young and the world was new,
Like the fresh bowers of Eden unfolding to view;
All—all now forsaken—forgotton—foregone!
And I—a lone exile remembered of none—
My high aims abandoned,—my good acts undone,—
Aweary of all that is under the sun,—
With that sadness of heart which no stranger may scan,
I fly to the Desert afar from man!

Afar in the Desert I love to ride,
With the silent Bush-boy alone by my side:
When the wild turmoil of this wearisome life,
With its scenes of oppression, corruption, and strife—
The proud man's frown, and the base man's fear,—
The scorner's laugh, and the sufferer's tear,—
And malice, and meanness, and falsehood, and folly,
Dispose me to musing and dark melancholy;
When my bosom is full, and my thoughts are high,
And my soul is sick with the bondman's sigh—
Oh! then there is freedom, and joy, and pride,
Afar in the Desert alone to ride!

There is rapture to vault on the champing steed,
And to bound away with the eagle's speed,
With the death-fraught firelock in my hand—
The only law of the Desert Land!

Afar in the Desert I love to ride,
With the silent Bush-boy alone by my side:
Away—away from the dwellings of men,
By the wild deer's haunt, by the buffalo's glen;
By valleys remote where the oribi plays,
Where the gnu, the gazelle, and the hartebeest graze,
And the kudu and eland unhunted recline
By the skirts of grey forests o'erhung with wild-vine;
Where the elephant browses at peace in his wood,
And the river-horse gambols unscared in the flood,
And the mighty rhinoceros wallows at will
In the fen where the wild-ass is drinking his fill.

Afar in the Desert I love to ride,
With the silent Bush-boy alone by my side:
O'er the brown Karroo, where the bleating cry
Of the springbok's fawn sounds plaintively;
And the timorous quagga's shrill whistling neigh
Is heard by the fountain at twilight grey;
Where the zebra wantonly tosses his mane,
With wild hoof scouring the desolate plain;
And the fleet-footed ostrich over the waste
Speeds like a horseman who travels in haste,
Hying away to the home of her rest,
Where she and her mate have scooped their nest,
Far hid from the pitiless plunderer's view
In the pathless depths of the parched Karroo.

Afar in the Desert I love to ride,
With the silent Bush-boy alone by my side:
Away—away—in the Wilderness vast,
Where the White Man's foot hath never passed,
And the quivered Coránna or Bechuán
Hath rarely crossed with his roving clan:
A region of emptiness, howling and drear,
Which Man hath abandoned from famine and fear;
Which the snake and the lizard inhabit alone,
With the twilight bat from the yawning stone;
Where grass, nor herb, nor shrub takes root,
Save poisonous thorns that pierce the foot;
And the bitter-melon, for food and drink,
Is the pilgrim's fare by the salt lake's brink:
A region of drought, where no river glides,
Nor rippling brook with osiered sides;
Where sedgy pool nor bubbling fount,
Nor tree, nor cloud, nor misty mount,

Appears, to refresh the aching eye:
But the barren earth, and the burning sky,
And the blank horizon, round and round,
Spread—void of living sight or sound.

And here, while the night-winds round me sigh,
And the stars burn bright in the midnight sky,
As I sit apart by the desert stone,
Like Elijah at Horeb's cave alone,

'A still small voice' comes through the wild
(Like a Father consoling his fretful Child),
Which banishes bitterness, wrath, and fear,—
Saying—MAN IS DISTANT, BUT GOD IS NEAR!

Makanna's Gathering

Wake! Amakósa, wake!
And arm yourselves for war.
As coming winds the forest shake,
I hear a sound from far:
It is not thunder in the sky,
Nor lion's roar upon the hill,
But the voice of HIM who sits on high,
And bids me speak his will!

He bids me call you forth,
Bold sons of Káhabee,
To sweep the White Men from the earth,
And drive them to the sea:
The sea, which heaved them up at first,
For Amakósa's curse and bane,
Howls for the progeny she nurst,
To swallow them again.

Hark! 'tis UHLANGA'S voice
From Debè's mountain caves!
He calls you now to make your choice—
To conquer or be slaves:
To meet proud Amanglézi's guns,
And fight like warriors nobly born:
Or, like Umláo's feeble sons,
Become the freeman's scorn.

Then come, ye Chieftain's bold,
With war-plumes waving high;
Come, every warrior young and old,
With club and assegai.
Remember how the spoiler's host
Did through our land like locusts range!
Your herds, your wives, your comrades lost—
Remember—and revenge!

Fling your broad shields away—
Bootless against such foes;
But hand to hand we'll fight today,
And with their bayonets close.
Grasp each man short his stabbing spear—
And, when to battle's edge we come,
Rush on their ranks in full career,
And to their hearts strike home!

Wake! Amakósa, wake!
And muster for the war:
The wizard-wolves from Keisi's brake,
The vultures from afar,
Are gathering at UHLANGA'S call,
And follow fast our westward way—
For well they know, ere evening-fall,
They shall have glorious prey!

The Forester of the Neutral Ground

A South-African Border-Ballad

We met in the midst of the Neutral Ground,
'Mong the hills where the buffalo's haunts are found;
And we joined in the chase of the noble game,
Nor asked each other of nation or name.

The buffalo bull wheeled suddenly round,
When first from my rifle he felt a wound;
And, before I could gain the Umtóka's bank,
His horns were tearing my courser's flank.

That instant a ball whizzed past my ear,
Which smote the beast in his fierce career;
And the turf was drenched with his purple gore,
As he fell at my feet with a bellowing roar.

The Stranger came galloping up to my side,
And greeted me with a bold huntsman's pride:
Full blithely we feasted beneath a tree;—
Then out spoke the Forester, Arend Plessie.

'Stranger! we now are true comrades sworn;
Come pledge me thy hand while we quaff the horn;
Thou'rt an Englishman good, and thy heart is free,
And 'tis therefore I'll tell my story to thee.

'A Heemraad of Camdebóo was my Sire;
He had flocks and herds to his heart's desire,
And bondmen and maidens to run at his call,
And seven stout sons to be heirs of all.

'When we had grown up to man's estate,
Our Father bade each of us choose a mate,
Of Fatherland blood, from the *black* taint free,
As became a Dutch burgher's proud degree.

'My Brothers they rode to the Bovenland,
And each came with a fair bride back in his hand;
But *I* brought the handsomest bride of them all—
Brown Dinah, the bondmaid who sat in our hall.

'My Father's displeasure was stern and still;
My Brothers' flamed forth like a fire on the hill;
And they said that my spirit was mean and base,
To lower myself to the servile race.

'I bade them rejoice in their herds and flocks,
And their pale faced spouses with flaxen locks;
While I claimed for my share, as the youngest son,
Brown Dinah alone with my horse and gun.

'My Father looked black as a thunder-cloud,
My Brothers reviled me and railed aloud,
And their young wives laughed with disdainful pride,
While Dinah in terror clung close to my side.

'Her ebon eyelashes were moistened with tears,
As she shrunk abashed from their venomous jeers;
But I bade her look up like a Burgher's wife—
Next day to be *mine*, if God granted life.

'At dawn brother Roelof came galloping home
From the pastures—his courser all covered with foam;
' "'Tis the Bushmen!" he shouted; "haste, friends to the spoor!
Bold Arend! come help with your long-barrelled roer."

'Far o'er Bruintjes-hoogtè we followed—in vain:
At length surly Roelof cried, "Slacken your rein;
We have quite lost the track."—Hans replied with a smile.
—Then my dark-boding spirit suspected their guile.

'I flew to our Father's. Brown Dinah was sold!
And they laughed at my rage as they counted the gold.
But I leaped on my horse, with my gun in my hand,
And sought my lost love in the far Bovenland.

'I found her; I bore her from Gauritz fair glen,
Through lone Zitzikamma, by forest and fen.
To these mountains at last like wild-pigeons we flew,
Far, far from the cold hearts of proud Camdebóo.

'I've reared our rude shieling by Gola's green wood,
Where the chase of the deer yields me pastime and food:
With my Dinah and children I dwell here alone,
Without other comrades—and wishing for none.

'I fear not the Bushman from Winterberg's fell,
Nor dread I the Caffer from Kat-River's dell;
By justice and kindness I've conquered them both,
And the Sons of the Desert have pledged me their troth.

'I fear not the leopard that lurks in the wood,
The lion I dread not, though raging for blood;
My hand it is steady—my aim it is sure—
And the boldest must bend to my long-barrelled roer.

'The elephant's buff-coat my bullet can pierce;
And the giant rhinoceros, headlong and fierce.
Gnu, eland and buffalo furnish my board,
When I feast my allies like an African lord.

'And thus from my kindred and colour exiled,
I live like old Ismael, Lord of the Wild—
And follow the chase with my hounds and my gun;
Nor ever repent the bold course I have run.

'But sometimes there sinks on my spirit a dread
Of what may befall when the turf's on my head;
I fear for poor Dinah—for brown Rodomond
And dimple-faced Karel, the sons of the *bond*.

'Then tell me, dear Stranger, from England the free,
What good tidings bring'st thou for Arend Plessie?
Shall the Edict of Mercy be sent forth at last,
To break the harsh fetters of Colour and Caste?

The Cape of Storms

O Cape of Storms! although thy front be dark,
And bleak thy naked cliffs and cheerless vales,
And perilous thy fierce and faithless gales
To staunchest mariner and stoutest bark;
And though along thy coasts with grief I mark
The servile and the slave, and him who wails
An exile's lot—and blush to hear thy tales
Of sin and sorrow and oppression stark:—
Yet, spite of physical and moral ill,
And after all I've seen and suffered here,
There are strong links that bind me to thee still,
And render even thy rocks and deserts dear;
Here dwell kind hearts which time nor place can chill—
Loved Kindred and congenial Friends sincere.

Frederic Brooks

Nature's Logic, or Isaak van Batavia's Plea for His Manhood. A True Story

Question.
Where do you live my Slave Boy, say?
I want to hire you by the day.

Answer.
Massa me no Slave *Boy* be;
Me be free *Man*, me be free.

Question.
Who gave you your freedom my black *boy?*
Will you not come to my employ?

Answer.
Yes *Massa*, me come, do every *ting*,
My hands, and feet, and heart, me bring;
But, when me come to your employ,
Me be a *Man*, me be no *Boy*.

Question.
A *Man!!!* a *Man!!!* who tells you so?
How far does his knowledge go;– *(aside.)*
Who gave you thoughts above your station,
To unfit you for your avocation?

Answer.
Massa, the Great Big Book did say,
When God from darkness made the day;
And Sun, and Moon, and Stars, so high,
Like twinkling diamonds in the sky;
That, by and by, by His own plan,
He spake to *dust*, and up rose *Man*.
Adam *my father* was, and *thine*,
O! let I pray your heart incline,
Without a wrangle and no bother,
To hail *me* as a *Man* and *Brother*.

For fleecy locks and black complexion
    Cannot alter nature's claim;
Skins may differ, but affection
    Dwells in *Black* and *White* the same.

The Emigrant Shoemakers; or, a Trip to Algoa Bay

Tune— 'Oh, cruel.' By W.J.P.

Two gentlemen shoemakers, my shopmate
Jack and me,
Took a start to Algoa Bay, a precious way
by sea;
We went among the blacks, to make our
fortins you must know,
For mayn't shoemakers *look* for trade, where
people *barefoot* go?
Tol de rol, &c.

We took a stock of boots and shoes, some
leather and that *ere,*
Took leaf of friends, and jump'd on board,
the wind and weather fair;
We had a quick sail to the Cape, (our ship
was a quick *hand.*)
And hoped our boots and shoes would have
as quick a *sail* on land.
Fol de rol, &c

When at Algoa Bay we landed, we *see* such
lots of blacks,
As neither had shoes to their feet, nor yet
shirts to their backs;
Caffres, or *Gaffers* they are call'd, or some
such sort of name,
And people *as* don't know 'em, says the
savages is tame.
Fol de rol, &c.

Algoa Bay is not like London, no houses
nor *no* streets,
You *has* to build your house yourself, dig
wells, and all *them* treats;
We built a house, and open'd shop, and
thought *as* we should *do,*
And so we did *do—nothink,* for we never
sold a shoe.
Tol de rol, &c.

No wonder *as we nothink* sold, for *Gaffers*
never *buys,*
They *comes* in droves, and *burns* your house,
and *steals* your *marchandise;*

They *comes* bang! with their *banging* clubs,
    and *bangs* your heads about,
Oh, *them's* the *Gaffer singing clubs, as*
    makes you soon *sing out.*
        Tol de rol, &c.

Ten thousand *Gaffers* storm'd our house,
    and robb'd and beat us too,
And we to save our lives *run out* and *out-run*
    all the crew;
And all the way we *run* from them, we heard
    great lions roar,
Which made us both expect *no less* than soon
    to be *no more.*
        Fol de rol, &c.

Then *setting* down to dine, two lions *came* to
    dine on us,
And soon they had their bellies full–*from*
    our blunderbuss;
It is the lions' custom to pop on you
    unawares;
We wanted *custom* bad enough, but wanted
    none of their's.
        Tol de rol, &c.

So much for emigration! we found it a bad
    spec;
And, coming home to England, we tasted a
    shipwreck;
But now in our own country safe, we'll no
    more castles build,
If we cannot make our *fortins,* we can *live,*
    and not be kill'd.
        Fol de rol, &c.

The Morality of a Printing House

The world's a *printing-house,* our words are thoughts,
  Our deeds are characters of several sizes;
Each soul's a *compositor,* of whose faults
  The levites are *correctors;* heav'n *revises;*
Death is the common *press,* from whence being driven,
We're gather'd sheet by sheet, and *bound* for heav'n.

Juvenalis Secundus

The Press

Of all the blessings England's sons possess
Give me that one—a free and manly Press:
That can, with gentle, yet unyielding hand,
Unveil each wrong, each grievance of the land;
A Press, the guard and champion of the law,
That will speak out and keep the rogues in awe;
As justice bids, will censure or applaud,
And hold the mirror up to truth or fraud;
That dares th' oppressor curb, th' oppress'd defend,—
The bond-slave's guardian, yet the freeman's friend.

But let the Press be sparing of abuse,
By no harsh feelings sway'd no *private* views;
Let no man's fame be sullied by its pen,
Averse to principles and things, not men;
Justice the only object of its zeal,
Its only aim and wish the public weal.

Let those who work this mighty engine, see
They deal its fearful strokes with clemency:
Oh! let them think awhile, how many a wound
Its pond'rous arm, perchance, inflicts around,
From one man's malice, may, from want of care,
No time can heal, no med'cine can repair.
'Tis good to have a giant's strength of limb,
But surely not to use that strength like him.

Consider well, then, whosoe'er thou be,
Who wield'st a Press that's English, fair and free,
How grand the path that opens to thy view,
How bright, how pleasing, and how useful too.
But if thou only tak'st thy ruffian pen
To stab the feelings of thy fellow-men;
If thou hast tried, by bold and fierce excess,
To make us bond-slaves of a *tyrant* Press;
If thou hast chosen one man for thy foe,
Or Slave, or Governor, or high, or low;

And all thy spleen, thy ruthless rancour shed,
On all *that* one man did, and all he said;
If thou'st pursu'd us with an adder's spite,
And stung with mad invective, wrong or right,
Himself, his children, friends, and all he lov'd,
And all who wish'd him well, or who approv'd;
If thou hast call'd the Press, its aid to bring,
And mix'd thy poison with its wholesome spring,
And made its wrong'd and profanated page
The public vehicle of private rage,
And us'd its power to spread thy noxious slime;—
Thy talent *then becomes* a curse and crime.

Andrew Geddes Bain

The British Settler

Tune – 'Oh what a row', or, 'The humours of a Steam-boat'.

Oh! what a gay, what a *rambling* life a
Settler's leading!
Spooring cattle, doing battle, quite jocose;
Winning, losing; Whigs abusing; shopping
now, then mutton breeding;
Never fearing, persevering, on he goes!

When to the Cape I first came out, in days
of Charlie Somerset,
My lands were neatly measured off, and
reg'larly my number set;
I strutted round on my own ground, lord of
a hundred acres, sir,
And said I'd plough, I'd buy a cow, the
butchers cut and bakers, sir.
Oh! what a gay, &c

On Kowie's banks I built a house, and made
a snug location there;
I fenc'd my lands with my own hands to keep
all tight;
The river rose, and fore my nose made awful
desolation there;
The Kafirs stole my only cow away that night!
I made a trip to Kafirland, in hopes to find
my cow again,
And tried to act the dentist then, which no
one can do now again;
I drew the Kafir's ivory teeth, at risk of
hempen collar, sir.
Which at Graham's Town on the market brought
me full 300 dollars, sir!
Oh! what a gay, &c

My second go was but so so, although the
trade was brisk enough;
The patrols nearly boned me in a secret maze;
I hid my load out of the road, and, faith, I
just had risk enough,

For this trade was hanging matter in those
good old days!
My stock-in-trade on pack-ox laid, I tried
my luck at *smouching* then,
But found the Boers were wide awake as
Yorkshiremen at chousing them;
They swapt me some rock chrystals – gems,
they swore, of purest water, sir;
And for *breeding* stock, a scurvy lot of
hamels and *kapaters,* sir!

Oh! what a gay, &c

Of fortune's frowns, smiles, ups, and downs,
I had a great variety;
I *smouching* drop. I open shop, then buy a
farm;
Doing charming with my farming, blest with
friends' society,
When all at once the Amakosa break the
charm!
Assegaing, yelling, crying – murder! fire!
and revelry!
Stealing cattle, bloody battle, every kind of
devilry, –
Helter-skelter, seeking shelter, wives and
children rustling in!
Husbands wounded, – lost, confounded, tender
friends are justling in!

Oh! what a gay, &c

Hopes are blasted, pale and fasted, now
reduced to beggary;
Burnt locations, public rations all we've left;
Names abused, of climes accused by agents
vile of whiggery,
Any sympathy withheld, when of our all bereft.
Compensation for spol'ation, after such
representation,
Seemed so futile and inutile, that 'twas
scouted by the nation!
And that we've still a dollar left, our thanks
be to no stingy-man,
Whose name's a charm our souls to warm, – THE
GOOD, THE BRAVE SIR BENJAMIN!

Oh! what a gay, &c

Kafirs lauded and rewarded for their savage,
fierce irruption,
By the folks of Downing-street and Ex'ter
Hall!
Then no checking Boers from *trekking*, fleeing,
seeing such corruption;
Hottentots and Fingoes, saucy vagrants all!
Such delusion and confusion seldom are exhibited,
When for convenience of the blacks the whites
are stabbed and gibbeted!
Yet, persevering through those ills, the storm
again I've weathered, sir!
My children married happy, and my nest again
well feathered, sir!
Oh! what a gay, &c.

'Tis four and twenty years, my friends, since
first on Afric's shore we landed!
And retrospections crowd my mind of that great
day;
Fear and doubt shut hope all out, for on a
desert we seemed stranded,
And dreary was our prospect then in Algoa Bay!
View contrasted, while they lasted, times of
which I'm now relating,
And our happy meeting here, this great event
commemorating!
Then may our hearts be grateful still, that
Heaven has so guarded us
Through all our toilsome pilgrimage, and now
so well rewarded us!
Oh! what a gay, what a *rambling* life a
Settler's leading!
Spooring cattle, doing battle, quite jocose;
Winning, losing; Whigs abusing; shopping
now, then cattle breeding;
Never fearing, persevering, on he goes!

To Choose a Wife by Lighting a Candle

In York, we're told, a wag his whims to please,
Once chose a wife by eating Cheshire cheese;
But he, whose tale I'm now about to handle,
Chose his alone by lighting of a candle.

Near Ludgate Hill, in London's famous city,
A haberdasher lived, both rich and witty;
Who, by civility, and care in trade,
A fortune of some consequence had made:
Tired of the eating-houses, where he daily
Paid eighteen-pence to fill his empty belly;
He wisely judged, that if he had a bride,
He'd dine in comfort at his own fire-side;
So Mr Bobbin swore that he in Co.
With some fair partner very soon would go,
And share with her in peace, the pleasant fruits
Of his well-earned industrious pursuits.
Three buxom ladies – handsome, young, and
  nimble,
Lived by the aid of scissors and of thimble;
All milliners in famed *Thread-needle-street,*
Who in good style made both ends closely meet.
The first, a lovely nymph, was called Miss
  Grace,
Blest with a beauteous form and smiling face;
The second, heavenly creature, sweet Miss Jess,
In point of beauty, surely, nothing less;
The third, Miss Jane, a prize that kings might
  die for,
Was all an honest tradesman's heart could sigh
  for,
Our Cit, with all the three at once enchanted,
Found he'd a couple more than should be
  wanted;
The English laws no more than one permitting,
Tho' Mahomet thought polygamy befitting;
Their charms united, Bobbin could but stand ill,
So picked out one – *by lighting of a candle!*
All three invited to his house one night,
He *dous'd,* as if by accident, the light,
And said, 'Miss Grace pray do excuse my
  rudeness,
To light the candle will you have the goodness?'
Poor Grace, but little conscious of her fate,
Soon lit the candle at the burning grate;
And in her best endeavours him to please,
She wasted nearly half a pound of grease!
Scarce was the light in being, 'ere our Cit,
In shamming snuffing, *re*-extinguished it;
And asked Miss Jessie next to try her art,
Who with an easy grace performed her part;

But, heedless, threw away the burning paper,
The moment she'd applied it to the taper.
Good Mr Bobbin was not yet content
Till each a trial fairly underwent;
Again he quench'd the candle's vital spark,
Which made Miss Jessie wittily remark,
'This strange behaviour seems a little *dark.*'
Miss Jane now rose, like beauty's lovely queen,
And volunteer'd to light the darken'd scene;
A slip of paper carefully she folded,
As ever nurse my pin-a-fore of old did,
And sooner than you could pronounce old Nick,
The flame was seen in contact with the wick:
Unlike her rivals – ever on the watch,
She anxiously preserved the burning match!
'Bravo!' exclaimed our Cit, in flaming rapture,
'Sweet Jane has power alone my heart to capture;
Grace is too greasy; – Jess I don't desire,
My house, and not my heart, she'd set on fire:
Long such a partner I have tried to catch,
Who'd light a candle, and *secure the match!*'
Friends! if with two, or more, you idly dandle,
Like Bobbin choose, by lighting of a candle!

Kaatje Kekkelbek
or Life among the Hottentots

My name is Kaatje Kekkelbek,
  I come from Katrivier,
Daar is van water geen gebrek,
  But scarce of wine and beer.
Myn A B C at Ph'lipes school
  I learnt a kleine beetje,
But left it just as great a fool
  As gekke Tante Meitje.

But a b, ab and i n, ine,
  I dagt met uncle Plaatje,
Aint half so good as brandewyn,
  And vette karbonatje.
So off we set, een heele boel,
  Stole a fat cow and sack'd it,
Then to an Engels setlaars fool,
  We had ourselves contracted.

We next took to the Kowie Bush,
   Found sheep dat was not lost, aye
But a schelm boer het ons gavang,
   And brought us voor McCrosty.
Daar was Saartje Zeekoegat en ik,
   En ouw Dirk Donderwetter,
Klaas Klauterberg, en Diederick Dik,
   Al sent to the tronk together.

Drie months we daar got banjan kos
   For stealing os en hammel,
For which when I again got los;
   I thank'd for Capt. Campbell.
The Judge came around, his sentence such
   As he thought just and even.
'Six months hard work,' which means in Dutch
   'Zes maanden lekker leven.'

De tronk it is een lekker plek
   Of 'twas not juist so dry,
But soon as I got out again
   At (Todds) I wet mine eye,
At Vice's house in Market-Square
   I drown'd my melancholies;
And at Barrack hill found soldiers there
   To treat me well at Jolly's.

Next morn dy put me in blackhole,
   For one Rixdollar stealing,
And knocking down a vrouw dat had
   Met myn sweet heart some dealing.
But I'll go to the Gov'nor self
   And tell him in plain lingo,
I've as much right to steal and fight
   As kaffir has or Fingoe.

Oom Andries Stoffels in England told
   (Fine compliments he paid us,)
Dat Engels dame was juist de same
   As our sweet Hotnot ladies.
When drest up in my voersits pak
   What hearts will then be undone,
Should I but show my face or back
   Among the beaux of London.

H.H. Dugmore

from: A Reminiscence of 1820

In the lone wilderness behold them stand,
Gazing with new strange feelings on the scenes
Now spread around them in a foreign clime,
Far from the sea-girt home that gave them birth.

They had been landed on a cheerless shore,
Dreary and solitary; and the hope
That erst had brighten'd all their visions, when,
O'er the blue waters looming afar,
They had seen Afric's mountains rise to view,
Had nigh been quench'd again. But they had left
The barren strand, and over hill and dale
Had slowly toil'd to reach a place of rest,
And give their children once again a home.
. . .
And this is now their home.
'Tis lone and wild;
But there is beauty in its wildness. See!
Yonder are mountains; in their deep ravines
Dark woods are waving, whence in noisy flight
While parrots issue forth, while loories hide
Amidst their deep recesses. Water springs
Send limpid streamlets down the mountain side,
Fring'd with bright evergreens, and brighter flowers.

Issuing from yonder dark and craggy gorge,
Where lurks the stealthy leopard, and where shouts
With loudly echoing voice the bold baboon,
Kareiga winds its devious course along
Between its willow'd banks; while here and there
The dark leav'd yellow wood lifts its proud head
In stately dignity. Along the vale
The wildwood's sheltering covert stretched, where
The bushbok barks; the duiker, sudden, springs;
The timid bluebok through the moonlight glides;
And monkey mimics chatter saucily.
And there are feather'd songsters in the groves;
Not with the thrush's or the blackbird's notes.
That flood Old England's woods with melody;
But short, and sharp, and ringing in their tones,
Responsive to each other from afar,
While telling of a life of light and joy.

In the green pastures on the sunny slopes,
Where the mimosa's golden blossoms shed
Gales of perfume around; and fertile soils
Promise the husbandman a rich return
To cheer him in his toil.

'This is our Home!
A spot on earth we now call our own;
A starting point for a new life's career.
Wake all our energies afresh! A brighter day
Has dawn'd at last upon us. Let us raise
A song of gratitude to Heaven,
And gird us for our duties.'

1870–1940

Albert Brodrick

Rorke's Drift

On the wild river's bank two horsemen appear –
They are bearers of tidings that fill them with fear.
'Haste! Put us across and prepare for the fight,
The Zulus are out in their uttermost might,
They rushed on our camp like a dark hungry flood
And their spears are all red with or countrymen's blood.'

We heard them. – A moment our pulses stood still,
Then we went to our work with a heart and a will –
Two stores to defend, with a hundred, all told,
And thirty sick mates – 'Come boys, let's be bold!
Let's fasten the waggons together with chain
And build up our ramparts with sacks full of grain.'

What is that coming on like a herd of black game
Round the hill to the south, with the speed of a flame,
With feathery plumes, like wild manes, flaunting high
And sound like a myriad wings in the sky?
The Zulus! – for now in the sun's glance appears
The quivering lightning-like sheen of their spears.

They are on us. Six hundred at first, with wild cries –
The lust of the battle still red in their eyes –
The blood of our comrades still wet on each blade,
And see! there come thousands behind to their aid.
But thanks to the heads that directed our hands,
All firm and unbroken our little camp stands.

It stands like a rock, the Atlantic's wild wave
Breaks over and harms not! We took and we gave.
They leap on our walls, they stab, hiss and yell;
They come on in thousands – dark legions from hell –
Our bayonets are ready, our rifles are 'there',
And their small tongues of flame tell there's death in the air!

They took half our fort – foot by foot, inch by inch
They lighted the roof – and yet none would flinch.
We threw up another redoubt with the maize,
And fought by the light of the Hospital blaze
When the darkness came down, and all through the night
Surrounded, we kept up the terrible fight.

Ah! Who shall declare the deeds that were done
Ere the world woke again to the light of the sun?
For twelve long, long hours we stood at our posts
And beat back (how often!) the enemy's hosts.
We had our revenge for the blood that was shed
At dark Isandhlwana – they paid for our dead!

Day broke and the devils had silently gone,
We counted their slain – more than twenty to one.
Our loss was fifteen, so we set up a shout
That frightened the vultures slow sailing about.

In the heart-thrill of nations will live your reward
Oh brave 24th, oh brave Bromhead and Chard. –

Jong Koekemoer

After Great Scot

Copied from the MS. of Jan Van der Schryff, Tutor in a Dutch Gentleman's family.

Oh! Jong Koekemoer from Marico's come out–
His schimmel Paard 'Ruiter' is sterk en gezout,
And, save some Peach Brandy, refreshment he'd none;
But he had his 'Martini,' that 'Son of a gun!'
So faithful a vryer, so fluks with his roer,
There ne'er was a Kerel like the Jong Koekemoer.

He never off saddled, nor stopped for Kanteen,
He swam the Hex River where no drift was seen,
But e'er he held still at old Crocodile Kraal
The bride had said 'ja' to an Englishman small–
For a wealthy old trader who had a 'tin' store
Was to wed the fair Sannie of Jong Koekemoer.

He entered the house just in time for the ball,
Met oompies, and tantes, neefs, nichtjes, and all;
Then spoke Sannie's pa–old Swart Dirk Coetzee
(A dapper old Krygsman and Raad's Lid was he):
'What make you now here, Hans, so warm on our spoor?
Will you drink, smoke, or dance with us neef Koekemoer?'

'Wacht Oom, waar is Sannie? her long have I vryd,
For in all Transvaal she's the mooiste meid–
Last nachtmaal we swore on the Bible to wed–

But now I will just drink a soopje instead—
There are girls in Marico—who still love a Boer—
That would gladly be vrouw to Jong Hans Koekemoer.'

The bride brought the glass (blaauw, with bloemetjes rond),
He drank the Peach brandy, but first cried 'Gezond.'
Poor Sannie, she trembled, and couldn't tell why;
Yet she smiled with her lips, and she winked with her eye!
He took her warm hand while her ma she gaat treur—
'Now let's have a reel, kerels,' said Jong Koekemoer.

So tall in his moleskin, so prim in her print
(While her sweet mouth was full of the Smouse peppermint).
They danced 'Afrika' to the fiddles' sharp sound,
While the guests were half blinded with dust from the ground;
And all the young nichtjes cried 'Mag! Hans is voor,
Zy is gek als zy loop niet met Jong Koekemoer.'

Quick. She pinned fast her skirts, and her kapje she tied.
They rushed o'er the stoep where old 'Ruiter' they spied,
He sprang in the saddle, she jumped up behind:
And away, through the Thorns, they flew, swift as the wind!
'Hold on to my belt, en moet niet achter loer,
They'll never catch "Ruiter",' cried Jong Koekemoer.

There was shouting of 'Opzaal' from all the Coetzees—
Doof Louw, Slim Hermanus, and Scheel-oog Du Preez!
There was chasing on horseback, in buggy, in wain—
But they never set eyes on sweet Sannie again!
Old Dirk, he 'looked daggers,' the Uitlander swore:
And now Sannie is married to Jong Koekemoer.

Wanted a President (1871)

According to a very low idea

Wanted a President, fitted to fill
The post of a Leader, with competent skill;
He must know how to drive an ass, ox or mule,
Draw the line when required,—yet not rule by rule.
He must always be civil—give each one the hand,
And the odour of moleskin must cheerfully stand.

Wanted a President (who'll act well as such),
He must understand English, and certainly Dutch,
He must know all the Laws that were ever invented,
A Roman-Dutch swell, (yet not highly scented).
He musn't be proud, there's no pride here. God knows!
And he needn't be over refined as to clothes.

Wanted a President: one who can plead,
And win us a case in a time of great need;
Who when Gold, or what not, besides us is found,
Can stop the 'slim' English from taking our ground;
And in fact, can, whenever we seek arbitration,
Go in like a bird, and prevent annexation.

Wanted a President, one who can speak
At a dinner or meeting, at least once a week.
He must live on his means, which means he must be
Dependent at times on his friends (you and me),
His religious opinions must roll like a ball,
'Hervormd,' 'Reformeerd,' 'English,' 'Romish,' and all.

Wanted a President, (this is our third),
A Cape man, or even 'Uitlander' preferred,
He must hold with the people, although bored to death,
He must speak of their faults only under his breath;
He must think them the wisest, and best in the world,
Or else from his seat by 'Besluit' he'll be hurled.

Wanted a President, one who can plough,
And govern as well, (Cincinnatus, knew how),
No German (oh Legion!) no Frenchman (my eye),
No Hollander (ready of pen), need apply,
No Englishman if he respects 'Union Jack',
Unless he has got a good Bank at his back.

Wanted a President, plucky, yet cool,
He must ever be wise, yet at times act the fool.
Be prepared for big meetings of Boers on his stoep,
Demonstrations,–Memorials–and take them–like soup,
With this saving clause, only known to a few,
Resign when too hot, and next morning renew.

Wanted a President—one who can eat
Raw biltong and biscuit, and still keep his seat;
He must drink, without sugar, burnt barley or corn.
He must wear a felt hat, and a coat overworn;
He must wear our own Veldschoens or boots ready made,
Unless a new Field shall be open to trade.

Wanted a President: age, rank, or name,
Don't matter a farthing, as long as he's game;
The payment is certain, as certain as truth,
But we don't want 'a raw, inexperienced youth';
We offer 800 per annum, (in notes),
And we'll chuck in, at times, some old trousers and coats.

Epitaph on a Diamond Digger

Here lies a digger, all his chips departed—
A splint of nature, bright, and ne'er down-hearted:
He worked in many claims, but now (though stumped)
He's got a claim above that can't be jumped.
May he turn out a pure and spotless 'wight,'
When the Great Judge shall sift the wrong from right,
And may his soul, released from this low Babel,
Be found a gem on God's great sorting table.

The Wheel of Fortune

There's many a slip
Twixt the 'stuff' and the scrip
Johannesburg Proverb

Round goes life's wheel, with constant spin—
    Some 'felloes' up, and others under;
And those who lose, and those who win,
    And those who're right, and those who blunder,
Succeed each other, day by day,
Till all, in time, are whirled away!

Here, 'neath these pleasant Afric skies,
    Some men get mended, though thrice 'broken';
And big men sink, and small men rise,
    And scarce a word of wonder spoken!
One moment—with a 'balance' great—
The next they're begging of a mate.

There's Jack, who, in the early days,
'Voorlooped' for some old Afrikander;
Now (though he spells in artful ways),
Signs cheques like any rich Uitlander.
And Sam, whose name still runs a Mine,
Is quite uncertain where to dine.

We don't want much, we want *enough;*
We don't want after coin to grovel:
We want the pleasant 'quantum suff'—
That keeps us from the pick and shovel.
Let's have enough, and well employ it—
And let some others, too, enjoy it.

There are some men with so much gold—
They're quite afraid to have much pleasure;
Like some old Boers, who, I've been told—
Sit with a gun to guard their treasure;
They've got so much they half detest it,
And howl, because they can't invest it!

Oh! what a life? and what is pelf?
And what's the good of always hoarding,
When very soon, just for yourself,
You'll only want some feet of 'boarding'?
You go—and your last will won't mend it;
They'll quarrel o'er your gold, and spend it!

Round goes life's wheel with ceaseless spin,
Some fellows up, and others under;
And those who lose, and those who win,
And those who're right, and those who blunder—
Succeed each other, day by day,
Till all, in time, are swept away!

D.C.F. Moodie

Storm in Tugela Valley, Natal

When once, at ev'ning's mellow close,
The round moon lit the sky,
And all beneath in calm repose
In slumber rapt did lie—

Seated on high upon the steep,
Amid the moonlight glow,
I looked upon a valley deep,
And on a river's flow.

Sudden, across the chasm wide
The heavy thunder growled,
While far below in sullen glide
The noble river rolled.

And now a thousand feet below,
Betwixt me and the stream,
The thunder-cloud, with lightning's glow,
Obscures the river's gleam.

Loud and more loud, and all about
The echoing hills among,
The spirits of the tempest shout
Their diapason song.

Full in the midst the cloud now parts,
And wars on different sides,
And through the gap the light moon darts,
Where bright the river glides.

William Selwyn

Hymn Written During the Zulu War

O Saviour throned in peace above
 Reveal Thy piercéd side,
And let the vision of Thy love
 Stay war's remorseless tide;
  Risen Saviour, hear!

For white, for black, alike didst Thou
 Low bow Thy fainting head;
For all of every clime and hue,
 Didst Thou thy heart's blood shed.
  Suffering Saviour, hear!

Behold fair Africa's sunny lands
 With reeking carnage strewed,
See God-made man with rigid hands
 In brother's blood imbrued;
  Sorrowing Saviour, hear!

O hear the Briton's dying groan,
 The Zulu's piercing wail;
O hear the famished orphan's moan,
 The Widow's sobbing tale;
  Pitying Saviour, hear!

In mercy stay the quivering spear;
 Avert the death-winged ball;
Pour balm for every scalding tear,
 And breathe Thy peace over all.
  Mighty Saviour, hear!

The Loss of the Six Hundred

With apologies to Lord Tennyson

Half-a-crown! Half-a-crown!
Every rap plundered;
All my dear Granny left,
  Sovereigns, six hundred.
Forward! the broker said,
Into the 'swim' he led,
Soon, winged by scrip, there fled,
  Three of six hundred.

Forward! the broker cried,
Flowing is Fortune's tide;
Hope and be undismayed
  Though you have blundered.
Mine not to make reply,
Mine not to reason why,
Mine but to sign and sigh
  O'er all my six hundred.

When will my Div's be paid?
O what wild fibs were made
While schemers planned their raid;
  E'en Satan wondered.
Bright visions all are flown;
From Granny's cold head-stone
Hear a deep reproachful groan
  O'er her six hundred.

A. G. E.

The Digger's Grave on the Vaal

He left for the land where the diamond gleams,
The siren had lured him along,
And whispered of wealth in his rapturous dreams;
He was charmed, he was tranced with the song –
He was soothed with the marvellous song.

The phantom he followed so fatal and bright.
The hopes he had cherished were vain,
The land he had traversed in vision of night.
Proved the scene of his death and his pain –
Of his pitiful anguish and pain.

In his rude hut he lay on the crystalline sand,
With the glare of the sun at his door;
The gems he had gathered were clutched in his hand,
But they will never gladden him more –
Their beauties will charm him no more.

Midst the tossings of fever that nothing can stem,
He looks on the glittering heap,
When he thinks of the treasure he's bartered for them.
His moanings are bitter and deep –
His wailings are fearful and deep.

He calls up a face as he wearily lies,
A vision enchantingly fair,
With the azure of heaven in her love-lit eyes,
And the hue of the sun in her hair –
Its glow on her golden hair.

Like the ripple of water in summer lands,
He murmurs the sound of her name,
And yearns for one touch of those delicate hands
To quiet the throb of his brain –
The fever and throb of his brain.

Lo! the vision is changed. See the Angel of Death.
Approach in Cimmerian array,
And bend o'er his form, whose lingering breath
Still clings to its temple of clay–
Its death-stricken temple of clay.

Uncoffined, unknelled, to his grave he was sped,
    Unwept, with irreverent haste,
No requiem was sung, nor ritual read,
    O'er his bed in the desolate waste –
    His grave on the terrible waste.

J. Spranger Harrison

Micky Doone's Last Jest

When old Micky Doone was lying
On his camp-bed slowly dying
From the phthisis he'd contracted seven years back underground,
He looked up at Doctor Golding,
Who his wrist was firmly holding;
Then his eyes took stock of each of twenty diggers standing round.
'Shure ut's honourin' me shack, here,
Aye, an' me upon me back, here,
An' ut's proud Oi am this momint, bhoys, to see ye standin' round.
And if on'y thim two buyers,
Izzie Greaves an' Duggie Myers,
Would turn up Oi'd shure die shmoilin', an' be happy onder-ground.
For Oi've sowld 'em all me shtones, bhoys, an' Oi call 'em each me fri'nd,
An' Oi'd loike to have 'em wid me for a moment at the ind;
Yes, Oi'd loike to have 'em sittin' wid me, one on oither hand:
An' Oi'd choose thim two from all me fri'nds Oi've got throughout the land.'

Well, you could have heard a tickey
Drop at these strange words from Micky—
Words that left the diggers stupified, for very well they knew
That Mick hated diamond buyers,
Called them 'Crimson thieves an' liars,'
And he swore they were the 'tit-bits av the divil's own black brew.'
Now, before them all there lying,
On the very point of dying.
Here he's wishing that two buyers, whom the diggers know he hates,
Would come in and join the meeting,
And he'd give them friendly greeting,
Can you wonder that such words should stun and stagger Micky's mates?
And the views of all the gathering were voiced by Silas Squeers
Who'd been digging with old Micky Doone for close on seven years:
'Waal, I guess that lil oration, Mick, would give us all the hump
If we didn't sort o' calculate that you were off your chump.'

'Shure ye'll have to have the hump, bhoys,
For Oi'm no-woise off me chump bhoys.'
Whispered Micky. And a smile lit up the hollows round his eyes.
'Oi wud give me owld dog, Jess, bhoys,
(An' she's all that Oi possess, bhoys),
For to see me fri'nds, the buyers. An' Oi'm tellin' ye no lies.'
Well, we'll have to get them buyers.

Izzy Greaves an' Duggie Myers.
If it's goin' to give Mick pleasure. Yes, they must be got somehow.
So we'd best dispatch a nigger
Into Bloemhof,' said a digger,
'With a note to tell the chaps Mick wants they got to come right now.'
So the nigger left for Bloemhof, and at 12 o'clock came back
With the buyers in a taxi, and they brought good Father Flack,
For they knew Mick was an R.C. and the padre was his friend.
And they thought the hard old digger might require him at the end.

'Ut's good mornin', Greaves and Myers.'
Said old Micky to the buyers.
'An' ut's proud Oi am to have ye here in me poor little shack.
An' ut's plazed Oi am to see, bhoys,
That ye gave a thought to me, bhoys,
Whin ye brought along His Riverince, me owld fri'nd, Father Flack.
For Oi fear Oi've gone the pace, bhoys,
An' Oi'd now be seekin' grace, bhoys;
So Oi'll bid yez all to leave me wid the Father for a shpell.
An' whin Oi've done confessin',
An' received the howly blessin',
Shure Oi'll call yez all back in agin. So wait ontil Oi yell.'
It was forty minutes later when the padre came and said,
'You may go and see him now, boys. In ten minutes he'll be dead,
And he wants his friends, the buyers, to sit one on either side.'
'Poor old Micky! But of course we shall,' the buyers both replied.

And they trooped inside, and found him
Sinking fast, and grouped around him.
And the buyers sat on packing-cases, one on either side.
'Och! ut's grand to have ye here, bhoys;
An' if on'y Oi'd some beer, bhoys,
Or a cask of whisky for a wake Oi'd be quoite satisfied.
But—bad luck!—Oi haven't any,
For Oi don't possess a penny,
So ye'll have to howld a wake wid tea an' coffee, bhoys, instead.'
Then he looked at both the buyers,
First at Greaves and then at Myers,
And a roguish smile lit up the dying eyes, as Micky said,
'Now, ye're wondhrin' why Oi chose ye two to sit on oither hand!'
(All the diggers bent to catch the words). 'Roight soon ye'll ondershtand:
Tho' Oi haven't lived as Jaysus did— (the glazing eyes sought Greaves)
—Shure (an' thanks to ye!), me *ind's* loike His—*betwane a pair av thieves!'*

C. & A.P. Wilson-Moore

Changes

'Tis startling in this humdrum world of ours,
  The curious changes circumstances make;
To see such changes (in a vulgar phrase),
  I really think the Goldfields 'take the cake'.

I passed the Rand; saw scarce a human face:
  Two years roll by, the old scene with it rolls;
Where once the Boer's humble cottage stood,
  Stands now a town, with twice ten thousand souls.

I met a man, —a timid curate—once,
  Who, from the pulpit, preached of sin and Heaven;
Now in a crowd, his shrill voice pipes on high,
  'I'll buy "Main Reefs", "Main Reefs" at forty-seven!'

He well might smile! A broker well to do;
  But now his face another aspect takes;
Flown is the jaunty air, the swagger sunk,
  With twenty thousand, in the 'Farewell Stakes'.

I met a maid, once, in the days gone by;
  A quiet country lass, was little Liz;
The timid glance is now a brazen'd eye,
  The once sweet voice, a constant croak, (for "Fiz").

Why does the wretched widow dry her eyes,
  And greet her prodigal with gentle smile?
Is it to have him back at home again,
  Or in those magic words, 'I've made my pile'?

Ah me! I know not! This howe'er I know,
  Changes for worse are more, for good are few;
Should you, perchance, find Fortune frowning darkly,
  I wish a speedy, happy change to you.

Lynn Lyster

Her Photograph

A song of the B.B.P.

At the door of his hut in the dim evening light,
In the 'lines' of the Border Police,
Sat a bronzed stalwart trooper, enjoying the night,
While his comrades were sleeping in peace.

Macloutsie was quiet. He heard not a sound,
Save the sigh of the slumbering Camp,
Or the stamp of some steed on the sun-hardened ground,
And the wind as it flickered his lamp.

He had opened his tunic of brown corduroy,
And bared his broad muscular breast,
That he might the cool breeze of the evening enjoy,
With its slumberous message of rest.

At his side was a table, a rough little stand,
Home-made you could see at a glance,
For it showed the black trace of the Milkmaid brand,
On the top of the table by chance.

In his hand was a Photo—a sweet winning face,
Framed in clouds of rebellious hair;
As he strained his tired eyesight her features to trace,
Did he sigh the sad sigh of despair?

As he looked down the lines to the officers' huts,
Did home-visions throng, thick and fast,
While the Book of the Present, Forgetfulness shuts,
And Memory opens the Past.

Did he think of the days when at Ascot and Cowes
He was never away from her side?
And with that safe licence which distance allows,
Did he think of her now as his bride?

Not at all! for this trooper at sentiment mocks
(Tho' his duty he never forgets),
But the Photograph? Oh! *that* he found in the box
When he opened his last Cigarettes.

Alexander Wilmot

In the Country of Mankoraan

North of the Vaal River, December 1882

Ah sad are our hearts,
  Our souls full of trouble,
Ruin's harvest has come–
  We are left as the stubble.

The white man is here
  For our fields and our cattle;
No hope is now left us–
  No chance in the battle.

We look on like men
  Who are used to disaster,
And see ruin's night
  Falling faster and faster.

Or like animals struck
  By the swift assegai,
We are sentenced to death,
  We have only to die.

From Limpopo to Vaal
  Has the mandate been given,
'From his veld and his home
  Must the black man be driven'

From the homes of our youth,
  Which our eyes love to scan,
We are forced from the kraals
  Of our chief–Mankoraan.

We starve in the veld
  So blooming and verdant;
The invader is Lord,
  The owner–his servant.

Christianity–lo!
  To your justice we fly;
Protect us at once,
  Or we perish and die.

William Charles Scully

'Nkongane

Old—some eighty, or thereabouts;
    Sly as a badger alert for honey;
Honest perhaps—but I have my doubts—
    With an eye that snaps at the chink of money;
Poor old barbarian, your Christian veneer
    Is thin and cracked, and the core inside
Is heathen and natural. Quaint and queer
    Is your aspect, and yet, withal, dignified.

When your lips unlock to the taste of rum,
    The tongue runs on with its cackle of clicks
That like bubbles break as their consonants come,
    For your speech is a brook full of frisky tricks.
You love to recall the days of old—
    That are sweet to us all, for, the alchemist, Time,
Strangely touches the basest of metals to gold,
    And to-day's jangled peal wakes to-morrow's rich chime.

But not like the past in a moony haze,
    That shines for us sons of old Europe, is yours—
You glow with the ardour of bloodstained days
    And deeds long past—you were one of the doers—
Of spears washed red in the blood of foes,
    Of villages wrapped in red flame, of fields
Where the vultures gorged, of the deadly close
    Of the impi's horns, and the thundering shields.

Strange old man—like a lonely hawk
    In a leafless forest that falls to the axe,
You linger on; and you love to talk,
    Yet your tongue full often a listener lacks;
Truth and fiction, like chaff and grain
    You mix together, and often I try
To sift the one from the other, and gain
    The fact from its shell of garrulous lie.

You were young when Chaka, the scourge of man,
    Swept over the land like the Angel of Death;
You marched in the rear when the veteran van
    Mowed down the armies—reapers of wrath!

You sat on the ground in the crescent and laid
   Your shield down flat when Dingaan spake loud—
His vitals pierced by the murderer's blade—
   To his warriors fierce, in dread anguish bowed.

And now to this: to cringe for a shilling,
   To skulk round the Mission-house, hungry and lone;
To carry food to the women tilling
   The fields of maize! For ever have flown
The days of the spear that the rust has eaten,
   The days of the ploughshare suit you not;
Time hath no gift that your life can sweeten,
   A living death is your piteous lot.

The White Commonwealths

Tomorrow unregarded, clean effaced
The lesson of unhallowed yesterday,
We rail against each other; interlaced
Albeit are our fortunes. So we stray,
Blind to the lurid writing on the wall,
Deaf to the words Fate's warning lips let fall.

A.K. Soga

Santa Cruz: The Holy Cross

The Cross; a symbol of that faith,
  That points to Calvary;
A living token of that Death
  That sets the guilty free.

Long hath it stood, so silently,
  Where Algoa's rock-bound shore
Beats back the waters of the sea
  With angry sullen roar.

It tells of man's belief in God;
  Of Diaz and his band,
Who braved the waters and the flood,
  At Christian King's command.

It speaks of Freedom's flag unfurled,
  For Christianity;
A beacon light, in this dark world,
  To God and liberty.

On Santa Cruz, long may it stand,
  As emblem, may it be
The cheer of Good Hope; in the land
  Peace and prosperity.

Rudyard Kipling

Bridge-Guard in the Karroo

'and will supply details to guard the Blood River Bridge.'
District Orders – Lines of Communication

Sudden the desert changes,
  The raw glare softens and clings,
Till the aching Oudtshoorn ranges
  Stand up like the thrones of kings–

Ramparts of slaughter and peril–
  Blazing, amazing–aglow
'Twixt the sky-line's belting beryl
  And the wine-dark flats below.

Royal the pageant closes,
  Lit by the last of the sun–
Opal and ash-of-roses,
  Cinnamon, umber, and dun.

The twilight swallows the thicket,
  The starlight reveals the ridge;
The whistle shrills to the picket–
  We are changing guard on the bridge.

(Few, forgotten and lonely,
  Where the empty metals shine–
No, not combatants–only
  Details guarding the line.)

We slip through the broken panel
  Of fence by the ganger's shed;
We drop to the waterless channel
  And the lean track overhead;

We stumble on refuse of rations,
  The beef and the biscuit-tins:
We take our appointed stations,
  And the endless night begins.

We hear the Hottentot herders
  As the sheep click past to the fold–
And the click of the restless girders
  As the steel contracts in the cold–

Voices of jackals calling
    And, loud in the hush between,
A morsel of dry earth falling
    From the flanks of the scarred ravine.

And the solemn firmament marches,
    And the hosts of heaven rise
Framed through the iron arches—
    Banded and barred by the ties,

Till we feel the far track humming,
    And we see her headlight plain,
And we gather and wait her coming—
    The wonderful north-bound train.

(Few, forgotten and lonely,
    Where the white car-windows shine—
No, not combatants—only
    Details guarding the line.)

Quick, ere the gift escape us!
    Out of the darkness we reach
For a handful of week-old papers
    And a mouthful of human speech.

And the monstrous heaven rejoices,
    And the earth allows again,
Meetings, greetings, and voices
    Of women talking with men.

So we return to our places,
    As out on the bridge she rolls;
And the darkness covers our faces,
    And the darkness re-enters our souls.

More than a little lonely
    Where the lessening tail-lights shine,
No—not combatants—only
    Details guarding the line!

Recessional (1897)

God of our fathers, known of old,
    Lord of our far-flung battle-line,
Beneath whose awful Hand we hold
    Dominion over palm and pine—
Lord God of Hosts, be with us yet,
Lest we forget—lest we forget!

The tumult and the shouting dies;
    The captains and the kings depart:
Still stands Thine ancient sacrifice,
    An humble and a contrite heart.
Lord God of Hosts, be with us yet,
Lest we forget—lest we forget!

Far-called, our navies melt away;
    On dune and headland sinks the fire:
Lo, all our pomp of yesterday
    Is one with Nineveh and Tyre!
Judge of the Nations, spare us yet,
Lest we forget—lest we forget!

If, drunk with sight of power, we loose
    Wild tongues that have not Thee in awe,
Such boastings as the Gentiles use,
    Or lesser breeds without the Law—
Lord God of Hosts, be with us yet,
Lest we forget—lest we forget!

For heathen heart that puts her trust
    In reeking tube and iron shard,
All valiant dust that builds on dust,
    And guarding, calls not Thee to guard,
For frantic boast and foolish word—
Thy Mercy on Thy People, Lord!

Amen

F.W. Reitz

Gods of the Jingo

A 'progressional' dedicated to 'Mudyard Pipling'.

Gods of the Jingo—Brass and Gold,
  Lords of the world by 'right divine'
Beneath whose baneful sway they hold
  The motto 'All that's thine is Mine',
Such Lords as these have made men rotten
  They have forgotten—they *have* forgotten.

The nigger, as is fitting, dies
  The Gladstones and the Pitts depart
But 'Bigger Englanders' arise
  To teach the world the Raiders' art
Such Lords as these have made men rotten
  They have forgotten—they *have* forgotten.

They've got the gold, the ships, the men,
  And are the masters of tomorrow—
And so mankind shall see again
  The days of Sodom and Gomorrah,
These are their Lords, and they are rotten
  They have forgotten—the *have* forgotten.

Drunken with lust of power and pelf
  They hold nor man nor God in awe
And care for nought but only Self
  And cent-per-cent's their only law
These are their Lords, and they are rotten
  They have forgotten—they *have* forgotten.

Their braggart hearts have put their trust
  In Maxim guns and Metford rifles
They'd crush their foes into the dust
  And treat what's Right as idle trifles.
For boastful brag and foolish 'fake'
  Th' 'Imperialist' must take the cake!

Amen?

Arthur Maquarie

Sniped

Last night I heard a sob
    Beside me as I lay;
I turned and fell asleep,
    I woke and it was day.

The bugle called to arms,
    We rushed and worked the gun,
Ten hours we fought unscathed,
    But we were lacking one.

At night we bathed our heads
    And laid us down to rest;
The one we lacked was there
    With blood upon his breast.

A little patch of black
    With pink around the rim—
We cursed our sniping foes
    And dug a grave for him.

G. Murray Johnstone (Mome)

Christmas, 1899

Something 'uddled 'gainst the sky
    Some poor devil dead,
And our squadron riding by
    Cursed his gaping 'ead—
Just a man and nothing more,
    Smudged across with red.

Wondered what they thought at 'ome,
    Wondered what they'd say—
'Absent friends and those that roam
    An' where is Jack today?'
Wondered if they'd drink his 'ealth,
    Wondered would they pray?

Something 'uddled 'gainst the sun.
    What's the odds or why?
Some poor devil's work is done—
    Might be you or I—
We wondered if it 'urt him much
    When 'e come to die.

G. W. M. Wore

A Tale of the Worcestershire Regiment
South Africa, 1900

I chanced to meet out Kroonstad way, a week or two ago,
A batch of veldt-stained khaki lads, soldiers from head to toe
And having ruffed it a bit myself, I could tell by the looks of these
They'd passed the time of the day with the Boer,
They'd been in the battle's breeze.
For I've seen them as came out of Kimberley
Whose stomachs had asked for food,
Who for weary weeks midst shot and shell
At death's open door had stood.
I saw Kelly Kenney's division, after four or five weeks of hell,
So when I see fighting soldiers, I reckon I'm able to tell.
And I knew that these lads I talked with
Were some who had chanced their skin,
And for many long nights in harness had slept,
And oft had little within.
I couldn't tell what they belonged to, badges and numbers gone,
For you haven't a thought for ornaments
When life counts no more than a song.
But I very soon learned 'twas the Worcesters, the famous old 36th,
And 'firm' as of old their motto is, in the 12th Brigade they are fixed.
And I'm sure in the County of Worcester,
Back in the dear old home,
The people have read with pride in their hearts
Of the work these lads have done.
From Wolverhampton and Dudley, Kidderminster, Stourbridge and Brum,
Across 7 000 miles of land and sea, these lads have willingly come.
Helping to drive the cunning Boer, out of the Orange Free State
Each of them doing his country's work, helping to wipe the slate.
And they told me it was back around Arundel way
Compliments first were paid, for the Boers dropped shells right into the camp;
Just as the dinner was laid.
'Twas only an ordinary dinner, with the usual allowance of sand,
'Of course,' said my friend of the Worcesters, 'we took it away in our hand.'
And quickly set about moving, as soon as the music begun,
For when you're only in Big Gun range, your magazine's not in the fun.
And it's better to keep ammunition, till your visitors get a bit close,
So we cleared away then,
But we've peppered them since, with many a leaden dose.
And now for months, long weary months, we've followed them up and down,
Foot after horse, and failing like the elephant after the clown,

If they're fighting men, as some people say, why don't they stand their ground
Let's have a chance to see them,
Let us be equal all round.
But they prefer to lead us a dance, these 'braves' you hear people call.
Oh, where the blazes does bravery come in, when they fight inside of a wall?
Put 'em out in the open, stick 'em up twenty to one
If we don't wipe them out in less than an hour,
I'd swallow my blooming gun.
But they haven't got that on their programme, they go in a different style,
And drop in a shot occasionally, perhaps once in twenty mile.
And when you have to foot it, and keep up to them that's on horse,
It makes you say Hallelujah, or other things perhaps that are worse.
But that's what we've been doing
Since we started from Bloemfontein.
And I guess you could fill a tidy book with the blooming sights we have seen,
Over hundred of miles of dreary veldt,
Over kopjes and in betwixt,
We've marched and marched, and now
We're called the Marching 36th.
Our shirts are getting ticklish,
And we kill 'em in ones and twos.
They ought to send in new ones, and we are sadly in want of shoes.
The trousers are turned to knickers
For the part that hung round the feet.
Why we had to commandeer it, 'twas wanted up round the seat.
Tommy's addicted to grumble, when things go a bit on the twist
If he hadn't something to grumble about, I believe he'd cease to exist.
Night and day you can march him, and he'll damn at every pace,
But pass a joke to his comrades, you'll see there's a smile on his face.
There's another Battalion of Worcesters,
Ficksburg and Ladybrand way, holding the hills round Thaba-Nchu,
Keeping the Boers at bay.
And here as I write of the old 29th, news comes into my hand
That shall live in the annals of history, the holding of Ladybrand.
Bravo 'Old Worcesters,' you've shown the world
How British Tommies can fight.
Though 1 500 surrounded you, you 150 sat tight;
All honour to you for you've paid 'em back
In a little bit of their own.
The advantage of boulders and kopjes, as 'Allies' you well have shown
Let the grumblers cease to grumble, let the public orators think,
Of the difficulties Tommy's mastered
While he's sat at home with his drink.
You've got a tale to tell them, those heroes who value their skin,
Tell 'em the tale of Ladybrand, where the motto was never give in.
Tell 'em of outposts, frosty nights and a biscuit or two in the day,

Tell 'em you did it to wipe a slate, and then we'll see what they say.
And so my Worcester comrades, I'll bring my song to a close,
Wishing this minute that each of you, had a pot beneath your nose,
But I bid you be of good heart lads
There are better days in store,
And loving hearts awaiting you back
On Fair Brittania's shore.
Send these lines to mother or wife, and then in the years to come,
You can look at them through your glasses
As you sit by the fire at home.
'Twill remind you of where you've been to
And what you have done and seen,
And you'll think with pride of what you've done
For country, home and Queen.

M. Grover

I Killed a Man at Graspan

(The Tale of a Returned Australian Contingenter done into verse)

I killed a man at Graspan,
  I killed him fair in a fight;
And the Empire's poets and the Empire's priests
  Swear blind I acted right.
The Empire's poets and Empire's priests
  Make out my deed was fine,
But they can't stop the eyes of the man I killed
  From starin' into mine.

I killed a man at Graspan,
  Maybe I killed a score;
But this one wasn't a chance-shot home,
  From a thousand yards or more.
I fired at him when he'd got no show;
  We were only a pace apart,
With the cordite scorchin' his old worn coat
  As the bullet drilled his heart.

I killed a man at Graspan,
  I killed him fightin' fair;
We came on each other face to face,
  An' we went at it then and there.
Mine was the trigger that shifted first,
  His was the life that sped.
An' a man I'd never a quarrel with
  Was spread on the boulders dead.

I killed a man at Graspan;
  I watched him squirmin' till
He raised his eyes, an' they met with mine;
  An' there they're starin' still.
Cut of my brother Tom, he looked,
  Hardly more'n a kid;
An', Christ! he was stiffenin' at my feet
  Because of the thing I did.

I killed a man at Graspan;
  I told the camp that night;
An' of all the lies that ever I told
  That was the poorest skite.

I swore I was proud of my hand-to-hand,
An' the Boer I'd chanced to pot,
An' all the time I'd ha' gave my eyes
To never ha' fired that shot.

I killed a man at Graspan;
An hour ago about,
For there he lies with his starin' eyes,
An' his blood still tricklin' out.
I know it was either him or me,
I know that I killed him fair,
But, all the same, wherever I look,
The man that I killed is there.

I killed a man at Graspan;
My first and, God! my last;
Harder to dodge than my bullet is
The look that his dead eyes cast.
If the Empire asks for me later on
It'll ask for me in vain,
Before I reach to my bandolier
To fire on a man again.

Olive Schreiner

The Cry of South Africa

Give back my dead!
They who by kop and fountain
First saw the light upon my rocky breast!
Give back my dead,
The sons who played upon me
When childhood's dews still rested on their heads.
Give back my dead
Whom thou hast riven from me
By arms of men loud called from earth's farthest bound
To wet my bosom with my children's blood!
Give back my dead,
The dead who grew up on me!

Wagenaar's Kraal,
Three Sisters.
May 9, 1900.

Arthur Shearly Cripps

Resurgat

For C.J. Rhodes

God be with you in your need!
When God's mills have ground you through–
All the coarse cruel chaff of you–
Be there left one grain to sow,
Which in season may unfold
Your visionary might of old!

Vine-dresser of the world-to-be,
Leave not one branch, yet leave the tree
Its life abounding, leave it free
Like some fecund vine to sprawl
On the widths of Sion's wall
In penitence imperial!

From: The Black Christ's Crusade

At Easter in South Africa

Pilate and Caïaphas
They have brought this thing to pass–
That a Christ the Father gave,
Should be guest within a grave.

Church and State have willed to last
This tyranny not over-past;
His dark southern Brows around
They a wreath of briars have bound;
In His dark despisèd Hands
Writ in sores their writing stands.

By strait starlit ways I creep,
Caring while the careless sleep,
Bearing balms, and flow'rs to crown
That poor Head the stone holds down:
Through some crack or crevice dim
I would reach my sweets to Him.

Easter suns they rise and set,
But that stone is steadfast yet:
Past my lifting 'tis, but I
When 'tis lifted would be nigh.

I believe, whate'er they say,
The sun shall dance one Easter Day,
And I, that through thick twilight grope
With balms of faith and flow'rs of hope,
Shall lift mine eyes, and see the stone
Stir and shake, if not be gone.

To me—as one born out of his due time—
To me—as one not meet to reckon in—
To me (of all injurious aliens chief)
Christ hath reveal'd Himself—not as to Paul
Enthroned and crown'd, but marr'd, despised, rejected—
The Divine Outcast of a terrible land,
A Black Christ with parch'd Lips and empty Hand.

Come, watch Christ—black against the daybreak's glow—
Tilling His rain-blest land with rhythmic hoe—
A bread-winner, who Bread-of-Life confers
On His few friends and fewer worshippers.

If aught of worth be in my psalms,
It in the Black Christ's Hands I lay.
In those Nail-groov'd, hoe-harden'd Palms
He holds to me now ev'ry day—
The Black Christ, in Whose Name I pray,
Yet Who (oh, wonder!) prays to me
In wrong and need and contumely.

If any gift-of-sight of mine
Our land's veil'd beauty should reveal,
My reader, to those eyes of thine,
That gift to Him Who gave assign!

To Him (Whose Feet unsandall'd steal
Over the granite tracks I tread)
Head-haloed by our rose and gray
Of twilights, or our gold of day;
Who, near my red camp-fire, will spread

His reed-mat, or on rain-bless'd days
Hoe deep His pattern-work of praise
Full in my sight!

O happy eyes
Are mine that pierce the black disguise,
And see our Lord! O woe of woe
That I should see, that I should know
Whom 'tis they use—that use Him so!

Cullen Gouldsbury

By the Roadside

Tattered, and torn, and rent, with ragged roof
And poles awry,
The hut stood silent, sombre and aloof
As I rode by.

Red cacti, too, twined out in fleshy bands
About the place,
That might, I thought, have scarred with groping hands
The dead man's face.

Through all the silence, there was ne'er a sound
of human life–
But rank, green grasses rioted around
And weeds were rife.

Only–I knew that one had built the place
With hopes afire,
Spurred by the memory of an absent face
and young desire.

And thought to wrest a living from the wild,
And, fancy free,
To call a woman–almost, then, a child,
Across the sea.

But those dim ghosts that suck the souls of men
Had drained him dry–
Had stretched his brain to snapping-point–and then
Had let him lie.

Silent and still. And yet, the hut stood there
In grim disdain
Of broken lives, and premature despair,
And useless pain.

So, in a senseless fury at the thought,
I set alight
The ragged thatch, and watched it,
as 'twas caught.

Red tongues of fire flickered overhead,
And forked, and shone–
'A funeral pile,' I muttered, 'for the dead,'
As I rode on.

Kingsley Fairbridge

Magwere, who Waits Wondering

I

Among the smooth hills of Manika,
Near the edge of the big swamp where cane rats live,
Grew Magwere the mealie.

The crows who nest on the Peak,
And the striped field-mice from underground,
And the tin-nosed shrew that dies on footpaths,
Had miss'd Magwere when she was sown.

Therefore the mealie grew
In the moist earth on the swamp edge
With many of her sisters;

And threw up gay leaves, yellow-green,
That glitter'd brightly in the sunshine,
And always laugh'd when the wind blew,
And lisp'd, day long, in the ears of her sisters.

And Madongwe, the red locusts,
Found not the green leaves of Magwere,
Who flourish'd on the swamp edge.

Kwagudu, the old wife, with her hoe
That was worn blunt-nosed with use,
Weeded all day the fields of her husband,
And hoed the weeds from the roots of Magwere.

And Wanaka, the young mother,
Left her baby in the shade of Magwere,
While she pick'd mowa for the pot.

And the fat baby laugh'd greatly
At the green leaves that waved so,—
So gaily in the cool wind
That set all the mealies a-rustling.

II

But Dzua the Sun, who lives beyond the sky line,
Laugh'd in the sky, and sent words by the wind,
And the Wind whisper'd in the ear of Magwere.

'O Magwere,' the Wind said, 'thus says the Sun:—
''Ha, ha, Magwere, by the swamp edge!
Smile now, Magwere, while you can,
For the time of harvest is very close.

''Then will your flowers die, Magwere,
Your brown leaves sing only of death,
And your shiny beard will wither and turn brown.

''Madzua Nipi, or some other maiden,
Hot and hard-handed, from the kraal,
Will pluck you from your stalk, and tear your sheath
That hides the softness of your golden grain.

''What will Madzua Nipi do with you?
Roast you upon the coals, and shred your grains
Into her hand, and throw them in her mouth!

''Or will Marumi come, the husbandman,
Saying, 'This cob is good,'—and put you by
To sleep awhile and wake again in Spring,
To blossom gloriously an hundred-fold?" '

III

Magwere answer'd nothing, standing still
And very rigid in the mocking sun;
And knew not any answer for the wind.

And very dry her leaves grew in the sun,
And very brown her stalk, her sheath, and beard;
And all her joy drew back into her heart
That swell'd so sorrowful beneath its sheath.

Burial

Among the Manyika, a dead infant is buried
by its mother without a ceremony

Yowe, yowe, mwanango duku!
I bury you here by the edge of the lands.

Under the scrub and the weeds I bury you,
Here in the clay where the bracken grows.

Here on the hill the wind blows cold,
And the creepers are wet with the driving mist,

The grain-huts stand like ghosts in the mist,
And the water drips from their sodden thatch.

And the rain-drops drip in the forest yonder
When the hill-wind shakes the heavy boughs.

Alas! I am old, and you are the last—
Mwanango, the last of me, here on the hillside.

The dust where you play'd by the edge of the kraal
Is sodden with rain, and is trodden to mud.

The hoe that I use to fashion your dwelling
Is caked with the earth that is taking you from me.

Where now is Dzua who ripes the rukweza?
And where now are you, O mwanango kaduku?

Alas! Alas! My little child!
I bury you here by the edge of the lands.

Perceval Gibbon

Jim

An Incident

From the Kei to Umzimkulu
    We chartered to ride,
But before we reached Umtata
    Jim turned in and died.
By Bashee I buried Jim.
Ah! but I was fond of him;
An' but for the niggers grinning,
    I'd–yes, I'd have cried.

'Twas a weary trek through Griqualand,
    And me all alone;
Three teams and a dozen niggers
    To boss on my own.
And I felt a need for Jim;
It was just the job for him,
Hazin' the teams and the niggers,
    Hard grit to the bone.

I lost a load at Kokstad:
    An axle fell through;
I hadn't heart to tinker it,
    So pushed on with two.
If I'd only had old Jim!
Axles never broke with him;
But I never could handle wagons
    Like Jim used to do.

I came to Umzimkulu
    With a pain in my head;
I ought to ha' bought med'cine,
    But I liquored instead:
Never used to drink with Jim;
There's a girl that asked for him;
But the jackals root at Bashee–
    An' Jim, he's dead!

Thomas Craig

The New Woman

On the Threshold flaunting, brazen,
   See the Coming Woman stands;
Bold her mien, absurd her garments,
   Harsh her speech and strong her hands.

Loud She prates at public meeting,
   Solid plants her massive foot;
Shrieks her message: 'Man, the tyrant,
   Of all evil is the root!'

Howls for equal rights for woman–
   Right to don divided skirt;
Right to swear, to smoke, to gamble–
   Right to drink, to woo, to flirt.

Dread Emancipated Female–
   Wants to make man share the 'Curse';
Wants to see him rock the cradle,
   Wants to wreck the Universe!

Wants man's vote, his pants, his latchkey,
   Wants *this* passed and *that* repealed–
Wants all sick'ning social festers
   To her morbid gaze revealed!

She-crusader, with a 'mission,'
   Let *her* motto be unfurled:
'Woman's will must sway the senates–
   Unsexed neuters boss the world.'

Ian Colvin

Elegy on a City Churchyard

On the second reading of Colonel Crewe's Bill to deal with the disused cemeteries in Somerset Road.

Dusty, neglected quarter of the dead!
Upon whose half-obliterated stones
From year to year no mourning tear is shed,
Whose monuments are crumbling with their bones,
And death himself has fled
To find new habitations more remote,
Thine end is near, for even graveyards die,
And mine, the only tributary sigh,
Poor unregretted victim of a vote!

Memento mori to the city clerk
In his diurnal journeys on the car;
The trysting-place of tabbies after dark,
Scene of fierce love and unmelodious war;
The temporary ark
Of some poor tattered Romeo down at heel,
Who shelters in thy 'detestable maw'
From the more real terrors of the law
And colder welcomes of the ne'er-do-weel.

And in the spring, when the geranium throws
A flush of scarlet on the dismal scene,
In white and gold the arum lily glows,
The dingy cyprus takes a livelier green,
The yellow cactus blows,
Then young invaders clamber from the street
To snatch the fragrant harvests of the grave,
Till, spite of best endeavours to be brave,
They scatter in precipitate retreat.

But, save for these rash visitants, thy ways
Are all untrodden, and the sculptured fane
Flaunts to the desert air its empty praise,
And all thy flattering epitaphs are vain,
No need for weather stain
To blot inscriptions that are never read!
None cares to know who lies beneath the stone,
Whether it be a Darby or a Joan,
Or whether Brown or Robinson be dead.

Yet these unmarked *Hic Jacets* are the sign
    That some once breathing pinch of valiant clay,
With thoughts and feelings just like yours or mine,
    Hoped, loved and hated in his little day,
        Danced, courted, and drank wine,
Played cards, backed horses, even as you or I,
    Engaged in every whirling chance of life,
    Schemed to win wealth or pleasure or a wife—
Poor devil! never dreaming he would die!

Commingled in this mortal dust-heap lies
    Another Cape Town, huddled layer on layer,
Inextricably mixed—the fools, the wise,
    The rich, the poor, the beggar and the Mayor,
        Grey hairs and beauty's eyes!
Whate'er they were they came to the same end,
    And we must follow in a little while
    Like answered letters stuck upon a file
And docketed by some officious friend!

Douglas Blackburn

The Converted Missionary

From the land of the White, to the Kraal of the Black,
Came Bigsby the Missionman, hot on the track
Of the Heathen in darkness all sitting.
All sitting at ease, free from care or disease,
With no want that their heathendom could not appease,
And a pitying wonder that White men should please
To consider hard labour more fitting.

Bigsby prospected round, and with horror soon found
That of progress barely the ghost of a sound
These regions of rest had invaded.
That for ages untold, ere the rivers were old
These Kaffirs had done without trousers or gold,
Had never of Sectarian squabbles been told,
But in scriptural ignorance waded.

So in Zulu as taught by the Mission School sort,
Bigsby clicked off a discourse the natives all thought
Would be vastly more clear if translated.
So they called up 'Slim Jack,' a Christianised Black,
Who had Civilisation's cat marks on his back
(Having strayed into Progress's dangerous track),
And optics and nose rum inflated.

'Well, Brother,' said Jack, smacking Biggs on the back
With a fervent familiar and rib-racking whack,
'Is it Whisky or Gospel your craze is?
If it's either, your samples you'd better not show,
For these heathen have very good reason to know
How these blessings of civilisation can blow
A Kraal of black saints into Blazes.

'I'm a pretty fair sample of what is produced
Through having by Exeter Hall been induced
To go back on the training of Mother.
Can read, write, and cypher, drink whisky, and fight,
In fact I've absorbed all the vice of the White,
But am neither fish, flesh, nor the other.
I'm sneered at by all, both in town and in Kraal,
I have not a creature I brother can call,
For to all I'm the rankest outsider.

'Now no sensible Kaffir prefers to remain
Perpetually out in the cold and the rain
Without rum or friendship to cheer him.
I've striven my best to bring into our fold
My chief who in Heathenish darkness grows old,
But of Civilisation's dark side he's been told,
And refuses to have Christians near him.

'So I want you to show the old sinner 'twere best
For his present and future salvation and rest,
To lay hold of some Christian connection.
You must lay it on thick, and at no trifle stick,
For the good of the cause justifies any trick
That will prompt him religion of some sort to pick,
And from some of the brands make selection.

'Then I want you to show, tho' a Christian and White,
You are perfectly able to act square and right,
And not here after loot or concessions.
You must stay here a week and no word ever speak
That would cause a suspicion you're anxious to speak
(While pretending it's only for lost souls you seek)
Our cattle and other possessions.

'If this trial you stand you then try your hand
At persuading my chief that your own happy land
Is fuller of bliss than all others.
You will let out the cat if you pass round the hat,
Or hint that collections make mission men fat.
And the wily old rascal will soon smell a rat,
If you call us your dear beloved brothers.'

Bigsby's Mission zeal rose, as he took off his clothes,
And defying outrages on sight, ears, and nose
Went pluckily through his probation.
Though at times he repined for good things left behind
And sometimes regretted his tastes were refined,
He was free to confess it was easy to find
A worse place than a Kaffir location.

At the end of the week, though less well groomed and sleek,
Bigsby felt he had well earned the title to speak
On the blessings of Civilisation.
While the Kaffirs confessed they were deeply impressed
By the way in which Bigsby had stood the hard test
And redeemed the bad name of his nation.

Since the ages had flown such a case was unknown
Of a White being left to prowl round all alone,
Never stealing or begging the worth of a bone,
Or seeking a personal favour.
So they came one and all to the Chief's royal Kraal
And called on Slim Jackie to kick off the ball,
By Investing Big.'s Mission–taught Zulu with all
That was needed to give it true flavour.

'Now before I let go,' whispered Jack, 'you must know
If my words you confirm with emphatic ''ye bo,''
It will help the old Chief to believe us.
But if you should fail to back up my tall tale
The game will be up and the risks you entail–
If you guessed them I'm certain you'd turn sick and pale
And become very anxious to leave us.'

Then Jackie began, and he spoke as a man
From whose mouth words of eloquence trickled and ran
That would credit a mob agitator,
For in mission school he had shown promise to be
Fair sample of goods to be sent over sea
To encourage subscribers, who in him would see
A real mission-field crop Irrigator.

'From the land where the sun goes to sleep every night,
This white man has come to give some of its light'–
Jack began–and young Bigsby said 'Ye bo.'
''Tis a land where the Christian gets all that is best
Because he's a Christian, of all men most blest.'
And dubiously Bigsby said 'Ye bo.'

'No sorrow is there and no care, and no work,
And nothing a rest-loving Kaffir would shirk;
For the hardest work's eating one's dinner.
All are happy and gay, with no hut tax to pay,
And this Mission man tells me he's happy to say
He's converted the very last sinner.
So he's nothing to do but come preaching to you
To give you a chance of accepting a few
Of the blessings of which he's so many;
Which have filled his own land, being plenty as sand
And made of his people one vast happy band,
And the price is to you not one penny.'

'Steady O! Do go slow!' yelled poor Bigsby 'No, no,
I cannot to that in my heart say "ye bo,"
For you've quite overlooked the collection.'
'Then if that be so you have capsized the show,'
Said Slim Jack, 'And the sooner you pack up and go,
The longer these niggers will be ere they know
Mission yarns won't stand serious reflection.'

Calm and slow spoke the Chief, much to Bigsby's relief,
Saying, 'Whiteman, I'm satisfied you are no thief,
But your cheek, baas, is truly tremendous.
You'd have us suppose that all happily goes
In the land that you come from, when everyone knows
That half of your own folk are needing the clothes
You wheedle old ladies to send us;–
That thousands of white folks are crushed down with woe,
That many are starving, and few of them know
A tithe of the comforts we heathen can show,
But live upon hope for the morrow.

'Go back to your people and teach them to live,
Help your own poor and needy, get rich men to give
Of their plenty to those who would borrow.
Get your priests to agree in what creed they believe
And so give us a reason why we should receive
Those dubious blessings your own people leave
And by taking them add to our sorrow.'

Bigsby felt the impact of the logic of fact–
An experience which those who had sent him all lacked–
And for once in his life saw truth clearly.
So he planned to go back, state the case of the Black,
Tell the good folks at Home that the Heathen's no lack
Of the comforts men value most dearly.
So to Exeter Hall he went straight from the Kraal
And with 'Truth about Missions' astonished them all,
Showing Jack as a shocking example.

Then a Bishop arose in his wrath to propose
That Bigsby be put in the Black List with those
Who of Wolves in Sheep's clothes are a sample.
Both Bigsby and Jack were given the sack,
And having no money to carry him back,
Jack toured as 'The Wild Man from Gogo.'
While Bigsby returned to the calling he spurned
When Mission field nonsense his callow head turned.
And is selling tea, coffee, and cocoa.

John Runcie

The Bells of Allah

Once in a beautiful valley,
  When the high noon drowsed in its heat,
I heard the Bells of Allah
  Ring out so clear, so sweet—
Silver Heath of Riversdale,
  Caledon Bells of blue,
And the triple bell of the Frieiza
  Rang out as I passed through.

'Hark!' cried the Painted Ladies,
  'The bells are calling to prayer';
'Come,' said the Moederkapjes,
  And they looked so quaint and fair,
And a beautiful sea-blue Disa
  Hung like a fairy star:
And fairy-like Periwinkles
  Were twinkling near and far.

Clang went the big Proteas
  As they swung on the hot noon's haze;
And my soul, with the pious people,
  Followed the prayer and praise
Till the trump of the Arum Lily
  Quivered and hung in the air,
While the eyes of the Zevenjaartjes
  Were full of the sun's white glare.

But then came the cool sun-under,
  And the hush of the ebbing-day,
And again rung the Bells of Allah,
  And again went the folks to pray;
But the folks were the stars of Heaven,
  And they did not call to me,
Like the little Moederkapjes
  That brushed against my knee;
Like the friendly Painted Ladies
  That nodded a bright 'Good-day,'
When I heard the Bells of Allah.
  And went with the folks to pray.

Three Phases

I saw three Crosses on a hill,
  Three bodies hung thereon.
And on the Midmost crucified,
  A beam of Heaven shone.

I saw three Crosses in the dusk,
  Where bones hung dry and white,
A vulture sat on the Midmost Cross,
  And screamed against the night.

I do not see these Crosses now,
  Mine eyes are strained in vain,
But that vulture's claws are on my heart
  And his beak is in my brain.

Denys Lefebvre (Syned)

A Reminiscence

The sun shone brightly
Showing the pale rose silken hangings,
Fine napery and glistening silver,
A smoking urn.

The woman poured a cup
And waited,
Smiling across the table:
'Last night, I passed her
Beneath a street lamp;
Waiting for love,
As I did once . . .
Like some men, she thinks more of money.'
(His paper rustled).

'You used to go for rides together—
You may remember?
A blue-eyed girl, with long shy lashes;
Hair, as if God had breathed upon it,
So soft and fragrant,
Or so you told her;
And rosy cheeks—
Last night her skin looked drawn and sallow;
And lurking, half concealed by powder,
I saw a wrinkle.

'You married me,
You may remember?'
(Her voice laughed smoothly)
'Not for my wrinkles.
How fortunate when love is wealthy!'
Her tone purred at him:
'Pâté-de-foie, dear,
Or eggs and bacon?'

Charles Ould

London, August

I am tired of London,
Foul city that sneers at the poor,
And all this life.
If I look at the ground,
The streets are up;
If I look at the people,
Their faces offend me;
If I look at the shops,
I perceive that their wares
Are reserved for the upper classes;
If I look at the sky,
I see written upon it
'Daily Mail.'
In such a town
It is good to remember
This is not all,
And to call to mind
A vacant, desolate, wind-swept place
Where the jackals cry to the moon.

Red

Hibiscus was red,
(It grew by the window),
And salvia,
Poinsettia,
The spikes of aloes,
And the Kaffirboom
In flaring splendour.
Here there are flowers,
Frail lives of loveliest name,
Daffodils, primroses, daisies,
Fritillaries, buttercups,
But nowhere in England
That pagan colour,
Nowhere that red
That flamed at the window.

Alice Mabel Alder

The Street of Peacocks

Down the blue chasm of the street,
Where the tall sightless houses stood
With walls of ice,.in solitude—
Its blue-green shadows, cold and sweet—
The vision of the peacocks came,
A murmuring river: in God's name
Some old lost bells remembered time:
And to the dreaming of that chime,
The stream of peacocks stepping slow,
Shadowed with gleaming blues and greens,
Clucking and rustling like a river,
And coroneted like old queens,
Flowed onward down the street for ever.

Far up the shadows of the street,
Between a rift of timbered walls,
A tender light of earthly sun
Bestowed a golden shaft of gleam,
And birds of snow, with unheard calls,
Passed on the ray, and, one by one,
Departed from the street of dream.

Then in the shadows of the street
A shadow rose and spoke to me—
Hands to my hands, with no words said,
Palms on my palms spoke silently
Among the houses of the dead,
Where, moving, rustling like a river,
The blue-green peacocks streamed for ever.

Francis Ernley Walrond

Eve

The grey of the morning
Creeps in the room like fear.
It is growing lighter,
But I sit crouched and shivering.

I dare not look at the bed,
Lest I laugh—
Or curse God.

How does it happen?
Yesterday my wife,
And now—a strange thing—
Anything—nothing.
A body without breath,
Arms without warmth,
Lips without kisses.

'Eve' was her name,
And the strangest part is
That I want to call—'Eve,
Come and look at this thing
That lies on your bed
And looks so like you.'

Cosmos

Bright flowers, of varied tender-tinted hues,
Red, white, and purple-pink,
And lightly poised upon your stems of green,
Like flame upon a candle.
Who would have thought the stern and sombre veld
Could nourish things so delicately fair?
It is as though a man morose and sad,
Whose thoughts are twilight-tinged and grey,
Should suddenly uplift a tuneful voice
And troll a love-song.

For, as some painter with a dream of heaven
May fill his background in with cherubs' heads,
Faces of lovely children

With dimpled smiles that only childhood knows,
So Nature, ever seeking new effects,
And tiring of old sameness, here
Has taken children's faces,
And breathing changed them into flowers,
And strewn them laughing o'er the barren veld.
You men of bounded lives,
Whose music is the clicking of the keys,
And all your colour painted scrip,
Leave these in God's name, who made Nature fair,
And for an hour at least,
Gazing upon this loveliness, forget
The buying and the selling of the world.
Come forth and view
These regiments of firm-encampèd flowers,
These dancing faces in their sea of green,
And ye shall know,
Unless your hearts be wholly dried
And squeezed of power to love the lovelier things,
A sweeter joy than any walls enclose.

F.C. Kolbe

The Sparrows of Little Jesus

They say, but no one need believe,
That little Jesus at his play
With other boys, one summer eve,
  Made sparrows out of clay.

They laid their sparrows side by side.
'Our birds,' the other laddies cried,
'Are just as good as yours, and we
Can do all things as well as you.'
Then Jesus clapped his hands in glee,
And lo! his sparrows flew away.
The bragging boys were left with clay:
  His sparrows flew.

Thus read the story, whoso will:
Thus let us read it, you and I.
The Child Divine has playgrounds still,
He and the world, with thoughts for toys.
They fashion fancies from our clay,
And side by side those fancies lie
And fill our hearts with rival joys.
'All pretty,' says the world, 'but mine
Are just as good and true as thine.'
Again he claps his hands in play,
And lo! his thoughts ascend the sky.
The world's ideas still are clay:
  His sparrows fly.

Harold Fehrsen Sampson

Murder in a Hut ('Nocemfu')

'Let us sew the breast-cloth of Nocemfu,
the marriage garment of our sister,'
the first wife said.
(A last flame struggled on the coals
tossing the shadows about the thatch-poles overhead.)
'Both cannot sew, for one would be idle,'
the other wife said.

The breast-cloth of Nocemfu!
Both cannot sew, for one is dead
with ragged stabs, and the other fled
into the night through empty lands
with trembling hands.

The troubled flame has wavered out
like the flame of life at the flash of a knife,
and no ravelled threads of hate and doubt
will perplex the breast of Nocemfu.

To 'Miracle', a Cat

Come, careful cat, come lingeringly,
Coying all chairlegs on the way.
So, wanton, so; be not afraid of me.
I am the patron of all honest cats.
Miracle, my beloved, my smooth one,
Relax this hard timidity,
You will not suddenly be suspent
Tailwise by me, who am the patron
Of proud and unsophisticated cats,
Of secret and leisurely ones.
Do I not give your fondled throat
Most stretchful drugging pleasure?

Francis Carey Slater

Lament for a Dead Cow

Chant by Xhosa family on the death of Wetu, their only cow

*Siyalila, siyalila, inkomo yetu ifile!**
Beautiful was Wetu as a blue shadow
That nests on the grey rocks
About a sunbaked hilltop:
Her coat was black and shiny
Like an isipingo-berry;
Her horns were as sharp as the horns of the new moon
That tosses aloft the evening star;
Her round eyes were as clear and soft
As a mountain-pool,
Where shadows dive from the high rocks.
No more will Wetu banish teasing flies
With her whistling tail;
No more will she face yapping curs
With lowered horns and bewildered eyes;
No more will her slow shadow
Comfort the sunburnt veld, and her sweet lowing
Delight the hills in the evening.
The fountain that filled our calabashes
Has been drained by a thirsty sun;
The black cloud that brought us white rain
Has vanished—the sky is empty;
Our kraal is desolate;
Our calabashes are dry:
And we weep.

*We weep, we weep, our cow is dead!

Captive

✓

Lament of sick Xhosa mine-labourer in a compound hospital

As a wild bird caught in a slip-knot snare—
The plaited tail-hairs of a dun-coloured cow,
Almost invisible—
So, tethered in the toils of fever, do I lie
And burn and shiver while I listen to the buzzing

Of flies that flutter vainly
Against cold, hard, deceiving window-panes:
Like them would I escape, and escaping hasten
To my home that shines in a valley afar,
My home—brightest tooth in the jaws of distance.

There, now, the cows I love are feeding
In some quiet sun-washed vale;
Their lazy shadows drink the sunlight
Rippling on the grasses;
There, through the long day, girls and women
Among the mealies chant and hoe,
Their swinging hoes are like the glitter
Of sunshine on water;
There, now, shouting, happy herdboys,
While they watch the cattle browse,
Are busy moulding mimic cattle
From clay moist and yellow.

There, when the sun has folded his wings that dazzle,
And has sunken to his hidden nest beyond the hills,
All shall group together gaily, around the crackling fires,
And chew the juicy cud of gathered day;
And greybeards shall tell stories of ancient battles,
And cattle-races of the days of old,
Of hunters, bold and fearless, who faced the lion's thunder
And stalked the lightning leopard to his lair.
—But here I burn and shiver and listen to the buzzing
Of flies against deceiving window-panes.

from: **Drought**

Powder is the grass, burnt powder,
Mingled now with the dust from which it sprung;
Dead are the lilies in the veld-pans;
The veld-flowers have vanished.

Naked is the veld, scorched and naked,
Charred is its coat, once brave and green;
Naked to the sun's lash it quivers—
A victim defenceless.

Silent are the streams, sad and silent;
Drought has sucked their shining souls away;
The stars have slipped from their fingers,
The moon has escaped them.

Dead are the blossoms and the berries,
The bright birds have departed,
Like poor-whites, they have fluttered to the cities,
And there they starve songless.

Dead are the friendly sheep and cattle:
Bleached bones whiten in the sun;
No soft lowing comes from the valleys,
No faint bleat from the hills.

Lonely is the veld, stark and lonely,
On its scarred breast no living thing is seen,
Save only a hawk that hovers,
Like doom o'er its shadow.

Drought—the dark vulture—hovers,
Desolation—his shadow—swings below,
Over the long-drawn anguish
And despair of the veld.

Upon a solitary farm,
Tucked away unobtrusively
In a tiny crinkle of the vast veld,
Dwells the tenant-farmer, Piet Bloem.
Piet's home is a three-roomed cottage,
A rough habitation of unburnt brick
Roofed with corrugated iron.
Piet possesses a small herd
Of companionable cattle—
Cows, calves, tollies, heifers and oxen—
Which he cherishes with the love of a mother.

Dwelling quietly on his lonely farm
Piet has caught at whiles sudden gleams,
Lovely as a crumbling rainbow,
Flashes from the elusive wings
Of the kingfisher, happiness:
And beside the door of his dismal cottage
He has noticed, absent-mindedly,
The slow, shy budding
Of the coy flower, contentment.

Iron Drought is now upon the land,
The bird of happiness has flown;
The flower of contentment is dead:
And Piet is despondent.
Daily he searches the skies,
The stark, pitiless skies,
For the flutter of a white-winged hope
In their blue, burning expanses;
Daily he watches and waits in vain;
Daily he sees his work wasted,
Sees his shining fields of mealies
Burnt up by an angry sun;
Shrivelled, too, is the grass,
And the distressed cattle
Huddle dejectedly around the homestead,
Sick with hunger.

Grimly Piet toils from dawn to dark,
Chopping branches from all trees
That have the slightest flutter
Of green leaves upon them;
Slicing prickly-pear and aloes
For his famished cattle;
Carrying water from the bore-hole
For those too weak to rise.
But his labours are vain,
The foodstuffs are exhausted;
The bore-hole dries up:
Huddled around the homestead
The cattle lie—too spent to stand:
They follow Piet with patient eyes,
Inquiring and suffering eyes.
Piet—the only God they know—
Can no longer aid them
And puzzled they die—despairing they die.

Feverishly Piet wanders in the veld,
As restless as unkennelled winds
That rustle night-long
Through coverts of silence;

Restless and distraught he roams
Under the blanched face of the moon:
Now he stumbles up a rugged koppie,
Wildly surmising that he sees his cattle—
Ghostly beeves browsing upon stones.

Bewildered he staggers homeward,
And after weary tossing
Sinks suddenly into the sea of sleep.
Sleeping he dreams:
Dreams that the long-delaying rain
Is sweeping and swirling over the veld,
And thudding softly upon the roof:
He awakes, sits up, and listening,
Hears only the dreary night-wind
Soughing dolefully amongst
The stripped, listless trees.

Helpless and heart-broken
Piet nails to his cottage-door
A message of despair:
'God has forsaken us.'
Then, with his wife and young children,
He trudges to the nearest dorp
And joins the legion
Of defeated, dispirited poor-whites—
Sands of an encroaching desert
Sullenly stifling the land.

Drought is upon the land,
And distress overshadows
The dwellings of the Dark People.
Huddled together in narrow spaces,
The Dark People are packed
Into pigmy habitations,
Into huts as innumerable,
And almost as unnotable,
As ant-hills that mottle
The wide stretches of the veld.
At the coming of Spring
The men toiled from dawn to dark,
Ploughing the lean, long-suffering fields
And scattering the golden mealie.
Then, after the bleached yellow-shoots
Stole furtively from the broken soil,
And bloomed into green, glossy plants—
Plants scintillating with hope—
Women and maidens hummed and chanted
As they toiled through long, hot hours,
Hopefully hoeing the shining mealie-fields.

But the longed-for rain came not,
And the people looked in vain
To the heavens for a sign.
Some there were amongst them
Who sought their temples
And prayed for rain:
The red-blanketed heathen did otherwise:
They killed the fattest ox
And prepared a feast for the witch-doctor—
The invincible Rain-maker.

But the Rain-maker manipulated
His dry dolosses in vain;
His medicines were ineffectual
And his incantations useless:
The shimmering fields of mealies
Became dull and bleached
As relentlessly they were scorched
By the sun's dragon-breath;
Slowly they shrivelled and crumbled,
With dry rustling whispers—
Ghostly as the midnight lamentations
Of a ragged newspaper
Caught in a rosebush—
They crumbled to dust.
Then the cattle died: and famine drew near.

The young men and the middle-aged men
Arose and journeyed northward,
Away to the Ridge-of-White-Waters,
There to labour and sweat
In the dark belly of the earth,
Shut away from the pleasant sunshine
And the free air of heaven.
Pity these poor, simple labourers—
Pastoral people, dwellers in the open,
Nourished on sunshine—
Now condemned to burrow like blind moles
In the inner darkness of the earth.
Grimly they toil through night-like days,
Dreaming of their sunlit kraals
And their hungry women and children.

Only the old men,
The women and children,
Now remain in the desolate dwellings

Of the Dark People.
The women rise, before the morning-star,
And hasten away to draw water
At distant wells, now daily drying up.
As they return dejectedly,
With cans of muddy water
Balanced upon their heads,
The few starved sheep and goats
(All that are left of the livestock)
Scenting the water
Totter after the women
Bleating dismally:
But that mud-stained water
Is more precious than pearls,
And the thirst-stricken animals
Cry for it in vain.

The brown calabashes—
The thin-necked, big-bellied calabashes—
Have long been empty and dry;
The stone-mouthed cellars
Under the cattle kraals,
Strong-rooms and treasuries,
Wherein reserve mealies are stored,
Have been sadly and reluctantly raided
And will soon be empty:
The last of the water-wells
Is almost dry: the people will perish.
Drought is upon the land,
And there is wailing and distress
In the dwellings of the Dark People.

Thus having sung of Drought,
Which is the hate of the sun,
Come, let us sing of Hate,
Which is a drought of the spirit:
For this blind serf of death
Lays waste our Land of Hope,
Strangling its springs of action,
Blighting its wistful buds,
Heralding sterile torpor
And desolation.

Hate crucifies this Land,
Hate more fell than Drought,
Malignant hate, implacable hate:

The hate of the ringhals,
That swift-darting, sharp-hissing serpent,
Who blinds his foe with venomed spittle
That he may strike at will.

Like our tortured Land,
We have suffered tribulation:
Droughts of hate have devastated us;
Erosions of the spirit have made us poor;
The waters of love, sweeping over us,
Have escaped unheeded.
How long shall we wander aimlessly
In deserts of drought and despair?
How long shall we walk blindly
In a land flooded with sunshine?
How long shall we insult the vast veld
With our mean thoughts?
And shatter its great silences
With the noise of our petty wrangles?

Roy Campbell

from: The Flaming Terrapin

Far be the bookish Muses! Let them find
Poets more spruce, and with pale fingers wind
The bays in garlands for their northern kind.
My task demands a virgin muse to string
A lyre of savage thunder as I sing.
You who sit brooding on the crags alone,
Nourished on sunlight in a world of stone,
Muse of the Berg, muse of the sounding rocks
Where old Zambezi shakes his hoary locks,
And as they tremble to his awful nod,
Thunder proclaims the presence of a god!
You who have heard with me, when daylight drops,
Those gaunt muezzins of the mountain-tops,
The grey baboons, salute the rising moon
And watched with me the long horizons swoon
In twilight, when the lorn hyæna's strain
Reared to the clouds its lonely tower of pain.
Now while across the night with dismal hum
The hurricanes, your meistersingers, come,
Choose me some lonely hill-top in the range
To be my Helicon, and let me change
This too-frequented Hippocrene for one
That thunders flashing to my native sun
Or in the night hushes his waves to hear
How, armed and crested with a sable plume,
Like a dark cloud, clashing a ghostly spear,
The shade of Tchaka strides across the gloom.
Write what I sing in red corroding flame,
Let it be hurled in thunder on the dark,
And as the vast earth trembles through its frame,
Salute with me the advent of the Ark!

. . .
Out of the Ark's grim hold
A torrent of splendour rolled—
From the hollow resounding sides,
Flashing and glittering, came
Panthers with sparkled hides,
And tigers scribbled with flame,
And lions in grisly trains
Cascading their golden manes.

They ramped in the morning light,
And over their stripes and stars
The sun-shot lightnings, quivering bright,
Rippled in zigzag bars.
The wildebeest frisked with the gale
On the crags of a hunchback mountain,
With his heels in the clouds, he flirted his tail
Like the jet of a silvery fountain.
Frail oribi sailed with their golden-skinned
And feathery limbs laid light on the wind.
And the springbok bounced, and fluttered, and flew,
Hooping their spines on the gaunt karroo.
Gay zebras pranced and snorted aloud—
With the crackle of hail their hard hoofs pelt,
And thunder breaks from the rolling cloud
That they raise on the dusty Veld.
O, hark how the rapids of the Congo
Are chanting their rolling strains,
And the sun-dappled herds a-skipping to the song, go
Kicking up the dust on the great, grey plains—
Tsessebe, Koodoo, Buffalo, Bongo,
With the fierce wind foaming in their manes.

The Zebras

To Chips Rafferty

From the dark woods that breathe of fallen showers,
Harnessed with level rays in golden reins,
The zebras draw the dawn across the plains
Wading knee-deep among the scarlet flowers.
The sunlight, zithering their flanks with fire,
Flashes between the shadows as they pass
Barred with electric tremors through the grass
Like wind along the gold strings of a lyre.

Into the flushed air snorting rosy plumes
That smoulder round their feet in drifting fumes,
With dove-like voices call the distant fillies,
While round the herds the stallion wheels his flight,
Engine of beauty volted with delight,
To roll his mare among the trampled lilies.

The Serf

His naked skin clothed in the torrid mist
That puffs in smoke around the patient hooves,
The ploughman drives, a slow somnambulist,
And through the green his crimson furrow grooves.
His heart, more deeply than he wounds the plain,
Long by the rasping share of insult torn,
Red clod, to which the war-cry once was rain
And tribal spears the fatal sheaves of corn,
Lies fallow now. But as the turf divides
I see in the slow progress of his strides
Over the toppled clods and falling flowers,
The timeless, surly patience of the serf
That moves the nearest to the naked earth
And ploughs down palaces, and thrones, and towers.

The Zulu Girl

To F.C. Slater

When in the sun the hot red acres smoulder,
Down where the sweating gang its labour plies,
A girl flings down her hoe, and from her shoulder
Unslings her child tormented by the flies.

She takes him to a ring of shadow pooled
By thorn-trees: purpled with the blood of ticks,
While her sharp nails, in slow caresses ruled,
Prowl through his hair with sharp electric clicks.

His sleepy mouth plugged by the heavy nipple,
Tugs like a puppy, grunting as he feeds:
Through his frail nerves her own deep langours ripple
Like a broad river sighing through its reeds.

Yet in that drowsy stream his flesh imbibes
An old unquenched unsmotherable heat—
The curbed ferocity of beaten tribes,
The sullen dignity of their defeat.

Her body looms above him like a hill
Within whose shade a village lies at rest,
Or the first cloud so terrible and still
That bears the coming harvest in its breast.

On Some South African Novelists

You praise the firm restraint with which they write—
I'm with you there, of course:
They use the snaffle and the curb all right,
But where's the bloody horse?

To a Pet Cobra

With breath indrawn and every nerve alert,
As at the brink of some profound abyss,
I love on my bare arm, capricious flirt,
To feel the chilly and incisive kiss
Of your lithe tongue that forks its swift caress
Between the folded slumber of your fangs,
And half reveals the nacreous recess
Where death upon those dainty hinges hangs.

Our lonely lives in every chance agreeing,
It is no common friendship that you bring,
It was the desert starved us into being,
The hate of men that sharpened us to sting:
Sired by starvation, suckled by neglect,
Hate was the surly tutor of our youth:
I too can hiss the hair of men erect
Because my lips are venomous with truth.

Where the hard rock is barren, scorched the spring,
Shrivelled the grass, and the hot wind of death
Hornets the crag with whirred metallic wing—
We drew the fatal secret of our breath:
By whirlwinds bugled forth, whose funnelled suction
Scrolls the spun sand into a golden spire,
Our spirits leaped, hosannas of destruction,
Like desert lilies forked with tongues of fire.

Dainty one, deadly one, whose folds are panthered
With stars, my slender Kalihari flower,
Whose lips with fangs are delicately anthered,
Whose coils are volted with electric power,
I love to think how men of my dull nation
Might spurn your sleep with inadvertent heel
To kindle up the lithe retaliation
And caper to the slash of sudden steel.

There is no sea so wide, no waste so steril
But holds a rapture for the sons of strife:
There shines upon the topmost peak of peril
A throne for spirits that abound in life:
There is no joy like theirs who fight alone,
Whom lust or gluttony have never tied,
Who in their purity have built a throne,
And in their solitude a tower of pride.

I wish my life, O suave and silent sphinx,
Might flow like yours in some such strenuous line,
My days the scales, my years the bony links,
The chain the length of its resilient spine:
And when at last the moment comes to strike,
Such venom give my hilted fangs the power,
Like drilling roots the dirty soil that spike,
To sting these rotted wastes into a flower.

The Sisters

After hot loveless nights, when cold winds stream
Sprinkling the frost and dew, before the light,
Bored with the foolish things that girls must dream
Because their beds are empty of delight.

Two sisters rise and strip. Out from the night
Their horses run to their low-whistled pleas—
Vast phantom shapes with eyeballs rolling white
That sneeze a fiery steam about their knees:

Through the crisp manes their stealthy prowling hands,
Stronger than curbs, in slow caresses rove,
They gallop down across the milk-white sands
And wade far out into the sleeping cove:

The frost stings sweetly with a burning kiss
As intimate as love, as cold as death:
Their lips, whereon delicious tremors hiss,
Fume with the ghostly pollen of their breath.

Far out on the grey silence of the flood
They watch the dawn in smouldering gyres expand
Beyond them: and the day burns through their blood
Like a white candle through a shuttered hand.

Rounding the Cape

The low sun whitens on the flying squalls,
Against the cliffs the long grey surge is rolled
Where Adamastor from his marble halls
Threatens the sons of Lusus as of old.

Faint on the glare uptowers the dauntless form,
Into whose shade abysmal as we draw,
Down on our decks, from far above the storm,
Grin the stark ridges of his broken jaw.

Across his back, unheeded, we have broken
Whole forests, heedless of the blood we've spilled,
In thunder still his prophecies are spoken,
In silence, by the centuries, fulfilled.

Farewell, terrific shade! though I go free
Still of the powers of darkness art thou Lord:
I watch the phantom sinking in the sea
Of all that I have hated or adored.

The prow glides smoothly on through seas quiescent:
But where the last point sinks into the deep,
The land lies dark beneath the rising crescent,
And Night, the Negro, murmurs in his sleep.

Overtime

To Peter Eaton

Amongst the ponderous tomes of learning,
Dull texts of medicine and law,
With idle thumb the pages turning
In sudden carnival, I saw,
Revelling forth into the day
In scarlet liveries, nine or ten
Survivors of their own decay—
The flayed anatomies of men:
And marked how well the scalpel's care
Was aided by the painter's tones
To liven with a jaunty air
Their crazy trellises of bones.
In regimental stripes and bands
Each emphasised the cause he serves—

Here was a grenadier of glands
And there a gay hussar of nerves:
And one his skin peeled off, as though
A workman's coat, with surly shrug
The flexion of the thews to show.
Treading a shovel, grimly dug.
Dour sexton, working overtime,
With gristly toes he hooked his spade
To trench the very marl and slime
In which he should have long been laid.
The lucky many of the dead—
Their suit of darkness fits them tight,
Buttoned with stars from foot to head
They wear the uniform of Night;
But some for extra shift are due
Who, slaves for any foot to blame,
With a flayed sole the ages through
Must push the shovel of their fame.

To the Sun

Oh let your shining orb grow dim,
Of Christ the mirror and the shield,
That I may gaze through you to Him,
See half the miracle revealed,
And in your seven hues behold
The Blue Man walking on the Sea;
The Green, beneath the summer tree,
Who called the children; then the Gold,
With palms; the Orange, flaring bold
With scourges; Purple in the garden
(As Greco saw): and then the Red
Torero (Him who took the toss
And rode the black horns of the cross—
But rose snow-silver from the dead!)

On the Martyrdom of F. Garcia Lorca

Not only did he lose his life
By shots assassinated:
But with a hatchet and a knife
Was after that—translated.

Song of the Horseman

Translated from F. Garcia Lorca

Córdoba
Remote and lonely

Jet-black mare and full round moon,
With olives in my saddle bags,
Although I know the road so well
I shall not get to Córdoba.

Across the plain, across the wind,
Jet-black mare and full red moon,
Death is gazing down upon me,
Down from the towers of Córdoba.

Ay! The road so dark and long.
Ay! My mare so tired yet brave.
Death is waiting for me there
Before I get to Córdoba.

Córdoba.
Remote and lonely.

Luis de Camoes

Camoes, alone, of all the lyric race,
Born in the black aurora of disaster,
Can look a common soldier in the face:
I find a comrade where I sought a master:
For daily, while the stinking crocodiles
Glide from the mangroves on the swampy shore,
He shares my awning on the dhow, he smiles,
And tells me that he lived it all before.
Through fire and shipwreck, pestilence and loss,
Led by the ignis fatuus of duty
To a dog's death—yet of his sorrows king—
He shouldered high his voluntary Cross,
Wrestled his hardships into forms of beauty,
And taught his gorgon destinies to sing.

The Volunteer's Reply to the Poet

'Will it be so again?'

So the Soldier replied to the Poet,
Oh yes! it will all be the same,
But a bloody sight worse, and you know it
Since you have a hand in the game:
And you'll be the first in the racket
To sell us a similar dope,
Wrapped up in a rosier packet,
But noosed with as cunning a rope.
You coin us the catchwords and phrases
For which to be slaughtered; and then,
While thousands are blasted to blazes,
Sit picking your nose with your pen.
We know what you're bursting to tell us,
By heart. It is all very fine.
We must swallow the Bait that you sell us
And pay for your Hook and your Line.
But when we have come to the Isthmus
That bridges the Slump to the War,
We shall contact a new Father Christmas
Like the one we contacted before,
Deploring the one he replaces
Like you do (it's part of the show!)
But with those same mincing grimaces
And that mealy old kisser we know!
And he'll patent a cheap cornucopia,
For all that our purse can afford,
And rent us a flat in Utopia
With dreams for our lodging and board.
And we'll hand in our Ammo and Guns
As we handed them in once before,
And he'll lock them up safe; till our sons
Are conscripted for Freedom once more.
We can die for our faith by the million
And laugh at our bruises and scars,
But hush! for the Poet-Civilian
Is weeping, between the cigars.
Mellifluous, sweeter than Cadbury's,
The M.O.I. Nightingale (Hush!)
Is lining his funk-hole with Bradburies
So his feelings come out with a rush,
For our woes are the cash in his kitty

When his voice he so kindly devotes
In sentiment, pathos, and pity,
To bringing huge lumps to the throats
Of our widows, and sweethearts, and trollops,
Since it sells like hot cakes to the town
As he doles out the Goitre in dollops
And the public is gulping it down.
Oh well may he weep for the soldier,
Who weeps at a guinea a tear,
For although his invention gets mouldier,
It keeps him his job in the rear.
When my Mrs. the organ is wheeling
And my adenoids wheeze to the sky,
He will publish the hunger I'm feeling
And rake in his cheque with a sigh:
And when with a trayful of matches
And laces, you hawk in the street,
O comrades, in tatters and patches,
Rejoice! since we're in for a treat:
For when we have died in the gutter
To safeguard his income and state,
Be sure that the Poet will utter
Some beautiful thoughts on our Fate!

Dreaming Spires

Through villages of yelping tykes
With skulls on totem-poles, and wogs
Exclaiming at our motor bikes
With more amazement than their dogs:

Respiring fumes of pure phlogiston
On hardware broncos, half-machine,
With arteries pulsing to the piston
And hearts inducting gasoline:

Buckjumping over ruts and boulders,
The Centaurs of an age of steel
Engrafted all save head and shoulders
Into the horsepower of the wheel—

We roared into the open country,
Scattering vultures, kites, and crows;
All Nature scolding our effrontery
In raucous agitation rose.

Zoology went raving stark—
To meet us on the open track—
The whole riff raff of Noah's Ark
With which the wilderness was black.

With kicks and whinnies, bucks and snorts,
Their circuses stampeded by:
A herd of wildebeest cavorts,
And somersaults against the sky:

Across the stripes of zebras sailing,
The eyesight rattles like a cane
That's rattled down an area-railing
Until it blurs upon the brain.

The lions flee with standing hackles,
Leaving their feast before they've dined:
Their funeral poultry flaps and cackles
To share the breeze they feel behind.

Both wart- and road-hog vie together,
As they and we, petarding smoke,
Belly to earth and hell for leather,
In fumes of dust and petrol choke.

We catch the madness they have caught,
Stand on the footrests, and guffaw—
Till shadowed by a looming thought
And visited with sudden awe,

We close our throttles, clench the curb,
And hush the rumble of our tyres,
Abashed and fearful to disturb
The City of the Dreaming Spires—

The City of Giraffes!—a People
Who live between the earth and skies,
Each in his lone religious steeple,
Keeping a light-house with his eyes:

Each his own stairway, tower, and stylite,
Ascending on his saintly way
Up rungs of gold into the twilight
And leafy ladders to the day:

Chimneys of silence! at whose summit,
Like storks, the daydreams love to nest;
The Earth, descending like a plummet
Into the oceans of unrest,

They can ignore—whose nearer neighbour
The sun is, with the stars and moon
That on their hides, with learned labour,
Tattooed the hieroglyphic rune.

Muezzins that from airy pylons
Peer out above the golden trees
Where the mimosas fleece the silence
Or slumber on the drone of bees:

Nought of this earth they see but flowers
Quilting a carpet to the sky
To where some pensive crony towers
Or Kilimanjaro takes the eye.

Their baser passions fast on greens
Where, never to intrude or push,
Their bodies live like submarines,
Far down beneath them, in the bush.

Around their heads the solar glories,
With their terrestrial sisters fly—
Rollers, and orioles, and lories,
And trogons of the evening sky.

Their bloodstream with a yeasty leaven
Exalts them to the stars above,
As we are raised, though not to heaven,
By drink—or when we fall in love.

By many a dismal crash and wreck
Our dreams are weaned of aviation,
But these have beaten (by a neck!)
The steepest laws of gravitation.

Some animals have all the luck,
Who hurl their breed in nature's throat—
Out of a gumtree by a buck,
Or escalator—by a goat!

When I have worked my ticket, pension,
And whatsoever I can bum,
To colonise the fourth dimension,
With my Beloved, I may come,

And buy a pair of stilts for both,
And hire a periscope for two,
To vegetate in towering sloth
Out here amongst these chosen few . . .

Or so my fancies seemed to sing
To see, across the gulf of years,
The soldiers of a reigning King
Confront those ghostly halberdiers.

But someone kicks his starter back:
Anachronism cocks its ears.
Like Beefeaters who've got the sack
With their own heads upon their spears;

Like Leftwing Poets at the hint
Of work, or danger, or the blitz,
Or when they catch the deadly glint
Of satire, swordplay of the wits,—

Into the dusk of leafy oceans
They fade away with phantom tread;
And changing gears, reversing notions,
The road to Moshi roars ahead.

William Plomer

Conquistadors

Along the Rand in 'eighty-five
The veins of gold were torn,
Red houses rose among the rocks—
A plundering city was born.

Some who under the diamond stars
Had sailed the gilt-edged veld,
Wearing across their prow-like breasts
The order of the cartridge-belt.

Above their dream-entagled beards
Had steely, rock-drill eyes,
Cash-box conquistadors,
Anarchs of enterprise!

Some stole or cheated, some
Made off with their feverish gains,
And many failed, and a foolish few
Blew out their bankrupt brains.

Pioneers, O pioneers,
Grey pillars sunk in real estate,
How funny when the years have turned
Swashbuckler prim and scamp sedate!

Too late in memory's recesses
To find the nuggets of your prime,
Or recover the payable ore of youth
From the worked-out reef of time.

The Big-game Hunter

A big-game hunter opens fire once more,
Raconteur, roué, sportsman, millionaire and bore—
But only shoots his mouth off, knowing how
He's safer on a sofa than on far safari now.

The Boer War

The whip-crack of a Union Jack
In a stiff breeze (the ship will roll),
Deft abracadabra drums
Enchant the patriotic soul—

A grandsire in St James's Street
Sat at the window of his club,
His second son, shot through the throat,
Slid backwards down a slope of scrub.

Gargled his last breaths, one by one by one,
In too much blood, too young to spill,
Died difficultly, drop by drop by drop—
'By your son's courage, sir, we took the hill.'

They took the hill (Whose hill? What for?)
But what a climb they left to do!
Out of that bungled, unwise war
An alp of unforgiveness grew.

The Scorpion

Limpopo and Tugela churned
In flood for brown and angry miles
Melons, maize, domestic thatch,
The trunks of trees and crocodiles;

The swollen estuaries were thick
With flotsam, in the sun one saw
The corpse of a young negress bruised
By rocks, and rolling on the shore,

Pushed by the waves of morning, rolled
Impersonally among shells,
With lolling breasts and bleeding eyes,
And round her neck were beads and bells.

That was the Africa we knew,
Where, wandering alone,
We saw, heraldic in the heat,
A scorpion on a stone.

The Death of a Zulu

The weather is mild
At the house of one of the dead.
There is fruit in the hands of his child,
There are flowers on her head.

Smoke rises up from the floor,
And the hands of a ghost
(No shadow darkens the door)
Caress the door-post.

Inside sits his wife, stunned and forsaken
Too wild to weep;
Food lies uncooked at her feet, and is taken
By venturing fowls:
Outside, the dogs were asleep,
But they waken,
And one of them howls:
And Echo replies.

At last, with a sudden fear shaken,
The little child cries.

A Transvaal Morning

A sudden waking when a saffron glare
Suffused the room, and sharper than a quince
Two bird-notes penetrated there
Piercing the cloistral deep verandah twice.

The stranger started up to face
The sulphur sky of Africa, an infinite
False peace, the trees in that dry place
Like painted bones, their stillness like a threat.

Shoulders of quartz protruded from the hill
Like sculpture half unearthed, red dust,
Impalpable as cinnamon softly sifted, filled
With heaped-up silence rift and rut.

Again those two keen bird-notes! And the pert
Utterer, a moss-green thrush, was there
In the verandah-cave, alert.
About to flit into the breathless air.

The strangeness plucked the stranger like a string.
'They say this constant sun outstares the mind,
Here in this region of the fang, the sting,
And dulls the eye to what is most defined:

'A wild bird's eye on the *qui vive*
Perhaps makes vagueness clear and staleness new;
If undeceived one might not then deceive;
Let me', he thought, 'attain the bird's eye view.'

Not Where We Came In

'This is not where we came in,
The story has all gone wrong.
Don't you remember, we saw
Terraces, vistas, marble urns,
Magnolias of human skin, a tall
Carved door, and that low superb
Smooth car? Between the two
The perfect girl was poised, to lead
With the scent of her physical pride
A millionaire playboy wolf
And a polished, lecherous duke.
It was what we had paid to see—
An epic of processed tripe.

'But the story has all gone wrong,
Her castle was pastry, her diamonds dew,
Her glossy hair is withered,
Her shoe-heels are abraded.
Just look at the girl, would you know her?
A refugee drab, she's lugging
A suitcase full of grudges
That nobody wants to buy.
Look at her now, she's pointing
Straight at us. She's armed. She's speaking.
"It's *you,* and *you,* and *you*
To blame. Take *that!* and *that!* and *that!*"
My God, she's real! I'm shot! It's blood!'

Stephen Black

The Soldier's Prayer

In memory of Armistice Day

I'm only a poor broken soldier,
I'm only a crushed bit o' clay;
But if you don't stop . . . well I'll hold yer!
You've got to hear what I say!

No . . . to fight I was never too willin' . . .
Except with my gal over 'ere!
And from bleedin' and woundin' and killin'
I've bleedin' well steered myself clear.

You see that bloke turnin' the handle?
A' grindin' out tunes with his stump?
My Captain he was – yus, a scandal,
It fair gives a feller a hump!

Well I might 'a been like him, an hero!
If I hadn't got out of the way
On that night with the glass down to zero,
When the orders was 'pray and then slay!'

The French with their very quick fire,
The British with all their big guns,
The Yankees behind their barbed wire
Made it thunderin' 'ot for the Huns.

I suppose they was all very brave sir–
Though I felt myself shake at the knee;
And I wasn't so anxious to save sir
Our civilisation as me!

Thank God I escaped on a lorry–
It was goin' like Hell to the base–
And I won't try to kid you I'm sorry
When I look at that pore hero's face.

No . . . I don't want no medal or job sir,
But a steak puddin' costs eighteen pence!
Well then spare a pore soldier a bob sir
For showing his bloody good sense!

(1929)

Mary Morison Webster

Rain after Drought

While talk circled about the room, circled heedlessly, from each to each,
A word there, and laughter, chairs moving, and then words again,
Above the casual interchange and interflow of speech,
I hear the rain.

I heard the rain beginning slowly to fall,
Quiet, heavy drops, one after the other, upon my thirsty tree,
And someone turned to the window and spoke: 'It's raining after all!'
They went on talking, but for me, for me,

The rain was like a secret; I did mark
Its measured progress, talked, observed, but heard the rain,
Laughed too, but all my senses roved the dark,
Beyond the room and the voices, beyond the dividing pane.

To those others, it was only raining; it was my secret; sad and brave
Travelled my thought two ways, and on separate errands, while it did fall;
I heard it patter quietly on the unquiet grass of a new grave;
I listened while, with patient assault, it fell on the roof of him I love, who never loved me at all.

The Quiet of the Dead

The quiet of the dead
Is as the peace of stones;
They lie dust-comforted,
In their still house of bones.

Some gentle, deep content
Their timeless slumber yields;
Such quiet as is lent
To stones in winter fields.

The Ox

This animal, this sleek and beautiful ox ambling along the pleasant road,
Is being led to the slaughter; a noose is about his head;
Is being led to the slaughter, to an unspeakable place of horror and blood,
In an hour or two, in a few hours at the most, he will be dead.

In the meantime, he walks lazily, contentedly sniffing the dust,
Delicately patterned still and darkly, with the drops of the baffled storm,
His hooves slipping heavily in his ease, his head, with its mild eyes, out-thrust,
His flanks shaken with their own weight, spattered oozily with dung still living
and warm.

An ox, most patient of beasts and most innocent.
His warm, brown glance appraises this and that fearfully as he proceeds;
Wherefore he travels this road he understands not, nor whither he is being sent;
Turning from side to side, he displays a troubled interest in the lush borders of
grass and the flowering weeds.

Yet in an hour or two, in a few hours at the most, he will be dead,
Will have suffered the final indignity at the hands of man in a pen of blood,
His quivering flanks stilled for ever on a dreadful floor, his nozzle red,
His cries, living and terrible still, hovering above the place where he stood.

Surely, although it remains unrecorded, along the hot roads to Jerusalem,
Christ paused in the dust, viewing sorrowfully the herds and the terrified flocks,
Raised His voice often times, in anger and protest, beholding them,
Was moved to pity at sight of the sweating camel, wept for the lamb taken for
slaughter, bemoaned the trapped fox,

And, watching the fishes tilting and tumbling in lively terror under His eyes,
Freeing themselves from the harsh nets, slipping and spilling in a heap of silver
on the quiet sand,
Winced, unsuspected by Peter, above them, knowing how hardly even the smal-
lest thing dies,
Troubled greatly in spirit by their glittering anguish, by the caperings of distress,
by the spent leapings from the hand.

O Son of Man, surely indeed Thou grievedst for such, and for all the things of
creation, of whatever kind,
Since even I do sorely grieve, and today stand on this roadside in the noonday
light,
Lost and incredulous, staring down at a pattern of hooves in a great darkness of
mind;
The ox, straining at his rope, bellowing loudly at last, breaking into a little run,
passed from my sight.

Herman Charles Bosman

Seed

The farmer ploughs into the ground
More than the wheat-seed strewn on the ground
The farmer ploughs into the ground
The plough and the oxen and his body
He ploughs into the ground the farmstead and the cattle
And the pigs and the poultry and the kitchen utensils
And the afternoon sunlight shining into the window panes of the voorhuis
And the light entangled in the eyes of the children
He ploughs into the ground his wife's brown body
And the windmill above the borehole
And the borehole and the wind driving the windmill.
The farmer ploughs the blue clouds into the ground;
And as a tribute to the holocaust of the ploughshare—
To the sowing that was the parting of the Juggernaut—
The earth renders the farmer in due season
Corn

The Poet

I don't say that the Fates were actuated
By any deliberate malice: I only say
That when they bestowed on me the gifts they did
They were careless. Why should I be fated
To bear the whole moon? Why could they not weigh
Out so much? Instead of a sky panoplied.
With flighted images I'd sooner have
A mealie-field to gaze on: I would try
To keep the growing earth within the sound
Of my blood. The Fates were careless when they gave
Me these banished things in superfluity—
Lost facts brooding like temples instead of ground
For seed and harvest. I would never seek at all
The poppied riot of imaginings
With summer dreams trampled under the wind's horses
And sorrow masked for a last carnival.
I want the sullied soil, not these fine things
That have their ends in water-lights, their sources
In old imperial desolations. Wings
Are angel's wear, not Jacob's. Why
Should I
Blond-pinion accoutremented be
In list in this most awful rivalry?

L.M. Hastings

Snapshot of Menelaus

Once in the long afternoon,
When Sparta baked in the sun,
She sprawled among the cushions
    The curled Helen—
    The oiled Helen—
Hot and relaxed and sleeping.
And he saw with accustomed eyes
Her white skin and her blue veins
(Slightly varicose, no doubt)
And the slack fold at her navel
    And sadly he remembered Ilium,
The long, lost years, the faded faiths,
The vivid beginnings,
The black boredom and dirt of it all,
The smell of the Camps,
The flies around the latrines,
The smart crowd boozing at the base,
And the dried dead among the jackals.
    And he thought: well, I was a fool,
But I fought for property, after all,
And one must keep one's self-respect—
    But Paris died for love,
He was the bigger fool of the two.
So he sighed, and went back to the office
And called a slave to bring him a drink.
    But she, the divine Helen,
Moved in her sleep and snored slightly,
For she was not so young as she was.

L.R.

'Civilised' Labour Policy

Hertzog is my shepherd; I am in want.
He maketh me to lie down on park benches.
He leadeth me beside still factories.
He arouseth my doubt of his intention.
He leadeth me in the path of destruction for his Party's sake.
Yea, I walk through the valley of the shadow of destruction.
And I fear evil, for thou art with me.
The Politicians and the Profiteers, they frighten me,
Thou preparest a reduction in my salary before me,
In the presence of mine enemies.
Thou anointest mine income with taxes,
My expense runneth over.
Surely unemployment and poverty will follow me
All the days of this Administration
And I shall dwell in a mortgaged house forever.

1940–1960

Peter Abrahams

For Laughter

Man's laughter is dead.

I have been peaceful,
Meekly obedient.
Humility spoke from my eyes,
Christ's reflection from my smile;
I craved their love,
They served me hate;
I yearned to be 'brother,'
But was paid with 'bastard.'
Humbly I accepted.
'Twas the 'Will of God.'

But I have witnessed
My sisters selling their bodies,
Thousands of them, everywhere . . .
  The factories are slow,
  The bosses want profits,
  My sisters must eat.

I have been awakened
By strange machines
Wiping laughter for ever
From the eyes of my regimented brothers.

I have been shaken,
And tears that I thought long gone
Brimmed my lids
When a starving white said 'Brother!'

I have seen in death
Hate fall away
And black fear and white fear
Twisted into human fear;
And black cries and white cries
Turned into human cries:
And black skins and white skins
Tortured into workers' skins.

I searched for laughter
In the eyes of children,

But soberly they went about
Digging peels from gutters.
Instead of laughter.
Death leered at me
From their hungry eyes.

I have learned to love
Burningly
With the fiercest fire;
And I have discarded my humility
And the 'Will of God'
And the stories of my wise teachers.
Arming myself with the wretchedness
In every plain man's life,
And all the tomorrows my soldiers
I battle on behalf of that freedom
That will restore the laughter of man!

H.I.E. Dhlomo

from: **Valley of a Thousand Hills**

A groaning wail from this dark Present breaks:
'O native Soul! art dead and ever flown?
Or art thou tame and lost in slavery?
For ages they have tramped, exploited you;
Forever you defy, escape, deceive,
And laugh at them! Forever blooming out
Into new beauties deep and fresh;
Forever chanting songs the Past exudes,
Of swarthy giant men, wise, kingly, proud!
Who midst these beauties of the Thousand Hills,
Forever strove and struck, themselves to wrench
From domination foreign,–shameful gadge!
Where is the Heart, the Soul, the Purpose of
Our blest ancestral bands? Ah! dig the Past!
Land of the Thousand Valleys if you live,
Still throbs the native Heart, still lives that Soul!
It lingers dumb but whole, unscathed if seared!'
Unsatisfied with tones all calm with hope,
Another in more poignant music thus:
'This beauty's not my own! My home is not
My home! I am an outcast in my land!
They call me happy while I lie and rot
Beneath a foreign yoke in my dear strand!
Midst these sweet hills and dales, under these stars,
To live and to be free, my fathers fought.
Must I still fight and bear anew the scars?
Must freedom e'er with blood, not sweat, be bought?
You ask me whence these yearning words and wild;
You laugh and chide and think you know me well;
I am your patient slave, your harmless child,
You say . . . so tyrants dreamt as ev'n they fell!
My country's not my own,–so will I fight!
My mind is made: I will yet strike for Right.'
With notes all dignified, in sweetness couched,
Still discontent a third now bellowed out
In screech of parlance modern, blunt and sharp!
    'We stood all ravished!
    And spite hope beheld no ray.
    All this is vanished
    For the poet had his say.

It is the poets lay
Will win the day!
It is the humble stock
No power can mock!
Let all the worker stock
Stand like a rock!
Let workers rise like stone,
Speak in one tone!
Our souls we wreck and soil
With useless toil.
Stand in united front!
Stop the affront
Of their fell boasted might!
Let's rise and fight!
United we can save
Those who now slave!
And we can reap the soil
Where we now toil.
Let peoples all unite,
Their evils right.
Let's rise and strike for Right
With all our might.

Agape burst all the holy graves!
Disturbed Ancestral Spirits rise
And call! A hush falls on the scene!
Obedient smiles the sun! The womb
Of life conceives, and life anew
Begins! Worms wind their way to light!
Wild-pulsings throb and course and give
New heart and blood into all tired flesh.
Buds burst into a flower of peace,
And coverts once again mean home;
New flowers midst all the dust are seen—
The flowers which tell the ever-blooming Soul
And Seed of this puissant race and young,
So quick to learn, at growing up so slow . . .
For long the youth of gods! Swift wild life tells
The unbroken roaming Urge in all black veins.
But best of all behold the winging birds
Take to the skies in song! It is our Soul!
It lives! It mocks! It sings! It soars! 'Tis great!
Rich fragrant odours grace the air;
And verdant plants figure their way to the crests!
All earth is purged, and we enthroned!
The picture from the Hills is painted full.

'As it began so never will it end!
And never will it last as now it is!
The Dawn comes soon! The Dawn—and you!'
Whispered the Valley of a Thousand Hills!

Not for Me

Not for me the Victory celebrations!
Not for me,
Ah! not for me.
I who helped and slaved in the protection
Of their boasted great civilisation:
Now sit I in tears 'mid celebrations
Of a war I won to lose,
Of a peace I may not choose.
Before me lies
Grim years of strife,
Who gave my life
To gain—what prize?
In land and sea my brothers buried lie;
The message came; they answered and they fell.
With blood and toil our rights they thought to buy,
And by their loyal stand Race fires to quell.
Now that the War is ended,
Begins my war!
I rise to fight unaided
The wrongs I abhor!
I see the flags of peace in joy unfurled,
And think of my position in the world
They say will come.
And I stand dumb
With wrath! Not victory in the battle field
Those precious things we crave for life will yield.
I see them gathered to decide on peace,
For War, they know, will lead to Man's surcease.
But, Lord, I am not represented;
My presence there is still resented.
Yet where I'm not,
There Christ is not!
For Jesus died and lives for all;
To Him no race is great or small.
And if they meet without the Lord to guide,
They cannot build a Peace that will abide.

The cause of war are Greed, Race, Pride and Power,
Yet these impostors sway peace talks this hour.
How long O Lord before they learn the art
Of peace demands a change in their own heart!
I'll fight! but pray, 'Forgive them Father,
Despite their boast and pomp they know not what they do.'
I hate them not; believe I rather
My battle will lead them discover Christ anew.
This is the irony,
This is the agony:
As long as those in power repentance need,
I sit upon the spikes of Wrong and bleed!
Not for me,
Ah! not for me.
The celebrations,
The peace orations.
Not for me,
Yes, not for me
Are victory
And liberty!
Of the Liberty I died to bring to need;
And this betrayal wounds and sears my soul. I bleed.

J.J.R. Jolobe

from: **Thuthula**

Love

Those days the chief vocation of the maids
It was to marry, find a lord and home.
Lobolo cows were paid for virgin maids.
To gain this end the mothers too did strive
To guard and foster innocence of maids.
Alas! again because of this same end
Their happiness was often sacrificed
To loveless marriages without a choice.
One day out there at this Mthunzana's kraal
A spear betrothal's sign was left in court.
Report was made it came from royal kraal.
The chief the regent Ndlambe at this time
Had wives who did not number less than ten;
Yea, they were more by many units then.
A wife for his old age now wanted he;
He saw this little dove, this charming maid;
He fell in love, and never stopped to ask
Where lay her heart, nor tried to win her love.
The master of the ceremonies too
As middle man between the parties worked.
A royal *khazi* in a day was paid.
Thuthula felt that loneliness which comes
To one who knows a secret known to none,
Which none can understand if told, perchance,
And in the depths of her young heart there was
A wail which issued from a saddened soul,
And seemed in groping yearning words to say,

'By night on my bed,
I sought him whom my soul loveth.
I sought him but I found him not.
I will arise now,
And go about the city in the streets
and in the broad way.
I will seek him, whom my soul loveth.
I sought him and I found him not.'

Anonymous

Shantytown

High on the veld upon that plain
And far from streets and lights and cars
And bare of trees, and bare of grass,
Jabavu sleeps beneath the stars.

Jabavu sleeps.
The children cough.
Cold creeps up, the hard night cold,
The earth is tight within its grasp,
The highveld cold without soft rain,
Dry as the sand, rough as a rasp
The frost rimmed night invades the shacks.
Through dusty ground
Through rocky ground
Through freezing ground, the night cold creeps.
In cotton blankets, rags and sacks
Beneath the stars Jabavu sleeps.

One day Jabavu will awake
To greet a new and shining day;
The sound of coughing will become
The children's laughter as they play
In parks with flowers where dust now swirls
In strong-walled homes with warmth and light.
But for tonight Jabavu sleeps.
Jabavu sleeps. The stars are bright.

Stuart Cloete

La Femme de Quarante Ans

I was born forty years ago.
I lived . . .
a little girl with blowing hair.
I grew . . .
like a flower
in that garden of security.
I knew no fear
in a world of five-per-cent security.
How superficially beautiful it was!
I married.
I was happy.
There was war.
He went for king and country.
He died for them.
He died with the other millions.
He left me with a son.
That was all that was left of him.
The boy grew up.
There was war.
He went for king and country.
He went in the air.
Like an eagle he went.
They shot him down.
And he died.
You have seen things fall
from a great height.
That is how he died.
Do you know who I am?
I am the woman of forty.
I am English.
I am French . . . German . . .
I am Russian . . .
I am the woman of forty
My men are dead.

Norman Clothier

Libyan Winter

There is so little earth, and so much cold
Grey sky clamped down upon us that we seem
Cut off from any kinship with the world,
That safe sane world we knew once in a dream.
We have been set apart like fallen souls
Without a past or future to fulfil
Blindly a driving destiny that hurls
Us on towards a goal beyond our will.
We only know that nights are long, and sleep
Comes slow to shivering men who lie
On cold hard ground, and dawn brings no respite,
Only the pallid sun and sullen sky.
Always on every side our trucks intrude
Their stark forbidding shapes above a plain
Of stones and yellow earth and grey dwarf scrub,
Bleak under wind and clouds that bring no rain.
The idle anxious days draw out their length
Into uncharted seas of time, and all
The urgent incidents that stirred us once
Are blurred and fading, lost beyond recall.
We know capricious death drones overhead,
And, more insistent as our column runs
Into the unknown battles we must fight,
Lurks in the thudding menace of the guns.
And we are trapped, for there is no escape
From this colossal tumbril as it reels
On its relentless way towards the fate
That waits us in the west before our wheels.
But still we trick ourselves with poignant dreams
Of half-forgotten days, and long in vain
For the old easy life we knew at home
In peace—that we shall never know again.
Those things are not for us; ours is the way
That lies over the desert under sombre skies
Past rusting blackened wrecks of trucks and tanks
And graves of men who blazed it in this guise.

Confession

Yes, I have killed
And I was wild with pride
And anger as they died.
High exultation filled
My heart and head like wine
With the sweet savage glory of success
And surging thankfulness
The forfeit was their lives, not mine.

And when I soberly surveyed
The things of silent horror they became,
Dead in the sunshine, things that I had made,
No pity stirred in me, I felt no shame.
Coldly I looked at them and coldly thought
'This is the end to which their striving led.
These were my enemies. We fought.
I live and they are dead.'

C. Louis Leipoldt (Pheidippides)

Recordatio

It was upon this heath,
   Now poppy pied,
That I came face to face with Death
   And knew men lied.
They called him 'Icy—grim—
   Austere—morose . . .'
I'd use a different name for Him
   Than one of those.

He came to meet my men,
   Who knew He came
Although they could not spy Him then;
   For smoke and flame
Obscured our view that night.
   But I could see
His quick hand greeting left and right
   His nod to me.

His face was like a boy's,
   Silk-smooth and fair,
Gladly serene as if all joys
   Were centred there.
His eyes were tender, mild:
   His smile was sweet;
So kind that every baby child
   Would crow to see it.

Where His white shadow fell
   Upon the ground
Peace came upon that clamant hell
   That raged around.
A nightjar fluttered by,
   And through the smoke
I caught a glimpse of starlit sky,
   And then He spoke.

I don't remember now
   What words He said.
His voice was very soft and low
   And comforted

My aching wounded pride,
My pain and fear;
I felt His presence at my side
So near—so near.

Then suddenly I lay
Prone on the ground.
My forehead touched the shell-scarred clay,
And from my wound
Blood mingled with the mire
And bleared my sight—
Then came a peace beyond desire,
And instant night.

How long I lay, God knows,
Upon that heath.
I only knew death had no throes
If this were death.
I raised my head. The moon
Rose o'er the hill.
Around, the men of my platoon
Lay quietly still.

Grandmother's Workbox

Inlaid with ivory from Indian elephants,
And mother o'pearl from Malayan seas;
A sandalwood sanctuary, finely carved
With beetles and Bhuddas arranged in threes.
It stands by the window, beside her mittens,
And Grandmother opens it now and then,
While we crowd around her to stare and wonder
At its quaint adornments of beasts and men.
It holds a motley, a rare collection
Of odds and ends of a time long fled,
The still loved remnants of what had meanings
Years, years ago, but that now are dead.

A fat jade idol with eyes of garnet;
A piebald toadstone, a seashell rare;
A shower of gemstones green and crimson;
A trifle of dainty porcelain ware;
Needles and knitting pins, foreign pennies;

A piece of eight and a golden doubloon;
Silk from Benares, a quiz from Paris;
And—bought at Burgos—her christening spoon;
Buttons and buckles her father wore—
He died at Florence, a Jacobite—
A Mulready card and a shrapnel bullet
Picked up on the field of some foreign fight;
Scents of sandal and opodeldoc
With orris and cinnamon bark combine;
Balsam of Tolu and attar of roses
With violets plucked on the German Rhine.
These and more in Grandmother's workbox
Screen and comfort what lies below,
Hidden from prying eyes and fingers
The ivorine portrait of Grandpa Joe.

Grandpa Joe, who came out, a settler—
Not that he settled, he roamed and ranged,
Seeking fortune and finding sorrow,
Bearing all with a faith unchanged.
Grandpa Joe who was tracked by Bushmen,
And shot a lion on Loubser's Hill
Raced a rhino on Troe-troe's townlands,
And planted the oak near the water-mill.
A fat faced youth in his father's suit,
Tight above and too wide below—
A clerk in the India Company's House—
Whatever made Grandmother love him so?

R.N. Currey

Unseen Fire

This is a damned inhuman sort of war.
I have been fighting in a dressing-gown
Most of the night; I cannot see the guns,
The sweating gun-detachments of the planes;

I sweat down here before a symbol thrown
Upon a screen, sift facts, initiate
Swift calculations and swift orders; wait
For the precise split-second to order fire.

We chant our ritual words; beyond the phones
A ghost repeats the orders to the guns:
One fire . . . two fire . . . ghosts answer: the guns roar
Abruptly; and an aircraft waging war
Inhumanly from nearly five miles height
Meets our bouquet of death—and turns sharp right.

This is a damned unnatural sort of war;
The pilot sits among the clouds, quite sure
About the values he is fighting for;
He cannot hear beyond his veil of sound.

He cannot see the people on the ground;
He only knows that on the sloping map
Of sea-fringed town and country people creep
Like ants—and who cares if ants laugh or weep?
To us he is no more than a machine
Shown on an instrument; what can he mean
In human terms?—a man, somebody's son,
Proud of his skill; compact of flesh and bone
Fragile as Icarus—and our desire
To see that damned machine come down on fire.

We've most of us seen aircraft crash in flames,
Seen how the cruel guardians of height,
Fire and the force of gravity, unite
To humanize the flying god and proclaim

His common clay; by hedge and field we came
Running through the darkness, tried to fight
The solid wall of heat. Only the white
Lilac of foam could get us near the frame—
That frame like a picked fish-bone; sprawled beneath—
Charred bodies, more like trunks of trees than men;
The ammunition began to go up then,
Another and more glittering type of spray;
We could not help them, six men burned to death—
I've had their burnt flesh in my lungs all day!

Lost World

In memory of E.C., died March 1959

She died in England, in the early morning,
A long experience from her starting-place.
The brilliant silver mirror of her death
Seemed the right symbol for her life, but gave
Too landlocked and unruffled an impression.

The simple commendation of one age
Is technicolor cliché in the next:

She was small and gay, with a hand for horses;
She rode side-saddle without a snaffle:
She turned the muzzle of her small revolver
To pierce, beside a panic of African women,
The flicker of a mamba along a verandah
Towards a child. In a lonely place
She grouped a caveat of holes on a target
For those who looked for a sign. These legends
That spark from the hooves of her earlier years
Wear the habit of a lost convention.

I was her first, and with her at the last,
The rôles reversed, but my help helpless
To halt or ease her difficult passage,
Her life-long habits of thought for others
Still there in flashes of maternity:
Her smooth white cap of hair recalling
The cape of comfort that brushed to the waist;
The worn hands, folded in death, out-reaching
My span of years to touch the legend.

She opened her eyes on the sleepy hollow
Of Rip-van-Winkle Pietermaritzburg,
Where waters ran under weeping willows

Through channelled streets. Her grandfather
Had written comparing it with Babylon
In layout, not in sin—the jail stood open,
The graves were few, he found the natives
Fine fellows 'shrewd as merchants upon "Change".'
He built a handsome house with an observatory
But lost it among the stars. Her father
Ran waggons up-country, built solidly-founded
Churches of character, gave sidelong glances
At diamonds and gold. At seven she saw
Water sold in the streets of Johannesburg.

She came home in plaits from her boarding school
To a veld at war. Her father and her brother
Took sudden separate ways to the frontier.
She, with her mother and the younger children,
Lived on a knife-edge of local friendship
And outside frenzy on a dwindling farm,
Where war requisitioned horses and oxen.
When a commando, boys they had known,
Rode in for food and songs round the piano,
She played a new song, 'Soldiers of the Queen'—
Her hands were merry but her eyes were tactful:
This is a story that fits like a glove
On the hands I knew. One moonless night
With waggon-wheels drawn up from the well
And thin mules lent by a friendly enemy
They crossed the nerve-taut lines. A chronicle
Where war draws in the lines of character
Must give a far too definite impression!

At seventeen she put up her hair
And trippled down in her riding-habit
To pass the barbed-wire picket of the new
Camp for burger families—innocent still
Of every overtone but improvisation.
In a marquee, equipped with shelter,
She led wild children and bearded youths
Through jogging songs and jingling tables—
Her riding-crop the symbol of order
But never of Empire. Among the waggons
She visited the families she had known,
Brought news to mothers of commando sons.

A photograph of not long after
Shows her as small and well-proportioned,
The face beneath the fantasy of flowers
Unformed as yet by suffering or fulfilment.
After the war her over-ridden heart
Sent her to Britain for recuperation
And lessons in painting. She married on her return
Out of the world that is now my legend
To the world I have come to share.

She was small and gentle, with a will of kindness.
She rode her love of animals and children
With easy rein, without a snaffle.
Her sensitive touch gave life to broken toys,
To oils on canvas, notes of a piano,
And all the kinder nuances of words.

The fountain of her gaiety spilled over
From family and friends to men and women
In thirty places in three continents
Her heart, which failed her at the last, had travelled
Through seas of every pigmentation, lands
Of every human contour.

A story that broke surface at her death
Tells of a solemn invasion of husbands
Into a laughing concourse of wives:
'The merry wives', she murmured, and the comment
Gives an exact impression.

John Howland Beaumont

Address Unspeakable

Soldier! Soldier!
Why do you walk with me?
Too short is life, too long the night
That follows on my little day.
O man without legs!
There's love, there's laughter yet for me,
And a singing bird in a tall green tree
Is singing me songs of life and light.
Why do you keep me company,
You of the sudden dark and the fatal night?
O brave young man without legs,
Do not come hobbling after
Spoiling my little laughter
With sounds of the rolling battle thunders.
Sweet is the singing bird in the tall green tree
And you bring me bitter company,
Fire and flame and fear and fallen cities
Tread on your heel,
And the final deathless ditties
Of bright cold steel
Go ringing down the centuries
Where the thudding drum and the marching soldier go.
Soldier! Soldier!
What have you to do
With a singing bird in a tall green tree?
You, who have no eyes for birds or trees
Or the urgent earthly wonders.

I cannot keep you company
With death for ever walking at your side
And sorrow going where you go.
The world is fair and wide:
Soldier! Soldier! Get you gone!
What have such as we to do
With such as you?
Take your hungry weeping companies
And get you gone!
You women and children of desolate lands,
Into the grave with you!
You dead of the desert sands,
You men without arms or hands.
Shades of the angry battle lines

And lords of shaken shrines
Into the grave with you!
What have you to do
With a dreaming brand-new world?
There's love, there's laughter still for me,
And a singing bird in a tall green tree
In a dreaming brand-new world.

Uys Krige

The Taking of the Koppie

No, it was only a touch of dysentery, he said. He was doing fine now thank
you . . . What the hell were the chaps grousing about anyhow?
He was sitting on the edge of the hospital cot clad only in a slip with both his
feet on the floor,
his strong young body straight and graceful as a tree, golden as any pomegranate,
but only firmer,
its smooth surface uncracked, gashed with no fissure by the burning blazing
sun of war;
and with his muscles rippling lightly
like a vlei's shallows by the reeds touched by the first breath of the wind of
dawn,
as he swung his one leg over onto the other.

He was telling us about the death of the colonel and the major
whom all the men, especially the younger ones, worshipped.
'The colonel copped it from a stray bullet. It must have been a sniper . . .
just a neat little hole in the middle of his forehead, no bigger than a tickey, and
he dropped dead in his tracks.
The major was leading us over some rough open ground between the gully and
the far koppie
when a burst of machine gun bullets smacked from the kloof, tearing him open;
he was a long way ahead of us all and as he fell he shouted:
"Stop! Stay where you are! Don't come near me! Look out for those machine
guns! There's one in the antheap and one on the ledge . . .
Bring up the mortars! The rest take cover!"
Then he rolled over on his back, blood streaming all over his body, and with a
dabble of blood on his lips he dies—Christ, what a man he was!'

The boy reached for a match box, then lighting a cigarette, he continued:
'We came on them about ten minutes later, three Ities curled up on some straw
in a sort of dugout
—as snug as a bug in a rug—and they were sleeping . . .
The two on the outside were young, I noticed. They were all unshaven.
The bloke in the middle had a dirty grey stubble of beard—and that's all I
noticed . . .'

As the boy stopped talking he moved, his hair falling in thick yellow curls over
his forehead, his eyes.
And as I caught the soft gleam of blue behind the strands of gold
I was suddenly reminded of quiet pools of water after rain
among the golden gorse that mantle in early summer
the browning hills of Provence.

'Then I put my bayonet through each of them in turn, just in the right place,
and they did not even grunt or murmur . . .'

There was no sadism in his voice, no savagery, no brutal pride or perverse eagerness to impress,
no joy, no exultation.
He spoke as if he were telling of a rugby match
in which he wasn't much interested
and in which he took no sides.

And as I looked at his eyes again
I was struck with wonderment
at their bigness, their blueness, their clarity
and how young they were, how innocent.

Addis Adaba, May 1941.

Harold Goodwin

Glorious?

(In the *Eastern Province Herald* of 21 September 1955, mention was made of the glorious battles of the Somme, Arras and Delville Wood)

In the days long gone by when the 1st S.A.I.
Took part in a battle arboreous,
Mid Delville Wood's trees with a vertical breeze
I don't recollect feeling glorious.

When the battle was o'er and we counted the score
We didn't feel very victorious.
With most of our band in a far better land
Not one of us said it was glorious.

When a pal fell down dead with no top to his head
We may have used language censorious,
But whatever we said as we looked at our dead
I'm certain we never said glorious.

At Ypres—call it Wipers—we cursed at the snipers
Whose accurate aim was notorious.
When we tried to attack up the old duck-board track
We didn't find life very glorious.

When at Wipers—call it Ypres—we were driven like sheep
To the slaughter, were we saltatorious?
The words we would choose as we sank in the ooze
Were varied, with never a glorious.

When we met with the stench of dead men in a trench
Friend and foe, decomposed and scorious,
There was mention, I think, of the horrible stink,
But we didn't describe it as glorious.

Our reactions to pain and to mud and to rain
Were perhaps somewhat subderisorious.
We mentioned the habits of white mice and rabbits
But nobody used the word glorious.

Now I think it is time that I ended this rhyme
Which is not altogether lusorious,
I'm inclined to get raw when some moron says war
Is noble, exalted or glorious.

Charles Eglington

The Vanquished

To Amelia Levy

With treble vivas and limp hedgerow flags
The children welcome us: again we meet
The fearful sons and daughters of defeat;
And through the town our dull compassion drags
The scarecrow of our greeting.

Brown-eyed brat,

Your dusty face and sapless, sapling limbs
Start in my blood a wave of anger that
Breaks hotly on my eyes in spray that dims
Your hungry, haunted smile but cannot drown
The image of a child you bring to mind
Who might be mine: If ever, thin and brown,
She, too, must some day wait to find
Bread and forgiveness on the conqueror's way,
May they advance defeated—as today.

A Sword for the Group-Captain

Sailor Malan : 3 X 1910 – 17 IX 1963

They always lacked grandiloquence,
The world's honours: and that was right:
Grandiloquence is right for fakes.
A hero's honours should be
Always personal, human that is,
Especially these days (1966)
When so many heroes (sic)
Are stuffed mess jackets
And medals pinchbeck.

Now they've dedicated a sword to you,
And this I think is logical.
Your element was air, your weapons
Machine guns. And yet a sword is fitting,
As is your nickname, recalling the sea.
I wouldn't know, being ex-infantry
And a groundling anyway—but I think
The air has the lustral flame of steel.

Anyhow, a good fighter pilot kills,
Quickly, cleanly as a good swordsman did
And is killed quickly, cleanly
As a swordsman was.
The sword is the symbol . . .

Lourenço Marques

Once, grave laodicean profiteer,
This harbour welcomed neutral ships
And warring secrets: enemies,
Remote from where fierce, fatal loyalties
Strode armed with death, strolled casually
And mingled with shut faces and tight hearts
In this pacific city, open then
To an ocean menaced by their conflict.
In still blue waters of flamboyant shade
Intrigue and treason, treachery and hate
Fermented like paludal slime. In febrile dreams
The city shared the stranger's destiny.

Yet, in that tense neutrality
There was a brooding innocence:
The war was far away and though the sea
Might wash a blaze of fire from the night,
The city knew the probabilities;
Its lassitude was old and wise;
The ocean it confronted was
(As backward-looking, sad Pessoa knew)
Salt with the tears of Portugal;
The mother-country's wars had all been fought—
How could there ever come a time
For guilt, expatiation and remorse?

Now (many years have passed) I sit
In still blue waters of flamboyant shade
And muse as sad Pessoa never could:
I lack blood knowledge of those bitter tears,
Those centuries when caravels
Caught storms of hazard in their sails
And left, in spastic writing on all maps
Directions to the unknown worlds of earth;
The city, grown and prosperous,

Exalts in me no backward-looking thoughts—
It has the future's brooding innocence.
I sense another taut neutrality.

Its world, though growing old, is young,
Its rooted heritage is germinal:
Behind its tall, proud back a continent
Throws out a challenge, like the oceans once.

F.D. Sinclair

Free State

'en stilte en dood lê weerskant soos die horison daar ver.'
—N.P. van Wyk Louw

Across the empty veld there creep
Red dusty roads that follow brave old names,
Marched by tall gums sunlit to windy flames,
Footless, and shrinking in the vast
Where all but wind and tree seems lost in sleep.

Here is more sky than you have seen,
Horizons flat and blue, or toothed with hills
That ever mock with distance; land that fills
Eagerly with light, and is
A loneliness, magnificent and mean.

Beyond this window, vaguely set
Where rocks break the dead grass and boulders lie,
A wind-wheel turns and the brown willows die
Point to red dust their stiffened leaves,
Defeated, without memory or regret.

Only the hard monotony
Of sound from the uneven turning wheel
Wakes upon unreality the real,
Gives the consuming secret out
Of brilliance that is steel and agony.

The man who built this house is dead
And all his youth and years gone by in vain,
A dull complexity of loss and pain,
In trafficking with dead beauty
That would not live for him, nor lift its head.

Now the man is dead, but yet
The house is here and from the window I
Can see the red road, the unending sky
And more, invisible to you,
By which his bitter labour was beset.

Look at this loveliness, and read
What heart is in it that can burst the rock,
What warmth this flame-red arrogance can lock
Deep in its jealous dust; and learn
What dead dreams in a darkening soul can seed.

Roy Macnab

The Hippopotamus

Out of the Zulu bush one day she came,
Without a by-your-leave, it was good-bye
To the hills of Mapamula, the herd and St. Lucia Bay,
Bellow on the wind and dust in the air,
Through broken mealies, the shattered stalks of cane,
Into our world the hippopotamus came.

Two years the journey, two thousand miles
In bush and swamp, cities, the pages of Punch
And The Times, stirred by ancestral memories, they said,
Searching for a long-lost ego, though once at night
In the dead-quiet street and the window's light,
She saw herself whole and took fright,

But never turned back to the past, the taste
Came soon for lights and fame, one day
At noon from the river's bed late rising,
She walked the square with councillor and mayor
And ate three fields of Pondo's fare, who thought
Thus to placate a much-feared witch.

Ours the accolade came next, the royal game, we too
Made much of her who on dignity and maize grew fat,
At many a muddy spa taking the waters, the sophisticate
Was quite unprepared for the denouement;
In the morning papers, with some surprise, we read
Of a sticky end, at Keiskama, two bullets in the head.

Questions in Parliament and mourning, the assassins
Brought to court, there was nothing mean, I remember
About the passing of Huberta, the celebrity's head
Stood firm on the courtroom table, later for posterity
With its nether self rejoined, was put down for parade
Here in the museum at Kingwilliamstown.

Now twenty-five years later as we stand, my child,
You in another generation, would that I could
Draw you but back beyond the taxidermist's art,
To where once and for once the fabulous tale came true,
When the great beast walked each night through the nursery dream
Only to leave, when daylight came, a garden of wrecked cabbages.

Rhodes

Rhodes is remembered in three places, in the Matopo Hills, on the slopes of Table Mountain and at Rhodes House, Oxford.

In these three places once you walked,
With heavy tread, a vision on each arm.

Where in the sun-scorched hills a grave
Lies white with meaning in the grass
And sits a Matabele boy and whistles for a bird,
Dreaming of the things his fathers told,
How night the crocodile with painted eyes
Was dreadful with *bayete* and the royal dead,
And the snake-tongued torches crackling out the song
Of lifting, lifting the white dreamer to his grave.

There, too, where a mountain casts a shadow
On a two-seas's conference your spirit moves,
And walks with giants across the stormy land;
Now all the earth goes trembling to the shore
And your guardian horsemen at the temple stair,
Rear up in terror and in terror turn to stone.

And in this house they built across the sea,
Where ancient towers still smile on dreams
As yours, where time's in step with all the world,
And only the bells will catalogue the years,
Here where the fire burned you thought of fire,
The dark red flame scorching a dusty map,
Fire that moulds a diamond in a digger's brain
Or sends him sentimental home again.

Here among these passages you walk,
And the white dust falls from your feet,
The Summer scents of vine and the warm surf sound,
A wandering spirit who finds no peace
Between the three—grave, temple, house,
The space-time image of a scientist's dream,
Fallen between two stools of life and death,
Unknown by either yet by both these claimed.

In these three places, with the world in bed,
I've heard your slow and measured tread
Along these paths where your bold schemes were led,
And whisperings of the wind have said
You plan some Cape-to-Cairo for the dead.

E. Vincent Swart

Casey Jones

Casey Jones has left today,
The decision was made in a desperate way,
Short as a wire and quick as a plane
And he isn't going to see any of you again.
There was no kind of good in staying on
When the delight was gone.

His hand at the welding was unsteady for months,
And the boss came very near sacking him once.
No rain for weeks: the old mower in pawn,
It was an impossible pastime cutting the lawn.
There was no kind of good in staying on
When the delight was gone.

Cries in the head were making him light,
He found it difficult sleeping at night,
The warmth of the women was a shocking reward,
And their unfortunate wishes were growing weird.
There was no kind of good in staying on
When the delight was gone.

O where did he head for? The wind in the wood,
And the goat on the tether was coughing up blood,
The clock on the church was pointing at ten
As he passed by the women and left the men.
There was no kind of good in staying on
When the delight was gone.

O where was he going? He didn't quite know,
For vague as a bandage the infected go,
And the mind must follow the deceived decision
Of the night before and the dream's incision.
There was no kind of good in staying on
When the delight was gone.

Walk on to Headland Height

Walk on to headland height, the naked cliff.
Here isn't lyrical fall, arms spreading
Like flowers, head handsome as bird, poised,
But a sharp nine hundred feet to the sea.

Should you walk nearer, where the abrupt edge
Nudges at death, topped by your own dizziness
Over, the surprised cry must give up
Midway, and the disgraced mouth know
Death of the whole head. Many as pores
Shall be holes in your body. Limbs,
Taken by air, before beach robbed of, buried as blood.

Read of your death. And read here, where wind like an axe
Cuts arms from summer, deprives seed of a signature,
And visiting teeth of salt bite rock-deep,
Famishing earth of water, O read here
That nothing is yours but the sharp granite,
The original bone. Let fall in the wind
That button from friend, this last week's letter from woman,
For nothing survives but to each his own private
Minimum of bone. The isolate cliff,
Shaking from shoulder earth, summer, and seed, alone is real.

Possess this private mastery with no sorrow.
That man who looks bare self in face
Discovers the gull's mystery, forgets his misery
And is safe. O black gull, black gull,
Whose effortless conversion into wind
Amazes, teach us from land release,
That sharp taking to air where no flattery is,
And we be as one, who drifting down there,
Is drifting as power would drift over sea face.

Elisabeth Eybers

Hagar

There is no quenching of the other thirst,
my son, my son. A woman's salt tears roll
corrosively: when as a babe I nursed
you at my breast, they seared your very soul.

Three lives have strangely shaped my destiny:
Abraham, promoting me to pride and shame,
briefly his favour did bestow on me,
Fertility my virtue and sole aim.

Then Sara came: how enviable remain
her easy laugh, her guile, her certainty,
to me, who tasted naught but infamy.

You are the third: my loneliness, my pain
have shed their wan submission and of late
been tempered to a man's defiant hate.

Adèle Naudé

Memling's Virgin with Apple

She is a person here in her own right.
This one forgets when the Child, the three wise men,
holy angels and shepherds share the light
with her. So often she's but part of the composition,
part of the scene.
                                        But here she's the centrepiece.
There's a Child, it's true, reaching a hand
for a glossy apple and rich embroideries
on His cushion. There's a cameo of a distant land.
But the landscape's far away, the trees
fading from the picture, the towers of the town
withdrawing themselves. The Child one hardly sees
although He is near. It is the blue of her gown
with the jewels, twin rivers of hair
held with a pearl-starred coronet, the glow
of the red cloak, the flowing hands. All is there
of purity in the lowered lids, the wide brow.

But there's a detachment and a strange withdrawal,
an aloneness in her serenity
taking her far away from us. It's unusual,
for mothers holding their children are not easily
disentangled. But she was different, I know.
There was no one quite like her. That's why,
Perhaps, the painter depicted her so—
a mother, but aloof, made lonely by the high
rôle she was playing. Special people would be
like that—kings and queens and very great
artists. Perhaps in this moment she,
for the first time, realizes her state
of separation. She was engaged before
with His hourly needs and the unfolding wonder
of motherhood. But here He is wanting more,
for He's older, wanting the shining object beyond her.
From this moment in the picture, onwards, her road
will be skirting the market-places, the cheering,
gossipy exchanges where a load
of strangers might be lightened in the sharing.
From now onwards her state will be a lonely one
all through her life and when the chapter ends
in darkness, she'll stand with the other Marys, alone
and weeping in a wilderness of friends.

Tania van Zyl

The Ballad of the White Camelia

I turned left and then right
and saw a mountain
on a black horse the mountain
was the earth moving away from me.
The black horse a space wind
coldly saddled for her use.

I turned right and then left
and saw a camelia tree
had cleft the sky with icy fire.
'Pick a camelia if you can!'
the earth said. To reach
so far a silver smith must hammer
and shape me into a star.

I looked right and then left
and climbed the tall camelia tree,
Two milk blossoms with silver
knees, two pale blossoms
with snow-cold breasts I picked.
The world said to me:
'Since you possess two camelias
with silver feet and golden crowns
What will you do?'

I turned left and then right:
the giant bones of the world
passed by on a black horse.
I knew she would pin on an empty
breast the silver flowers
or hang their buds in her hollow
eyes! What could I do?

Lewis Sowden

Hosea

I took a wife who went with men
And laughed when I entreated her—
Come live with me and be my own,
And I shall make your bed of down
And hold you till the sun is high
(And both of us resent the day),
Till morning drops in night, and I
Return your body's comforter.

And you shall bake my meats (I said)
And weave an awning for your head,
Where we shall find contentment when
No longer we resent the day,
Watching the flower blow, the fruit
Increase upon the trees, till ours
Be riper than the garden flowers
And dearer than all summer sown,
When summer robes are underfoot.
So come with me and be my own.

She laughed again, but unsedate
I led her to my garden gate.
And there I made her bed of down
Beneath a bower, and there we lay
On summer nights and summer noons,
Without resentment of the day,
Of autumn winds and winter moons
That trembled in the midnight spray,
Till summer danced with us again
And harvest brought its joyous yield
For me with richer blessing filled,
And I was happy with my own.

And then I found she went with men
Who laughed when I entreated her—
You are my home, you are the strength
Of me that gives my length of days
End and beginning, and repays
My labour in the world with rain
You are the mother of my son

In whom I see myself renewed
And hope recalled against decays
And hungry time withstood. Be still
A mother to him and me. Refill
His nights with rest. Restore my will
At mornings when the world accosts
And I resentful of the day
Am ready all morning to forego;
Who am your body's comforter,
Receiving most when I bestow.

But she her laughter joined to theirs
And shook her tresses at her own.
She made a jesting of my prayers
And bade me cancel what was gone,
To save a laugh out of the past
As she did, and remember last
The thing enjoyed, that nevermore
Would bloom again. For her new skies
And newer songs, as heretofore,
And other roses in her hair.
For me, she said, old lattices
And older thoughts, and God aware
Beside the door.

So unsedate,
I wandered to my garden gate,
Where I renewed her bed of down,
And more resentful of the nights
I kept a vigil on the days,
Of derelicts and castaways.
For when her summer days were done
She lingered at my garden gate,
Looking along the gloomy ways
Which autumn leaves had overblown,
To see what welcome waited her,
To see, perchance, a comforter,
And at her breast an alien one.

She lingered till the shadows grew,
And then she found her bed of down
And me beside it unsedate,
Looking the wanton through and through,
Impatient of the penitent,
While she would rather laugh than sue
And I would rather strike. She knew
And covered the alien at her breast.

But when my angers all were spent,
I let her in the shadows rest.
When morning came she ate my bread.
She baked my meats; she swept away
My heap of autumn doubts; she dressed
My winter nights. I sought her bed.
And as for the alien at her breast,
Him I accepted as my own.

For now I knew what I had known.
Two men my garden shared, and two
Contended for the residue:
The beast asleep upon my bed,
The dreamer with his dreams unread
Who looked for God and found instead
His yearning for a wanton one;
Who listened for the word and caught
The laughter shaking in his head
And ringing echoes from his own.

The beast upon his feather bed,
The dreamer on his straw, each fought
To fetter me to his desires
And each by other was waylaid.
The heavy jowl from dreaming spires
Looked when the dreamer most had prayed,
But when my lips were deepest dyed
The other dashed the cup aside
And led me to his starry stair—
To find the wanton waiting there.

And so, my wife was one who went
With men, making my daily torment
Between the having and having not
Which is the unresolved lot
Of man in two worlds misbegot
Whom neither will ever satisfy.
But daily torment was my school—
That there where love of God begins
I love a woman for her sins.
For I am all men, all men I,
And who so proud who dare deny
Another's seed before his own,
Or tread the seedling down by rule
That makes the morning his alone?

For life renews its sacrament
From purity to purity,
Destroying from corruption clay
And building altars from decay;
And nothing flawed, and nothing vain,
But God will make it whole again.

Lord, teach me then to be content
With this woman, in whom I see
Answered my own infirmity;
In whom a longing for the dust
Betrays my own unquiet lust;
Whom nothing flawed, and nothing vain,
Shall from her victory detain.

Teach me to know this fallen state
In which I may expect to find
(Unaccepting, unsedate)
God and a wanton close behind.

Be my example, be my spur,
Be my defence and comforter
When I refuse to pillage her.
What honour would I do your name
If I her weakness should proclaim?
What credit would on you confer
To choose a people free of blame?

Alan Paton

Dancing Boy

Small boy I remember you
I remember you used to dance here
By the roadside
And the white people stopped in their cars
And when you had finished dancing
Gave money to you,

Sir, I am the one indeed
I remember you stopped in your car
And when I had finished dancing
Gave money to me.

Small boy you are the one indeed
But why are you not dancing?
Do you not dance here any more?

Sir, I do not dance here any more
For one day when I was dancing
A white man stopped here in his car
And he came at me trembling
Like nothing I had seen before
And he thrust money at me
Great piles of paper money
Into my very hands and cried
For God's sake and for Christ's sake
Do not dance here any more.

I took this money to my father
And he said to me
It's a deep thing and a dark thing
And I do not understand it
But you must not dance there any more.

Sir, that is why
Although I am the one indeed
I do not dance here any more.

To a Small Boy who Died at Diepkloof Reformatory

Small offender, small innocent child
With no conception or comprehension
Of the vast machinery set in motion
By your trivial transgression,
Of the great forces of authority,
Of judges, magistrates, and lawyers,
Psychologists, psychiatrists, and doctors,
Principals, police, and sociologists,
Kept moving and alive by your delinquency,
This day, and under the shining sun
Do I commit your body to the earth
Oh child, oh lost and lonely one.

Clerks are moved to action by your dying;
Your documents, all neatly put together,
Are transferred from the living to the dead,
Here is the document of birth
Saying that you were born and where and when,
But giving no hint of joy or sorrow,
Or if the sun shone, or if the rain was falling,
Or what bird flew singing over the roof
Where your mother travailed. And here your name
Meaning in white man's tongue, he is arrived,
But to what end or purpose is not said.

Here is the last certificate of Death;
Forestalling authority he sets you free,
You that did once arrive have now departed
And are enfolded in the sole embrace
Of kindness that earth ever gave to you.
So negligent in life, in death belatedly
She pours her generous abundance on you
And rains her bounty on the quivering wood
And swaddles you about, where neither hail nor tempest,
Neither wind nor snow nor any heat of sun
Shall now offend you, and the thin cold spears
Of the highveld rain that once so pierced you
In falling on your grave shall press you closer
To the deep repentant heart.

Here is the warrant of committal,
For this offence, oh small and lonely one,
For this offence in whose commission
Millions of men are in complicity

You are committed. So do I commit you,
Your frail body to the waiting ground,
Your dust to the dust of the veld,–
Fly home-bound soul to the great Judge-President
Who unencumbered by the pressing need
To give society protection, may pass on you
The sentence of the indeterminate compassion.

N.H. Brettell

African Student

Shakespeare for 'A' level

The pressure lamp hisses into the silence
The narrow radius of sufficiency.
Mousefoot, moth-flutter, batswing, fumble and twitch
The foolscap shadows of the thatch.
Black scholar, intent, impassive still, you have no place
In time or language: as, pages rapidly flicking,
You turn from text to gloss to commentary,
Or now, as one listening to music might
Stare through the face of a friend,
You with poised pencil point look up, question the night,
Midnight, Twelfth Night, or what you will.

Or what you will: Illyria or Arcady,
The polity that never was but could be now,
Built with the measureless cubes of want and wit;
After the wit-weary exit of the courtiers,
The lonely envoi of the clown's last song
Leaves questions hung like cobwebs. Can you then
Sort out the faceless fragments into place,
Print on the dark your projects' clean impress,
With ridge and furrow the uncouth landscape combing,
To every Hodge his acre, every Jack his mistress—
O mistress mine where are you roaming?

Roaming: keep your wild hills for roaming; rest
Within the enormous solace of their thighs.
Still pick your ditties out of the wind's teeth,
Wind and the rain, the clean and bitter east
That shakes the bright drops from the flinching leaves
To twitch and fall like notes of harpsichord
To the nimble tissues of the cricket's fiddle:
Each untouched thing that still is but a toy;
The land is innocent still: so, keep innocency,
Keep the half-naked thing you were
When that you were and a little tiny boy.

Boy now no longer. Eye for eye we stare
Into the dark that tilts towards some dawn.
Can we accept these half-surmised replies,

That benign irony that still could make
Its chorus of the necessary clown,
Strolling aloof through knot-garden and gallery,
Accosting duke and dunce indifferently—
Accept the final self-withdrawn surrender,
The grim staff snap, the ruthless hands recall,
The god-like hands that jerked the puppet strings;
Could you, or I, with honesty endure
That golden franchise that embraced them all—
The knave, the gull, the Jew, the blackamoor?

Giraffes

Framed in the sedan windows, the tall triangular faces
Watched us with distant interest above the green-
Fringed parasols of the immense acacias
That scattered their point-devise in shady places
And the heat shimmer lay between.

Out-focused through lorgnette or quizzing-glass,
Neck inter-crossing neck, glance backward from between
Serpentine vertebrae, harmless and mild as doves,
With velvet hornlets topped, leisured they pass,
Innocent epicene.

Till with their five attenuated limbs
With gesture of a slowly geared machine,
They pick up distance on an enormous hand,
Outpacing my fantastic synonyms:
The sedan windows quivered in between.

Slowly the sedans pass:
With lamp-light and link-light bobbing on the strings
Of smooth blond faces down the boulevards,
With paint and patch behind the discreet glass
Attend the whispered tryst, the slow pavane, the cards,
The coy queens and complacent kings,
All the brocaded faded go-betweens,
And centuries remote beyond the sedan windows.

Your grave quaint harlequins, to deceive us
With the gay curves of kirtle and crinoline
In a grey wilderness. Reluctantly leave us,
While the incessant grasshoppers scissor away the minutes;
O lost arcadian scene,

O happy groves, centaur and unicorn prances
Across the hourless wastes that lie between
Our watchful present and the wistful bygones,
When the bland century and our budding fancies
Were both eighteen.

Guy Butler

Karoo Town, 1939

In a region of thunderstorm and drought,
Under an agate sky,
Where red sand whirlwinds wander through the summer,
Or thunder grows intimate with the plain, and rain
Is a great experience like birth or wonder:
By the half-dry river
The village is strung like a bead of life on the rail,
Along whose thread at intervals each day
Cones of smoke move north and south, are blown
By the prevailing winds below the clouds
That redden the sundown and the dawn.

Here the market price of wool
Comes second only to the acts of God:
Here climate integrates the landsman with his soil
And life moves on to the dictates of the season.

It seems that farmers discussing the weather,
Arguing prices round the cattle pens,
Might well repeat the ritual
On the last stock fair in time.

In the magnesium light of summer,
Behind the colours comes the column
With solemn tread to the thud of the drummer,
Six foot tall, in a leopard skin.

The call to arms!
The cry for recruits!
Europe asserts
Her infallible remote control,
Demands decisions
From us among our wool and lucerne bales,
Among our memories of hard rebellions and wars.
Drawing the entire village in its wake,
The catalysing sight and sound move on,
Past shutters closed against the noon
And bluegums drooping in the heat,
Crystallizing loyalties, hardening hates
Of a village lost in the plain, unknown
To the gods of London and Berlin.

The trumpets bay in unison
Imperative demands upon our lives.
Echoes ricochet between hot whitewashed walls,
Divide
The father from the son,
The child from the home,
Bring
The parting kiss,
Death in the desert

But cannot shake the rockstill shadows of the hills
Obeying remote instructions from the sun alone.

Myths

Alone one noon on a sheet of igneous rock
I smashed a five-foot cobra's head to pulp;
Then, lifting its cool still-squirming gold
In my sweating ten separate fingers, suddenly
Tall aloes were also standing there,
Lichens were mat-red patches on glinting boulders,
Clouds erupted white on the mountain's edge,
And, all insisting on being seen.
Familiar, and terribly strange, I felt the sun
Gauntlet my arms and cloak my growing shoulders.

Never quite the same again
Poplar, oak or pine, no, none
Of the multifarious shapes and scents that breed
About the homestead, below the dam, along the canal,
Or any place where a European,
Making the most of a fistful of water, splits
The brown and grey with wedges of daring green—
Known as invaders now, alien,
Like the sounds on my tongue, the pink on my skin;
And, like my heroes, Jason, David, Robin Hood,
Leaving tentative footprints on the sand between
The aloe and the rock, uncertain if this
Were part of their proper destiny. Reading
Keats's *Lamia* and *Saint Agnes' Eve*
Beneath a giant pear tree buzzing with bloom
I glanced at the galvanised windmill turning
Its iron sunflower under the white-hot sky
And wondered if a Grecian or Medieval dream
Could ever strike root away from our wedges of green.

Could ever belong down there
Where the level sheen on new lucerne stops short:
Where aloes and thorns thrust roughly out
Of the slate-blue shales and purple dolerite.

Yet sometimes the ghosts that books had put in my brain
Would slip from their hiding behind my eyes
To take on flesh, the sometimes curious flesh
Of an African incarnation.

One winter dusk when the livid snow
On Swaershoek Pass went dull, and the grey
Ash-bushes grew dim in smudges of smoke,
I stopped at the outspan place to watch,
Intenser as the purple shades drew down,
A little fire leaping near a wagon,
Sending its acrid smoke into the homeless night.
Patient as despair, eyes closed, ugly,
The woman stretched small hands towards the flames;
But the man, back to an indigo boulder,
Face thrown up to the sky, was striking
Rivers of sorrow into the arid darkness
From the throat of a battered, cheap guitar.

It seemed that in an empty hell
Of darkness, cold and hunger, I had stumbled on
Eurydice, ragged, deaf forever.
Orpheus playing to beasts that would or could not hear,
Both eternally lost to news or rumours of spring.

Ayliff and the Lepers

Wednesday, March the thirty-first, eighteen thirty.

After attending my English appointment, I took
a circuit round some distance to visit the lepers
who live on the banks of the Great Fish River.

I had not been before. The sun was declining.
Passing through a wood of mimosa trees
I came upon them suddenly in a group
on the banks of the river, sitting before their house,
regaling themselves in the sun before the close
of day and the autumn cold should compel them to retire.

I must confess that I was filled with pity,
astonished at seeing such objects of misery.

Restlessness — they seemed unable to sit still,
kept rubbing themselves continually, and one
poor creature bordering on stupor
paying little attention to what was passing;
yet they consider their greatest suffering to be
their social isolation; what afflicts them most
the exile of the heart and not their rotting flesh.

I never saw anything like it, no not even
in the sick-bays of the Navy, nor hospitals where I
have seen so many miserable sights, but none like these.
I now see why our Saviour in the days of His flesh
was touched to the quick by the lot of the leper.

Tuesday, September the seventh, eighteen thirty.

At intervals all through the winter I have seen
the lepers who live on the banks of the Great Fish River.
Some call me a fool for wasting my time on those
whom the world has already forgotten, as good as dead;
others tell me it is not healthy, that I
might bring the disease from them to others; but
I cannot pass by on the other side.

Today when I reached the desolate place I found
poor Antje Rautenbach sitting alone. She seemed
strangely at peace. Moved by I know not what
I asked her to tell the entire company
what had befallen her. She said:
'I cannot utter what I feel.
The first that I felt in my mind was two months ago:
it was so strange and sweet, so costly, like gold
that I was afraid of being caught with something
that did not belong to me by rights and would
perhaps be punished for having it. These things
were striving different ways in my heart. I felt
no desire for anyone's company; that hunger
had ended at last; instead I kept on calling
on Jesus to come.' She paused, then pointed to a spot:
'Two days after, when I was standing there, just there,
I felt a great light come into my heart; my troubles
all left me and I was happy at last.'

I questioned her then from the catechism
as contained in the Book of Common Prayer, in the Form
of Baptism for those of Maturer Years.
Her answers being sound, I requested one of the company
to bring me water in a gourd from a pool.
Then, blessing it, I baptised the Hottentot leper,
Antje Rautenbach, in the name
of the ever-blessed, the glorious Trinity.

It was indeed a solemn time to my mind:
several things conspired to make it so:
First, the order of the sacrament, the great
enfranchising words; Second, the person baptised,
a leper woman nursing a light within her;
Third, the congregation, outcast lepers
of an outcast race; Fourth, the place, a scrub-grown
river frontier under a wintry sky.
Yet I, I felt that the angels of heaven were present
rejoicing over another heir to salvation;
that desolate place was the house of God,
the gate of heaven was in that place.

Tourist Insight into Things

I've often thought, well, our big black underdog,
you can't expect to turn him into a spaniel
simply by feeding him sugar cubes, even
the very best sugar, the most refined.

And anyway, I'm sick of spaniels. Once
you have shed your British sentiment
for dogs and other animals, once you've felt
your own dark life-blood pulsing like a drum,
you'll find our big black brother has much, so much to teach you—
because, you see, he's still in touch
with all the old gods in a way
that makes one wonder
why D.H. Lawrence wasted all that time
in Mexico and Down Under.

Africans, like their continent, are not dark
for nothing. Their darkness is alive.

Compare, for instance, the various ways
we and they kill beasts. No priest in the West these days
leads the heifer (silken flanks with garlands dressed),
to the efficient abbatoir. The whole thing's done
by an hygienic machine. Not quite nice of course;
witness our treatment of butchers; but we take no moral notice,
the life of a calf not being sacred to us.

All over Africa all cattle are sacred
and the killing of an ox
is a ritual, a ceremony.
In a tribe that I know well
twelve of the best and glossiest young braves
are chosen for the task. Unarmed, naked,
they enter the kraal. The strongest, glossiest bull
lowers a horn-span five feet wide at them.
Black, pink-palmed hands leap, seize,
wrestle the beast to its knees.
He bellows helplessly.
The more he bellows the better; fathers, chieftains, ancestors
remember the deep bull voice long after they have forgotten
that silly sophistication, speech.

Next, with courage and cunning, the young men
lift the left hind leg over the left horn;
careened on its right side now
the great beast cannot heave itself erect.
Helpless, it bellows in throes, and its eyes
roll, roll, and its breath in spurts
blows up a smoke of powdered dung.
All round it sweating black bodies
glisten under the stinging sun.

The best of the glossy braves
with a specially sharpened assegai
now drops to one knee, and deft, quick,
slits the midriff open. Smiling ivory,
he thrusts his right hand through the diaphragm
right into the thorax, more than elbow deep.
The young men chant; outside the kraal
there is a communal clapping of hands by old and young
and a great wave of singing like a seventh breaker
rising, deepening, as the bull roars louder, louder.

The thrusting fingers and thumb
have found the titanic heart.

He holds a bull's heart beating in his hand.
Thrusting deeper, deeper, he finds
the root of life, root of the arteries, the aorta itself
beating out its dithyramb.
Blind in the dark bull body man's fingers seize and squeeze it shut.
In the great beast, the great heart shudders, bursts.

While hills and echoes carry the bull's last bellow
to the last of the ancestors, the laughing-singing-clapping wave
tumbles, sparkles, spreads in bubbles and spume
through the veins and the brains,
the nerves and the bloods of all that is African
on both sides of the grave.

White settlers, of course, don't like this way of killing,
cattle not being sacred to them. And they haven't
imagination enough to be tolerant about it;
they call it barbarous; and no anthropologist as yet
has got them to understand.

Anthony Delius

from: **The Last Division**

The Ethnic Anthem

'Ethnasia will last a thousand years,
Our land is studded with its glories,
Its monuments are separate bars
And segregated lavatories.

'God has through us ordained it so
Post Offices are split in two
And separate pillar boxes fix
That correspondence does not mix,
No one has ever managed better
To guard the spirit—and the letter.

'O ethnic trains and buses daily hurry
Divided hues to earn divided bread,
The races may not fornicate or marry,
They even lie apart when they are dead.

'God may award his just damnation
For mixed or unmixed fornication,
Down here we warn the citizen
With whom it is a crime to sin,
And no man takes, with our cognisance,
A liberty without a licence.

'Yea, in our law men stand or fall
By rule of thumb or finger-nail,
So sensitive's our Roman-Dutch
It notes if lips protrude too much.

'We've split all difference so fine
No wider than a hair or skin,
To foil the trick of traits and needs
So shockingly the same in breeds—
For such success in our researches
We thank Thee, Lord, in separate churches.

'How wondrous is our work, our way,
And thine as well, Great Separator,
Who separating night from day
Left us to sort the rest out later.'

The English South Africans

These million English are a vague communion
Indifferent to leadership or goal,
Their most accomplished children flee the Union,
Search other countries for their cause and soul,
And to the pioneer premise of their fathers
Add on no better moral, finer story,
Leave our crude glaring sun and savage weathers
To bask, reflect in other peoples' glory.
Most able men, not all, who stay behind
Fix loyalty to man upon shareholders,
The other whites are voters of a kind
And blacks are some statistics in their folders.
Man may diminish while they make their pile,
Black generations brew in new diseases,
What if the legislation stinks of guile?
What? If the supertax reduction pleases . . .
Their language is looked after by the Jews,
Their politics thought out by Afrikaners,
Their colleges embalm enlightened views,
While they get on with business and gymkanas.

The Lament of the Liberals

Ten little liberals waiting to resign,
One went and did so, and then there were nine.

Nine little liberals entered a debate,
But one spoke his heart out, and then there were eight.

Eight little liberals saw the road to heaven,
One even followed it, and then there were seven.

Seven little liberals caught in a fix,
One stayed liberal, and then there were six.

Six little liberals glad to be alive,
One turned a somersault, and then there were five.

Five little liberals found they had the floor,
One spoke for all of them, and then there were four.

Four little liberals sitting down to tea,
One choked on a principle, and then there were three.

Three little liberals looking at the view,
One saw a policy, and then there were two.

Two little liberals lying in the sun,
One turned dark brown, and then there was one.

One little liberal found nothing could be done,
So he took the boat to England, and then there were none.

Lady Anne Bathing

I have grown used to the retreat of seasons,
South-Easter, slow hail of different stars,
I can confront the threat of noosed horizons
Accept Napoleon's or another's wars

Are all my own, and no war has an end
Though evil changes sides. See, waters whiten
On the mountain face, whisper rage, descend
Till they step, pretty as a leopard's kitten

To fill my pool. In Town I dance my reel,
The Lady or the Poet, whatever is expected.
Existence caged in rooms or on parole
Will play the proper part that's to be acted.

The Burghers watch me from their placid lust
That has no naked eye. The officers
Dispense official gaiety, hate thrust
Away beneath the weeping chandeliers.

But dread of tame civility will grow,
Silk hiss against the flesh—until I flee
The twinkling clavichord and wine to show
My nakedness in hostage to a tree.

I stand here pale upon the mountain, dream
In panic at the bare baptismal step,
See water take my body without shame
And merge the shadow as the substance in its lap,

Wait poised above the sky within the shock,
The ecstasy caught in this cornered river,
And in exploding quiet watch the rock,
The tree, the peak and all beyond it shiver.

David Wright

Monologue of a Deaf Man

Et lui comprit trop bien, n'ayant pas entendu.
Tristan Corbière

It is a good plan, and began with childhood
As my fortune discovered, only to hear
How much it is necessary to have said.
Oh silence, independent of a stopped car,
You observe birds, flying, sing with wings instead.

Then do you console yourself? You are consoled
If you are, as all are. So easy a youth
Still unconcerned with the concern of a world
Where, masked and legible, a moment of truth
Manifests what, gagged, a tongue should have told;

Still observer of vanity and courage
And of these mirror as well; that is something
More than a sound of violin to assuage
What the human being most dies of: boredom
Which makes hedgebirds clamour in their blackthorn cage.

But did the brushless fox die of eloquence?
No, but talked himself, it seems, into a tale.
The injury, dominated, is an asset;
It is there for domination, that is all.
Else what must faith do deserted by mountains?

Talk to me then, you who have so much to say,
Spectator of the human conversation,
Reader of tongues, examiner of the eye,
And detective of clues in every action,
What could a voice, if you heard it, signify?

The tone speaks less than a twitch and a grimace.
People make to depart, do not say 'Goodbye'.
Decision, indecision, drawn on every face
As if they spoke. But what do they really say?
You are not spared, either, the banalities.

In whatever condition, whole, blind, dumb,
One-legged or leprous, the human being is,

I affirm the human condition is the same,
The heart half broken in ashes and in lies,
But sustained by the immensity of the divine.

Thus I too must praise out of a quiet ear
The great creation to which I owe I am
My grief and my love. O hear me if I cry
Among the din of birds deaf to their acclaim
Involved like them in the not unhearing air.

from: **Notes on a Visit**

November 1976

Arrival

I landed at Jan Smuts at noon;
A cousin met, and drove me home;
The early summer smiled
Where I was born, and am exiled;
Green willows wept, jacarandas
Blew over windy verandas
While morning glory crept
Up pergola and parapet
Whose engardened villas slant
White roofs below Witwatersrand,
The suburbs of an earlier time,
Once gimcrack, now uncertain.
Uncertainty's what I read
Upon those tatty and beloved
Arcades of bottle stores and fruit
Merchants, pharmacists, estate
Agents, dog beauty parlours, and
Italian delicatessens,
The bioscope, half derelict,
And flyblown cafes that sell ostrich
Biltong as well as Coca Cola,
Pavements of dust and torn paper.
Yet I see no change in the day:
The black and gentle passers-by
As if they had no use for anger
Still greet with courtesy the stranger.
Only the human silhouette
Offered as a revolver target
In the sports-outfitter's window
Remembers June in Soweto.

Black poet

I met him in a room with more
Books in it than furniture.
What was it we had in common?
Each of us was Jo'burg born;
The same language that gave him
Words for verse had served my turn.
Humane, in himself consistent,
The eye and brow magnanimous,
His words quiet, few, and meant,
And his quality, gravitas;
Each of us the wrong colour,
He for now, I in future,
Each disabled by a skin.
Where I shall never be he's been,
His world is locked close to me
Although, as now, he enters mine;
Both natives of the one country,
I have been made, like him, alien.

Weather report

Thunder masses in the air
Northward, toward Pretoria;
The sun, about to disappear,
Sharp on the sun-coloured bricks
Of a long slab, the police barracks,
Throws a black shadow of some trees,
Oude Meester brandy in my glass,
I contemplate a summer
Storm assembling. Heavier
Cumuli range a fading sky.
The sun rolls under suddenly.
Has the night come, or the storm?
A flicker-crackle of lightning
Illumines a falling curtain,
Rain spilling on Magaliesberg
From the burst belly of a cloud.
'How fast the darkness falls,' we say.
'There's no twilight in Africa.'

1960–Present Day

Douglas Livingstone

Sjambok

An Essay

A whip of plaited leather terminating
in a single thong, you pronounce the thing
shambok and you can buy them at
the Victoria Falls or any tourist trap
but a hundred good cracks and you are left holding
a cheap skein of lousy Egyptian cotton
wilting at unstrategic and weathered
corners, and whoever heard of a leather
whip with corners? These are not really
properly cured: chew them and they
are not salty enough and with the faint
rancid flavour of animal fat
which should have been eliminated in
the diligent scraping and an indulgent sun.

Nowadays, paradox this, the best ones
are made in Australia, out of kangaroos
—strange pouched upright giant mice—
or, hell! what does a kangaroo look like
anyway apart from a gonetoseed prize-
fighter, too heavy in the arse?

Perhaps you have heard the old sjambok tales:
bleeding and crucified on wagon wheels,
the early farmers flayed their blacks into death;
soandso's grandfather kept
five men equipped with the stabbing assegai
—a marauding Matabele patrol—at bay
with a twelvefooter; and somebody else sliced
his brother into thick crimson strips
with one for loving his wife too well. Shades
of Cain and Abel and all that jazz.

The sjambok was a subcontinent's tool
and like the freemason's trowel
has been promoted or relegated,
depending on which side of all the elevated
wrists your granddaddy stood, to a symbol.
It looks good on a wall and is still

the only goad the phlegmatic oxen apparently
understand. Of course, it is excellent
for killing snakes—the oldest symbol—lifts
off their heads in one if you are in practice.

Stormshelter

Under the baobab tree, treaded
death, stroked in by the musty cats,
scratches silver on fleshy earth.
Threaded flame has unstitched and sundered
hollow thickets of bearded branches
blanched by a milk-wired ivy. Choleric
thunder staggers raging overhead.

'Never stand under trees in a storm.'
Old saws have an ancient rhythm
in them, but these dry, far from bold
norms and maxims are scalpel-severed
by the sharp, needle-thin lightning,
frightening reason behind the eye,
slivered into lank abstract forms.

Steel spears, slim, yielding and stained
lightly with water, rattle their points.
Jointed the hafts swing, tufted brightly,
maiming invisibly. The shafts reel
through the streaked Impi from Nowhere.
There is only one thing to do—
wheel, stamping, into that brittle rain.

Lake Morning in Autumn

Before sunrise the stork was there
resting the pillow of his body
on stick legs growing from the water.

A flickering gust of pencil-slanted rain
swept over the chill autumn morning:
and he, too tired to arrange

his wind-buffeted plumage,
perched swaying a little
neck flattened, ruminative,

beak on chest, contemplative eye
filmy with star vistas and hollow
black migratory leagues, strangely,

ponderously alone and some weeks
early. The dawn struck and everything,
sky, water, bird, reeds

was blood and gold. He sighed.
Stretching his wings he clubbed
the air; slowly, regally, so very tired,

aiming his beak he carefully climbed
inclining to his invisible tunnel of sky,
his feet trailing a long, long time.

Johnny Twenty-three

I guess the others I never read
(returning the compliment as it were)
had the obit-blocks ready
for some time, date blank.
And the slickflicks like *Time*
worried delicately whether a delicate wit
was permissible in this grave time.

I'm late, John, but hail and farewell,
stout Caesar of Christ, from an unbeliever,
disbeliever and perhaps deceiver.

(Always thought, I did, the Pantheon
remarkably adequate
for the crumbling aqueduct of man,
carrying the joke of life from
in the beginning to the end.)

You were a good guy, it seemed,
from out here.
You didn't see any more visions
than those presented from inside prisons
where your love took you to the masses.
You never rose into the air
being far too fat for that.

A jolly bosun, you steered the whaleboat
of the Church on pre-atomic seas;
a gardener among the stones and yards of weeds
of men's rank disunity.
I don't know whether you were cynical about it
—you appeared to know humanity.
A rustic bailiff, you were locked in
and given the deadly keys to hold.

We should have crucified you or lionized
you for all this; but we have learnt
to mask our cruelty better with indifference.

I will send you fair thoughts from
here and there and now and then
though strictly pagan—
ones like the sun
on Roman flagstones,
and, lovers, moonlight, sea.

The end was tough, this return to dust,
but not so dusty, John;
I find I care as if I must, goodman Peter,
Thou Johnny twenty-three.

Gentling a Wildcat

Not much wild life, roared Mine leonine Host
from the fringe of a forest of crackles
round an old dome-headed steam radio,
between hotel and river—a mile of bush—
except for the wildcats and jackals.

And he, of these parts for years, was right.
That evening I ventured with no trepidations
and a torch, towed by the faculty
I cannot understand, that has got me
into too many situations.

Under a tree, in filtered moonlight,
a ragged heap of dusty leaves stopped moving.
A cat lay there, open from chin to loins;
lower viscera missing; truncated tubes
and bitten-off things protruding.

Little blood there was, but a mess of
damaged lungs; straining to hold its breath
for quiet; claws fixed curved and jutting,
jammed open in a stench of jackal meat;
it tried to raise its head hating the mystery, death.

The big spade-skull with its lynx-fat cheeks
aggressive still, raging eyes hooked in me, game;
nostrils pulling at a tight mask of anger
and fear; then I remembered hearing
they are quite impossible to tame.

Closely, in a bowl of unmoving roots,
an untouched carcass, unlicked, swaddled and wrapped
in trappings of birth, the first of a litter stretched.
Rooted out in mid-confinement: a time
when jackals have courage enough for a wildcat.

In some things too, I am a coward,
and could not here punch down with braced thumb,
lift the nullifying stone or stiff-edged hand
to axe with mercy the nape of her spine.
Besides, I convinced myself, she was numb.

And oppressively, something felt wrong:
not her approaching melting with earth,
but in lifetimes of claws, kaleidoscopes:
moon-claws, sun-claws, teeth after death,
certainly both at mating and birth.

So I sat and gentled her with my hand,
not moving much but saying things, using my voice;
and she became gentle, affording herself
the influent luxury of breathing—
untrammelled, bubbly, safe in its noise.

Later, calmed, despite her tides of pain,
she let me ease her claws, the ends of the battle,
pulling off the trapped and rancid flesh.
Her miniature limbs of iron relaxed.
She died with hardly a rattle.

I placed her peaceful ungrinning corpse
and that of her firstborn in the topgallants
of a young tree, out of ground reach, to grow: restart
a cycle of maybe something more pastoral
commencing with beetles, then maggots, then ants.

Steel Giraffes

There are, probably, somewhere
arms as petal-slight as hers;
there are probably somewhere
wrists as slim;
quite probably, someone has
hands as slender-leafed as hers;
the fingers, probably
bare of rings, as thin.

Certainly, there is nowhere
such a dolour
of funnels, mastings, yards,
filaments of dusk ringing shrouds
woven through the word goodbye,
riveted steel giraffes
tactfully looking elsewhere,
necks very still to the sky.

Giovanni Jacopo Meditates

(on Aspects of Art & Love)

The Poet's or Playwright's Function
Is to embark physically

Upon the Consciousness of his Generation;
Not merely as the Conscience

Of his Time; nor solely to reflect
Disintegration, if Disintegration

Is the Shaker of his Time's stormy Seas.
But to anchor a Present,

Nail to its Mast
One Vision, one Integrity

In a Manner so memorable
It fills Part of a Past.

A Poet's or Playwright's Enthusiasms,
These. The proper Pursuit

For a Gentleman remains to master
The Art of delaying his Orgasms.

Giovanni Jacopo Meditates

(on his Weighting in The Last Great Scorer's Book)

When my Corpse and Soul unwind
In that final Dialysis
& my case is being divined
Will the Charge be 'Satyriasis'?

At the Moment of Trans-shipment
When the Bench takes Quill & Vellum,
Will 'Sins' head such Equipment
As this Leg-hooked Cerebellum?

Are 'Napes of Necks' an Issue
To be raised at my Correction?
Is 'Dawn's erectile Tissue'
An inadmissible Connection?

Will there be an outraged Ripple,
Forensic Chins in Lapels tucking,
As each non-maternal Nipple
Is called where I've lain sucking?

Should the First-Cause prove Feminist
—Madame-Generalissimo!—
Will the Alternates be 'Chauvinist',
'Oral Hang-Ups' & 'Machismo'?

At the End of this Compacture,
In my new Rôle of Deponent
I must plead Non-Manufacture
Of each happy strange Component.

Map Reference

You cannot capture precisely the nature
    of love for it is an oblique advance
upon a hill by a skirmishing soldier

    who moves this way or that, up, past thickets,
bush, rocks and streamlets, boulders and braced thorn-trees;
    running breaks for cover, ever upwards;

exposed at times, pretends the taut guerilla
who—peasant's clothing on a sheepish wolf—
loiters alertly to the nearest corner

to crouch reconnoitre the snaked ascent. . .
the summit gained, lies panting and bewildered,
bemused or drunk from knowing he is safe;

rolls on his back to smile up at the ceiling
of sunlit blue and harmless clouds; light up
or picks his teeth with an adjacent grass-stem;

to swing off down the hill, while behind him
tomorrow's detail waits: same hill, the assault
more affable, the not-so-sure terrain.

A Natural History of the Negatio Bacillus

i *Definition of Negatio*

The distance between emotion and intellect, or heaven and earth, when such distance constitutes pathogenesis.

Thought to be caused by a gram-negative, anaerobic, spore-forming bacillus, probably growing readily on artificial media, it is known to arrest psychogenesis.

ii *Origins of Negatio*

In the beginning was a world quite naturally in contact with the principle of its creation.

One man stood up, like a tree, followed by others: their heads in the clouds, feet on the ground, unaware of such facts. Emotion and intellect enjoyed some unification.

One man stood up and held the principle off from the world exactly the height of a man. It is thought this had something to do with the cant or size of his head or fists.

His stance caused unnatural disturbances: adjustment was required in the principle and from the deprived surface: both wreathed themselves in the mists.

iii *Epidemiology of Negatio*

One man felt that by standing on stilts he could elevate himself further from the common ground.

One man felt that by standing on stilts he could elevate his head to a higher place. Heaven retreated a little without a sound.

One man felt that by otherwise using his stilts he could clear more room for himself, employing them to back up his demands as somewhat unsubtle hints.

Heaven and earth had to get out of range fairly quickly. The Q, or quarantine principle became mandatory and has been applied ever since.

iv Aetiology of Negatio

Natural immunity to the negatio bacillus is exhibited by those wholly of the earth or of the sky as these touch where those are, although this population steadily decreases.

It comprises all animals except the rabid; small children observing fireworks; certain women and a few primitive societies unravaged by starvation or other diseases.

Also by some saints and prophets, except the rabid, and a few isolated and inexplicable souls who have discovered the hidden itinerary.

Onset of negatio usually occurs at puberty and there is no known cure, except perhaps an awareness of itself but this is usually temporary.

Short-term alleviation is obtained by lying very flat upon or under the earth or its natural waters; but this has been known to be hazardous in both execution and function.

The disease is highly contagious as the bacilli are readily absorbed, resisting all modern techniques aimed at their destruction.

Certain older remedies, now under reinvestigation, may prove efficacious.

All cases, without exception, terminate fatally, the cadaver invariably becoming double infectious.

v Diagnosis of Negatio

When the patient's hand curls compulsively: aggressive knuckles up or acquisitively down, in whichever plane it is put.

When heaven is gone forever and earth gathers itself to flinch from the patient's foot.

vi Prognosis in Negatio: a case-history

There was a man with a soul which had arms holding on to whatever piece of earth he was on to wherever it is that the gods live.

The arms became attenuated as his mind questioned the task of linkage. (Note: linkage is a discipline or it can be instinctive.)

He stopped holding, commenced pushing, and failed to grow fast enough to occupy his expanding vacuum.

Vertiginous from the distances at hand, he complained of a terror of drowning. And proceeded to do so, flailing, clutching at nothing in that continuum.

Or at artefacts which do not float in this medium which is nothing at all whatsoever. Besides, his musculature had deteriorated and his grasp, though avid, functioned somewhat weakly.

His corpse is now an important corpse in one of those corporations of lesser importance that deals with corpses obliquely.

vii Prophylaxis: 'Contra-Negatio' mantra

'O father in heaven and my mother earth, love each other and keep contact with each other through me thy child.

Divorce not over me, condemn me not to the void between, and let me not be by nothingness beguiled.'

Locus

No, there is no going back;
and everything ahead
is earned with painful slowness.

There is not much can be said
except 'Sorry . . .' or 'Welcome . . .'
The stillnesses are themselves

self-contained, solitary,
quite uncommunicative.
A sort of spectre lies dead-

centre of these, face covered.
Of course, there is always bread,
or the sky on a clear night.

Under Capricorn

The first dominated from
the crest of a roadcutting.

Fecund, fornicatory;
hairy flank tun-tight; yellow
mad intelligent eyes bright
under quick horns; shaft damp still
from spraying his angled wives,
he wheeled and the last of him
was a leathery scrotum.

The road doubled back down and
there he was, or his brother,
rocking-horsing it down then
up the scarred embankment face.

As mist boiled up, they were all
about: rearing, threatening,
menacing the car windows
with split hooves; Fu Manchu tufts
below foolish horse faces
bobbing and weaving, bat-ears
flapping until the car seemed
ringed, by short ardent devils.

Another turn of the road,
and only an old man there:
mist coiling his thin ankles,
headdress flapping, both arms raised
like Moses; smiling, bowing
from the edge of the highway,
bleating the loud ironic
blessings or curses of a
temporarily deprived
if most patient Lucifer.

Sonatina of Peter Govender, Beached

Sometime busdriver
of *Shiva's Pride*, *The Off-Course Tote*,
The Venus Trap and *The Khyber Pass Express*.
I've fathered five bright, beguiling,

alert-eyed but gill-less children.
I had to fish:
first, surf; then the blue-water marlin.
(I heard a Man once
walked water without getting wet.)
Old duels for fares:
The South Coast road—all we could get;
my left hand conning the wheel.

My last was *Dieselene Conqueror*
—night-muggings, cops,
knives, that coked and jammed injector
—right hand nursing in me a reel,
the cane cracking at the start of the day,
things of the land becoming remote.
My prime as oarsman:
heroics of the offshore boat,
catching all that steel slabs of sea could express.
My porpoise-wife is gone, seeded,
spent, queen among curry-makers.
I'm old now, curt.

I've monosyllables for strangers
who stop by asking
questions while I repair my net.
Things learnt from the sea
—gaffing the landlord, the week's debt,
scooping in the crazed white shads,
twisting the great transparent mountains
past a wood blade—?
Contempt for death is the hard-won
ultimate, the only freedom
(—cracking the cane at the end of the day—):
not one of the men I knew could float.

The Zoo Affair

With some it is water shrugging, bunched and oily
at the quayside—the cold welcome of lewd carpets;
for others, the pineal-sucked lure, dragging dizzy
and out from windy skyscraper parapets.

With him it was the tiger: beautifully slack,
indifferent; sleep and captivity thinned;
lying on a fat pole like a striped rug, back-
legs adangle, forepaws crossed under chin.

He even learnt a few words of Bengali (culled
from Tagore) and leapt the ditch to press
long and urgently at the bars, mad to scratch unpulled,
tortoise-shelled and round furry ears.

Angry keepers and others ordered him back and he
went, backwards, arms out, aching and bent
about air the size of a tiger, and thought of his granite-
faced and quite unfurry apartment.

To shed his love one night he broke in, sat his
city trousers a moment on a foliage-crusted stone wall,
jumped running for the beloved bars, fumbled latches
and reverently entered the shrine through the feed-door.

For perhaps one second he felt it, face buried in rank
cat's fur: the sleepy response. Then the rasped purr
meshed with metallic springs. The barrelling flanks
pumped an outraged blast from alien vaults of power.

They found him on the floor early next morning, his head
a split and viscid watermelon; loosely the wet tufts
of combed brains spilled, his smile quiet through the red;
beside him, for warmth, the cosy sprawl of his love.

Dust

The bundle in the gutter had its skull
cracked open by a kierie.
The blunt end of a sharpened bicycle
spoke grew a solitary
silver war-plume from the nape of his neck.
I turned him gently. He'd thinned to a wreck.

It was my friend Mketwa. He was dead.
Young Mac the Knife, I'd called him,
without much originality. Red
oozed where they'd overhauled him.
An illegal five-inch switchblade, his 'best'
possession, was stuck sideways in his chest.

He had been tough; moved gracefully, with ease.
We'd bricked, built walls, carted sand;
pitting strength against cement-bags, we'd seize

and humpf, steadied by a hand.
I paid the regulation wage plus fifty
per cent, his room, his board. He wasn't thrifty.

We were extending the old house I'd bought.
Those baked-lung middays we'd swill
the dust with cans of ice-cold beer. I thought
he must be unkillable,
except by white men. Each night the beerhall
took him: stoned wide, he would not stall or fall.

I don't think he learnt anything tangible
from me. From him, I learnt much:
his mother, cattle, kraal; the terrible
cheat that repaired his watch; such
and such pleased a woman; passes; bus queues;
whereabouts to buy stolen nails and screws.

His wife in Kwa Mashu, a concubine
in Chesterville, a mistress
in town: all pregnant. He'd bought turpentine
but they wouldn't drink it. This
was the trouble with women. Letters came
we couldn't read. He found another dame.

He left—more money, walls half-done, him tight—
to join Ital-Constructions.
Perhaps it had been white men: I am white.
Now, I phoned the ambulance
and sat with him. It came for Mac the Knife;
bore his corpse away; not out of my life.

Ruth Miller

Spider

No spider struggles to create
The beautiful. His tensile arc
Knows mathematics in the dark;
A Michael Angelo of air
Who weaves a theory that states
Ultimatums on a hair.

Born to the purple of his need
He has no unsolved problems. He
Suffers no dichotomy,
But wakes to work and works to kill;
Beauty empiric in his greed,
Perfection in a villain's skill.

Ragblown summit of the ooze
Of soft warm mud that split and stirred—
I hold within my skull the word
Sealed and socketed; yet my hands
Fashion with artifice and ruse
Not wily web, but witless strands.

But when the poor cold corpse of words
Is laid upon its candled bier,
I, vindicate, will shed the tear
That falls like wax, and creep unheard
To weave in silence, grave and bowed,
The pure necessity—a shroud.

Birds

The lion, even when full of mud, with burrs
On his belly, tangled, his great pads heavy
And cracked, sends such a message on the dry air
As makes all smaller animals wary, their fur
Rising in silken shivers, their horned heads
Up with the wind, reading its tragic story.

There is nothing majestic about death. Yet the king
Remains royal, and knows it; is accepted,
Though fled. Only the tiniest things—

The birds, whirr down from the tall sky, fling
Their feathered softnesses at shadows, dare to move
In his company, dare to sing.

Suppose a million birds could once shake loose
From the tops of trees, from the white horizon,
Veering in a soft outflinging noose,
Clouds in their clouds, lightning in their claws—
To peck out his sagging heart. How royally they would bedizen
His beggarman bones with the charity of their wings.

Aspects of Love

1

Green things grow in the wrong places.
They unfeather in the emphasis
On noughts in the sum.
Love is no logician, hears the argument
Blandly, never to profit
By the Socratic method,
And puts forth greenness on outlandish stone.

2

Love? We should smother it
And push it up the chimney—
He said, half meaning it.
We know now what he intended
For finding love at their door
On a cold night, people—if they are wise—
Will push it up the chimney into the smoke before
It wails at them with such clenched desire
As will bring into the quiet house
The significant ecstatic loss.

3

On the high hill in the cold wind
On a sunless day
You brought me a bird seeking to unsay
Its vulture moments. Though I was afraid
I felt its warmth undo my startled hand.

Across

Across the chalk line
Sketched down the centre of the cluttered room
Across this line they dare not tread
But, carefully, may look
Look at each other in the clotted gloom.
May speak. Speak? Yes, if they turn
A deaf ear in a blind eye, may find
What otherwise they could not seek.

Out of the catchpenny cloth
The scissoring phrase cuts ragged
Emperor's clothing for the naked.

Thus they remain
Robed in the correct phrases
And gaze
At the dying light
And say—and say?
What was it you were saying, dear, what was
The word missed, when we were so enthralled
Shaping and cutting our imperial palls.

Words, cut quickly! Stitch, stitch
Bright needle, furiously, the cloth!
Soon we may not be able to recognise which
Is spider, which breathing, which a folded moth.
Across the chalk line, invisibly, the soft dust quests.

Those lips which once so rapturously
Kissed, those breasts
Wait for the moment. Wait . . .
The chalk in a gritty puff may one day be erased.
Then palm to palm, mouth to mouth, they'll meet
At last, their shameless clothes at their naked shame-less feet.

Voicebox

I have known her since I was a child.
I recall her in the suffusion of one morning
With her firstborn in the incredible bed,
Its white horizon steppes stretching flatly
Past the headlands of the two fat pillows,
Furrowed with grooves of valley legs and loins;

Biblical birthing of the dark damp fur,
The cracked egg of the baby's skull repeating
'In, out breath; save me from harm
I am egg thin, have mercy on me Lord.'

I remember her as ineffable,
I who gawked in my teens at the useless father
Occasionally hovering, shamed as an old bull.
Beautitudes filled each crevice of the air,
We were afloat, she and I, on revealed meanings.
Even the purse of the baby could spill nothing further.

Last week this woman walked into exile.
She is on her way to a defined Siberia.
The membrane that giddily gauds the delicate throat
Is dying or dead—the distinction belongs to Time.

She has not spoken for months except in a whisper.

Soon they will take away the little toy
The fragile mechanical toy that says—I am,
I want, I must, I shall—the song each singer
Sings with his pulse.

Beast grunts, dog barks, cat mewls.

The drunkard curses unintelligibly in the dark.
But she who is as gentle as milk
Must lie in the ward like a baby and beat out breath
Against the obdurate granite of our voices.

Tomorrow we'll order the bacon, remember the eggs.
Cracking the skull of the egg into the pan
We'll watch the pure globe grow out of God's hand
And praise him for all his mercies.

Now we must place our hands upon her throat
Pulsing like a skull, to hear the guttural
Guttering quenching of a fluted candle.

In the bat-soft cave we were afraid
And forced the word up—Aagh! into the dark.
Now we are afraid to enter her.
We stay outside at the entrance and long ineptly
To make, for the first time, fire,
To call, for the first time, Come.

Beast grunts, dog barks, cat mewls.

Perhaps she will learn to nod, to nod her head
Like a circus horse tossing; perhaps she will learn the patience
To wipe with a damp cloth the fear from our mouths
Before we kiss her on her breaking lips.

Submarine

Icarus swaggered into his dandelion death
Knowing the wings were strong, being his seed-maker's.
When he plunged, the crumpled sea was deathless.

But within depths so dense that even fishes
Abandon the domelid pressure to slow, dark
Lumpish things, or reeling threads
Lamped with a million moons in the seasonless weather—
Atom on atom, fathom on fathom, the lords
Of the earth and sky in their sleek phallus ram
Through forests of throttled night and rubber weed,
Packed with steel on steel, to hang there driftless.

The sea humps, thick and crammed.
Itself upon itself pressed in coiled weight;
Gathers a muscled push, one huge Laocoon heave.
Rivets melt like motes, bulwarks sway gelid,
The steel is mothed and butterflied. There are no more men.
The swaying list in the impacting solid
Thins, miles high, onto a white beach
Where Heaven is always Up.

While the persistent tides
Wait secretly to smash
Those whom dark hells in privacy corrupt.

Long Journey

A slotted arrowhead, the thrumming train
Threads through the angry scrub, turns to the North,
Where rows of mealies stream in tasseled strands.
Wind will devour them and the white worm tunnel
Their sweetest hollows, yet the grain
On speckled green will seed, munching cows will snuff

The goodness from the sourest stalks, grow fat
In heavy milk on the cold bitten bales.
Nothing is lost but time which comes like the worm
Again and yet again.

Along the spearing rails the eye is drawn
Toward the double vista of a dream
Which binds horizons down. We recognise
The station that we passed a year ago.
The trees are taller now; the dust remains.
Corrugated iron dazzles in the sun.
A dog barks, the chickens scratch in the dust. A child
Dumps sand from a pail and does not lift her head.

Threaded with iron frets, the bridges fling
Black parentheses across the mud
Of dried-up rivers. Occasionally a stream
Thinly repeats the sunlight's shaking glare.

Into the vacuous yawn of tunneled dark
We creak, and yellow-wedged the walls lurch past.
Sound solidified in masonry.
Breath stops. Ears tauten. Memory
Tries to forget the tonnage of the hill.
Almost too late the air grows clean, the arch
Widens on sanity. The hills look small again,
Each tunnel's shining pinpoint piercing sight
With pain but not with vision.

We pass through fields of sunflowers, shabby old women,
Each wearing the bright face of a golden virgin,
And starring the veld the pointed aloes, making
Asterisks on the reading-line horizon.
What was the sentence there unsaid: was the message urgent,
Or reading it would we find ourselves once more mistaken,
Waking one morning in the cindery darkness
Stiff and cold on the platform, never having moved,
Or opening our gritty dreamer's eyes
On streets we never knew, on hills unmapped?

Through the bony continent of skull
Cave-socketed our minds reach rag-bound cities
And sidings where the train stops for a while
Hot in the noonday veld, bare as a cloth with crumbs,
Silvered with milk-cans in the clattering dawn.
(Through the dark shutters the slatted sunlight draws
Thin lines of neon-like intensity.)

Thus one cold morning we may reach awareness
Of destinations, having learned to survive
Distances immense with nothingness;
While sullen with time the yellow rivers gather
Each bordered province in a shrivelled pouch
Within which we, the cunning bones of witchcraft,
Shake and stir.

The Stranger

The light plays tricks upon the senses—
Dense dark things—that can't unlearn
The first lesson, the stern
Reality of the uncorrected vision.

Coming up Cavendish Road, in the late evening, saw
Under a lamp-post, on the lifting corner
His feet set against the flight of the lifting hill—
Bare legs astride—a Japanese Samurai.

In the shadow of the lamp he glares
At invisible, invincible legions,
Their teeth bared, flashing curved metal,
Lust in their eyes, salty, bleeding

Ready to flash, move like a snake, sting—
Bring history into the quiet suburban streets
Where the grass grows and the red lilies
Burst like blood.
Samurai? One would be mad
To think it. Look again: It is only the old
African cleaner, in the late evening, at ease,
Slack, quiet, unassuming, his hands resting.

Passers-by flick him with a disregarding glance,
No more acknowledging him than they would
The Samurai in their own blood.

Tree

Shake the tree. The leaves
Cackle like red cockerels. The leaves
Shake out their russet wings and leap

From their bright summer perch
To the winter dayground.
The handsomest cock still crouches, sleeping

And the longest lasting leaves fail to fall
When one shakes the tree.
Therefore though it is now winter

There is a small crown of fire like fingers
Sketching a ruddy arabesque on the hard line.
The eye slumbers dreamily in the warmth of the dream.

The cruellest month then serves to reveal
The wiliest beauty proudly flexed to resist.
These few leaves remain the toughest-muscled.

What matter that the loudest song they sing
Will be cackled from a dungheap—for the dung
Smells of another hot summer.

Pebble

Down to the pebble
of me, I can hardly now
be eroded—only cracked open.
In the millionaire fields
this stone is a dead beggar.

The smooth pebble in one's hand
scooped from the wish-washing sea
is a toy to be treasured or a tool
to paperweight the dreams of a fool
or a grocer's demands.
It is abraded but smooth
while the pebble in the road is
as damaging as finished-and-done-with love.

Down to the pebble of me
though I acknowledge the atoms
and accept the void, a latter-day Galileo
recognising that This goes round That
or That round This
I am aware finally
that there are no heights, that a
packed and condensed spirit, Libido,—

call it what you will—
even a canticled cantankerous soul
is worn down to the nub, on which
no soft moss will grow. This is a shorn
sheared thing, too small
and insignificant to be pouched in a sling.
Goliaths walk unharmed. This is a dead stone
left in the road to rub and sting
a raw foot in a shoemile trampling of the hills.

Down to the pebble of me
when the dreams in the dreaming flesh
have been dammed and double-damned
what is left
is bone.

Sydney Clouts

Of Thomas Traherne and the Pebble Outside

Gusts of the sun race on the approaching sea.

In the air Traherne's Contentments shine.

A jewelled Garden gazed at him.

What shall be said of Paradise?

Obscure vermilion heats the dim pebble I hold.

The long rock-sheltered surges flash with spume.

I have read firm poems of God.

Good friend, you perceived bright angels.

This heathen bit of the world lies warm in my palm.

Epic

Metaphor and metaphysics
two old men:

'In the long barn of life we have turned over
and sleep on the streaked straw:
fire, fire and smoke.

This is the piled harvest.
I . . . and I . . . have seen
the knower and the known become the wood
of the roaring skyline of this neighbourhood.'

Within

You look long about you
intent on the world
on a midsummer day;
the sea flames hard
it is rumpled like tin,

the sun is burning
dimension away.
If you cast a pebble down
it will clatter on the waves,
your eye can not go in.
And it cannot find a tree
standing generous and full
or a house or flower
with individual power;
and it must not look within,
hardness afflicts you,
flat is the world you'd find:
a row of wooden rooftops
that can easily topple
and bring the heart down
and bring down the mind.

After the Poem

After the poem the coastline took
its place with a forward look
toughly disputing the right of a poem to possess it

It was not a coast that couldn't yet be made
the subject of a poem don't mistake me
nothing to do with 'literary history'

But the coast flashed up—flashed, say, like objection
up to the rocky summit of the Sentinel
that sloped into the sea
such force in it that every line was broken.

and the sea came by
the breaking sea came by

Intimate Lightning

Too succulent for quinces comes
this fresh quo vadis,
    Africa

    the bud
    the blossom
    the scent
    of intimate lightning.

Tusks traded for cash lie somewhere staling under hessian,
to be fetched for another buyer at the coast.
Tusks, skins, rhinoceros horn.

What I want, Zambesi's
abler darkness fools with:
the full penetrant
eye, and more, much more:

eye in whose obstinate dusks and rains
the forest opens;

truths of the long lianas tense with dew.

It promised these
once, but lost them
in me. I
now, in a scooped log, ride
upon More, More, the River of Night.

The Discovery

The heartbeat! the heartbeat! Be,
but, if, how, when, between.
Every drop of blood speaks by,
the soul in concept
storms the strings.
Here's the expedition, knot by knot,
the rigging and the prow.

Canary Islands, brightly;
Bojador, in darkness
darkness
esperança!

Rounding the Cape, the sodden
wooden grumble of the wheel.

Dawn Hippo

The size of a cavern for men to crouch in
by fire trickling small;
for demons uttered by name
to crowd like tropical thunder
and crackle against the wall,

he domes the birth of day;
built moving on the river,
shrubless mound of weighty sheen,
a large derisive slope
hammering back each ray,
he floats his quiet hilltop
he sizes up the morning;
a zone of bubbles happens round his head,
streaks of his glitter spear them dead,
breaking the break of day.

A fine froth scums his sides like primitive acid,
birds with sharp beaks fly over him;
he bulges landward
choosing a shelved approach,
the water shallows where he wants it to,
pushes in savage rings that smash
high reeds and rock the river. Mud swarms,
mud slimes his paddling belly as he climbs
heavily wagging the water away.
The full ridiculous splendour mobs the stones:
thunder and lightning jostle on his bones.

The Sleeper

for Marge

When you awake
gesture will waken
to decisive things.
Asleep, you have taken
motion and tenderly laid it within,
deeply within you.
Your shoulders are shining
with your own clear light.
I should be mistaken
to touch you even softly,
to disturb your bold
and entirely personal devotion
to the self that sleeps
and is your very self,
crucial as when you hasten
in the house and hasten through the street,
or sit in the deep yellow chair
and breathe sweet air.

Unaware of the stars
outside our window
that do not know they shine,
as well as of the wild sea
that can have no care,
as well as of the wind
that blows unaware
of its motion in the air,
sound be your rest
and gentle the dreaming
of your silent body
passionately asleep.
Can a cloud stay so still?
Can a bird be so lonely?
It seems you have found
great patience in your breath:
it moves with life,
it rehearses death.

Idiot Child

for R. V.

A solemn reverberating gold
sullened the sky and that is why
I took my tireless dolt
to run on the grass,
my dear dumb human colt
to thud on the green grass
looking up wild at the wildness he loved
of the tearing sky.

He leapt like a big stone
that starts at the brink
of a crude slope loosened by water.
Hardly could I bear to see
though I had watched him
a multitude, tiring never at all
to see him lock his clumsy hands
and fall on the ground with glee.
Good child, I said, though he never will hear me,
dearest child, when you were long ago born
unrespectably silent,
I did not hate you at all with such painful tenderness.
I was a long time preparing for my love.

What sealed you when you were born?
I stood in the dawn room
praying death into your cot where uninhabitant
you lay unborn.
Unborn?
O manless child, play wild
reverberant stones into the holes of snakes,
more perfect than your being and yet not made
even with such balked purposes:
torn edges of a dream that cannot sleep,
of sleep whose dreaming flares on a moonless mound.
Go wriggle your lenient fingers in the grass
sparing the snails with terrible natural sense:
ballooned your jaw with subtle symmetry,
unfeebled grace, yet feeble beauty blown
into disreputable clownishness.

O severed race, blood nearest, sinless child,
watch me if you can watch me one slow
second as I stand upon the ground,
this actual spot of balance where I suffer
eyes that so painfully
love and respect your driven dance,
that living I must undesperately fall
the direst slope that any man can fall
the cruellest desperation that you fall
in stricken silence falling as you fall.

For the Thunder

He salts and he strings the foreleg's
curled congealing gallop
to a branch
where it swings as it gently rots, releasing
buck to the full taste, turning
in the russet of the curing hook, the oaktree.

He turns in the shade.
Close by are the sheds hushed thick and forceful
with their childlike mountains of grain.
They gape their fullness as he walks up to the house,
his eye slow on the black man.
'Izak, are the horses fed?'
'The horses are now fed, baas.'

His 'ja' hangs low in his breast.
The gable's cloud, the stone-white curls that receive

the doorclick as it shuts below them, speed the shades
as the shadows fly, the shades that turn the globe;

and his townish children pain him,
the blacks bring in the harvest:
he endures the truth of movement, but he can shoot.
Something always moving away,
his children or his quarry
or the powerful speck that has edged into his sight
running from camouflage clear into space.

His angry rule alone has only begun
and history must rot for him.
Bowls of purple, bowls of red
in the big bright room.
At evening he will take down the buck's leg.

Perseus Adams

The Leviathans

'The South African Museum may claim to have one of the best collections of whale skeletons in the southern hemisphere'— From the official Guide Book by Dr K.H. Barnard

Foliage or flesh can sheathe a blade;
never the pure winter,
the honed and scolloped cold
of a liberating truth

and because of this and the strata,
the roots of space they promote,
the thoroughfares of height,

I visit the whale-house. They hang there
ready to share in a calm, galactic drift,
their empty bodies' inexhaustible braille
yielding to the mind's fingers
the architecture of silence,
the blue-print of timelessness and weight.

And slowly, majestically, their kin appear:
Redwoods, glaciers—
zones of the earth-held sun-birds
whirling on the latest Apollo;
the homesteads of projecting care
when two friends meet and walk

moments mounting to fullness, then overflowing
Strait-laced cumulus, moonscape
whose stillness spears my poise
then heals it bloodlessly—
as you draw me deeper in
my gaunt mime prods what it will soon outwear;
bone reaches up for bone
as if death were trying to stage a ballet

I had not known steep zeros could be
so strictly omnific,
so augmenting in what they do.
Right Whale, Sperm Whale, Fin Whale,
proud behemoths all,

you teach me this over and over
but cut me with another vista:

You alive—fathoming the dew
lifting your fountain in joy
to curl the sky, a thundering hill
a dark cloud
sending back rain into the sea.
Against the blaze of your presence there
how poor this is, how icily thrifty,
purged of genesis, light's veiled fever
and all that nails one
in dire loyalty to the bruising hour
and it's because of this,
a sense of so much
                                        gone astray
that I'm glad finally to forgo

your draughty X-ray's incisive exposure,

this mute act of your
tumultuous
involuntary strip-show.

The Cafe Bioscope

In the smoking darkness
    before films that jump and flicker,
assaulted by sound
    itself nicked, skinned, suddenly
hollowed—
    I muffle time, I strangle it
sometimes losing track of it with other
    drop-outs, drifters, the incurably
lonely. We come in and we sit down.
    We are glad to be cavemen
    around our twentieth century fire.

The beam from the back struggles slightly
    to mesmerise us, to thread us
like beads onto its second-hand necklace,
    eventually wins through. Its victory
is undercut by harassed waitresses
    bringing cooldrinks, tea, coffee
and by shadowy newcomers thickly brushed

with pollen of sunlight, fresh air
the tangled coldness of the indifferent city.
Ahead, six-guns continue
to flash, to roar—

Until once more we subside, give way,
till our bruised or broken dreams
realign themselves in the cooped night
that levels us, then folds us
quietly into its blaring eye. An outlaw
gallops off to a whiff of cheap
perfume. A man (probably queer)
nudges me with his knee. At the end
my drug imbibed, I make for the door
leaving many who still cling
to the sad merry-go-round.

Dollar Brand (Abdullah Ibrahim)

from: **Africa, Music and Show Business**

blues for district six

early one new year's morning
when the emerald bay waved its clear waters against the noisy dockyard
a restless south easter skipped over slumbering lion's head
danced up hanover street
tenored a bawdy banjo
strung an ancient cello
bridged a host of guitars
tambourined through a dingy alley
into a scented cobwebbed room
and crackled the sixth sensed district
into a blazing swamp fire of satin sound

early one new year's morning
when the moaning bay mourned its murky waters against the deserted dockyard
a bloodthirsty south easter roared over hungry lion's head
and ghosted its way up hanover street
empty
forlorn
and cobwebbed with gloom

life in a national park/or – take five

last night two monkeys stumbled onto an
AMAZING
COLOSSAL
FANTASTIC
secret

on the outskirts of an african village
where they had been sleeping off a drunken stupor
they discovered an ancient clock
ticking away in 1979
(they worked it out)

they were jubilant

after much deliberation
as to who the rightful owner was
(they even casted lots)

they finally decided that the whole world should know of this
amazing phenomenon and that by using their usual 'pay-while-
you-hear' ritual, they could ensure themselves a life time of
happiness and if it came to the push they would
DISCOVER
EXCAVATE
and even
INVENT
more clocks

this morning for some obscure reason (they thought)
the clock decided to change to 4/4
they were furious

learned gorillas were called in on this appalling example of disobedience

the suggestion that the clock's mechanism be studied was accepted, half
heartedly

but alas, it was too late
for when they touched the spring, there occurred a terrifying explosion
and the whole monkey kingdom was blown to bits

the resultant itch woke up TIME
and she scratched vaguely under her armpit

Robert Dederick

On a Theme of Tennyson's — Mariana Farther South

She drove along the only street,
Post in the boot, newspapers rolled,
Leather smelling of humming heat,
The wheel almost too hot to hold;
And by the one hotel she turned,
The ribbed road jabbing at her tyres,
And all the unconsuming fires
Of summer round her baked and burned;
  'The farmer took a wife' she said,
  And *'Gosh!'* she said, *'Gosh, what a change!*
  No more for me the broken shed,
  The blackened sluice, the moated grange!'

When winter lowered the northing arc
Of sun and dusted koppies white
And closed a caul of chilling dark
About the homestead's warmth and light,
And bedroom windows were frost-starred,
And static—as she brushed her hair
And draped her slip across a chair—
Crackled its tiny fusillade,
  'The farmer took a wife' thought she
  And *'Gosh!'* thought she, *'I was re-born!*
  No more that hot high balcony,
  No living forgotten, loving forlorn!'

Oh, there were bad days when the world
Lay parched and panting, days when all
Seemed one dry dam, clay-petals curled
Within a cracked and crumbling wall;
Then would begin some homing beam
To hum in her of far-off things:
Of cloud, soft shadows, emerald Springs,
Summers fleeting as a dream;
  And she would rage about the house:
  'These shimmering wastes I will exchange
  For flitting bat and shrieking mouse
  Within the lonely moated grange!'

But no, she never did; she stayed
With goats' pained faces and curving horns
And clank of turning windmill-blade
And sweet-thorns' white and bitter thorns;
And often along the only street
And the ribbed road where the axle rings
With flung-up stones, often she sings
In knifing cold or dizzying heat:
    'The farmer took a wife' sings she,
    And *'Gosh!'* sings she, *'Gosh, what a change!*
    Never again that balcony!
    Never again that moated grange!'

Whilst Walking in a Dry River-Bed

Though walking in the middle of a road
Becomes unsafe as more and more there is
Too much too at me pricking like a goad
Toward one or other of extremities,

Some primitive in me lies not too deep
To nudge me out from under boundary-trees
Whence any creed or anti-creed could leap
To jar off-balance my antitheses;

And here for once his nudgings not in vain,
Between high banks rare waters swirling round
Gouged as an earnest of their swirl again
Over these stones more bleached meanwhile than drowned.

Here to the primitive in me his due:
Plumb down the middle I can walk, and do.

Keorapetse Kgositsile

Notes from No Sanctuary

1

There are no sanctuaries
except in purposeful action;
I could say to my child,
There are wounds deeper
than flesh. Deeper and more
concrete than belief in some god
who would imprison your eye
in the sterile sky instead of
thrusting it on the piece of earth
you walk everyday and say,
Reclaim it.

But I let it pass since
it is really about knowing today and how.
This is what it has come to. Daughters
and sons are born now and could ask,
you know: Knowing your impotence why
did you bring me here?

I could say:
Life is the unarguable referent.
What you know is merely a point
of departure. So let's move, But we have
been dead so long and *continue*. There will
be no songs this year. We no longer
sing. Except perhaps some hideous
gibberish like james brown making believe
he is american or beautiful or proud. Or
some fool's reference to allah who, like
jehovah, never gave a two-bit shit about niggers.

I could say, like Masekela,
We are in jail here. Which is
to say, We have done nothing.
I could say, . . . but see,
What difference does it make
as long as we eat white shit?
no matter what it is wrapped up in!

2

How many deaths and specific
how or when ago was it
the rememberer said, where
to go is what to do?

Still we talk *somuch!*

And cold black hustlers of my generation claw
their way into the whitenesses of their desire
and purpose. Here a slave's groan and shudder
is a commodity the hustler peddles newly-wrapped
in *brother, sister, revolution, power to the people . . .*

So now having spoken our time or referent,
a people's soul gangrened to impotence,
all the obscene black&whitetogether kosher
shit of mystified apes . . . Where then is
the authentic song? The determined
upagainstthewallmotherfucker act?

So say you say you float above
this menace, having violently tasted
white shit past the depths of any
word you know. Say you float above
the dollar-green eye of the hustler whose
purpose is cloaked in dashikis and glib
statements about revolution.

Say you float
untouchably above this menace, does
your purpose, if there be one, propose
to be less impotent than this poem?

Mazisi Kunene

The Civilisation of Iron

I saw them whose heads were shaved,
Whose fingers were sharpened, who wore shoes,
Whose eyes stared with coins.
I saw them
In their long processions
Rushing to worship images of steel:
They crushed the intestines of children
Until their tongues fell out.
I saw iron with sharp hands
Embracing infants into the flames.
They wandered on the roads
Preaching the religion of iron,
Pregnant with those of blood and milk.
I saw milk flowing
Like rivers under the feet of iron.
The earth shrank
And wailed the wail of machines.
There were no more people,
There were no more women,
Love was for sale in the wide streets
Spilling from bottles like gold dust.
They bought it for the festival of iron.
Those who dug it
Curled on the stones
Where they died in the whirlwind.
I saw the worshippers of iron
Who do not speak.

The Gold-miners

Towers rise to the skies,
Sounds echo their music,
Bells ring backwards and forwards
Awakening the crowds from the centre of fire.
Attendants at the feast glitter,
Wealth piles on the mountains.
But where are the people?
We stand by watching the parades
Walking the deserted halls
We who are locked in the pits of gold.

Arthur Nortje

Waiting

The isolation of exile is a gutted
warehouse at the back of pleasure streets:
the waterfront of limbo stretches panoramically—
night the beautifier lets the lights
dance across the wharf.
I peer through the skull's black windows
wondering what can credibly save me.
The poem trails across the ruined wall
a solitary snail, or phosphorescently
swims into vision like a fish
through a hole in the mind's foundation, acute
as a glittering nerve.

Origins trouble the voyager much, those roots
that have sipped the waters of another continent.
Africa is gigantic, one cannot begin
to know even the strange behaviour furthest
south in my xenophobic department.
Come back, come back mayibuye
cried the breakers of stone and cried the crowds
cried Mr Kumalo before the withering fire
mayibuye Afrika

Now there is the loneliness of lost
beauties at Cabo de Esperancia, Table Mountain:
all the dead poets who sang of spring's
miraculous recrudescence in the sandscapes of Karoo
sang of thoughts that pierced like arrows, spoke
through the strangled throat of multi-humanity
bruised like a python in the maggot-fattening sun.

You with your face of pain, your touch of gaiety,
with eyes that could distil me any instant
have passed into some diary, some dead journal
now that the computer, the mechanical notion
obliterates sincerities.
The amplitude of sentiment has brought me no nearer
to anything affectionate,
new magnitude of thought has but betrayed
the lustre of your eyes.

You yourself have vacated the violent arena
for a northern life of semi-snow
under the Distant Early Warning System:
I suffer the radiation burns of silence.
It is not cosmic immensity or catastrophe
that terrifies me:
it is solitude that mutilates,
the night bulb that reveals ash on my sleeve.

Apology from London

Only at the particular moment how
disappointment hurts. It is another scene
that hears the lark at dawn in boughs of lush
green—we must all return & break more stone

south over the sea to where the diseased wind
rages in the dockyard of the soul.
In an English spring we litter our sorrows
following each other in a muddied file

or grouped in Highgate round a dead philosopher's
bust on a tomb, harsh-featured. Rain
washed the garlands. Your tears
eroded me. This is the short & plain

says Chaucer, Bodley. Do not sorrow wise man
goes Beowulf in an Oxford dialogue.
An apology arrives at breakfast:
your last non-appearance makes you beg

mercy. You are my blood as much as he, she,
you have as much right as any other.
There are those in that sun & rock country
who wouldn't dare call me brother.

Not over the marmalade that I'm surprised
or fierce because of trivial error.
'The long love that in my thought doeth harbour':
it is the larger suffering symbolised.

Elias Pater

The Madman whom Jesus Cured

When I first came forward to take my place,
Once again, in your society,
You set the village curs barking at me,
Your women-folk eyed me with suspicion.

Why? Had I not combed my hair and my beard?
Did my tunic not hang in the best of taste?
My answers, were they not judicious?
Or were your demands on me more radical?

Listen to me, you men! you elders!
I have lived too long amongst the dead;
I have known too many demons by name;
I have been touched by the finger of God.

You must continue to live, decay, die,
By the measure of your village wisdom;
See! I seize my wooden, vagrant's staff
And journey back into loneliness.

Anne Welsh

That Way

That way. He went that way.
The pink road through the brown hills,
The path across the yellow grass
Towards that lifted place
In those stone folds.

Bleak, they say,
The wind has no caress
But strips and burns.

The journey will be dusty,
Footfall after footfall.
And first the ash of evening
Will put out colour
Then nightfall overtake him.
The going is blind at times
For rock engulfs.

Moments of shelter
And of peace, perhaps—
When torn land is consoled,
The broken earth grows whole
And hills are loved by light.

Those coming back?
It's difficult to say—
Worn by weather,
Exposure under stars.

But that rock marks. It makes.
They look the same but have a different shape.
They say, when nothing is withheld
Rock takes them on,
Takes over, gives itself.
They say that terror goes,
That after night,
The shining of the morning is most marvellous.

Lionel Abrahams

Professional Secret

The voice between fashion notes and the serial
did not dispel the tea-time calm of Woman's Hour:
distinguished visitor, senior international nurse,
kindly recalling episodes from an interesting career.
'. . . Arriving while the guns could still be heard,
our first job in the Camp
was to sort out those we could save'
—the rest about the rest she left unsaid.
'Next came delousing:
we wore overalls, turbans, gloves,
trousers tucked into high boots,
worked on marble slabs
applying hard brushes all over the naked skins
—some like paper, but several surprising cases survived.
The lice once gone, the typhus death rate fell
to only twenty a day,
and within five weeks none from that cause.
We ran the whole Camp, of course, as a hospital:
those who weren't ill were in a bad way from starvation.
We had to feed them all on milk and honey
or they'd have died . . .'
This expert on aftermaths,
mileposting her life with disasters,
was undistracted by distinctions one might draw
between the natural and the calculated cataclysm:
Skopje as much her job as Nagasaki.
She trailed death's binges with a minimum of disgust
('. . . Still miles away we began to smell the stench . . .')
to clean-up-after, make all possible repairs,
bringing to the business her special indifferent vigour
and no questions about Causes.
The smokestacked signs of automated rage
stirred no answering rage for her to tremble with;
for routines of hate she presumed no compensatory
paralysing love;
tenderness would have chained her useful hands,
prevented Red Cross holy work.
I wonder if intended listeners inferred
the same brute hint that stalks me through her story:
The theoried overmen
who cater death's gross feasts, do more

—infect the whole race so
our hands must be as hard as those that kill,
and scrubbed clean of the carrier, passion,
to bring the living milk and honey.

For Charles Eglington

A land without ruins
is not where you easily learn that to fall
or be felled is the only condition of victory.
The triumph that survives the fighting,
flaunts and takes the spoils
is easy purchase, Pick & Pay,
and stoics, assured their aspect of virtue endures,
scholars who have caught a corner of the scheme
and can explain (or explain why there's to be
no explanation), saints, heroes, stars
are neon flash.
The maths-man or the mystic in the void
or the clown juggling apples, punning on the news
to no one, down in chaos
breathes Buddha breath,
Fall singing, die and laugh,
praise the gone gods,
philosophise when you have understood
that none's meaning stands.
While your contracted decades wrinkle to the lines
of the only binding clauses, blindly be.
Not because life is One
or truth accumulates
like the cells of a foetus.
Going on is because the habits do this,
the hormones do that.
Poet's lines, thus, are star courses and climates,
and the poet's suicide is death by natural causes.

Shabbir Banoobhai

echoes of my other self

echoes of my other self
forever keep haunting me

the mind always logical
the blood speaking differently

by your own definition

by your own definition
i drink too deeply
the blood of roses

    lean on a leaf
    for comfort

    mistake mysteriously
    a thorn for a star

when the world curls itself
around my fingers
seas gather in my palms
trees sustain the sky

    my life lifts to loving
    love leaps to living

    and without words i strive to answer
    questions you have never asked

oh making you understand
is like trying to crush
the skull of a mountain

for my father

for my father

days
    when you roughshod your way
through town and village and countryside

when your father bought the radio
    he had promised so long ago
and the laughter of the child rippled in his eyes

when the boy cracked the whip of exuberance
    and the mother stayed quiet
for she knew he was young

when the man emerged
    from the hideout of the boy
and caught the blast of life on his face

when the man spat on his hands
    and ploughed the land
and watched the sky for rain

when wife and child
    sat by his side
and lit the fire that was once his pride

nights
    when the light of a full, full moon
seemed dull against your bright, white face

when we still hoped
    held your hand
tried to breathe our strength into you

when you faltered at last
    slipped from our grasp
lost your will in the hills

the border

the border

is as far
as the black man
who walks alongside you

as secure
as your door
against the unwanted knock

Ridley Beeton

The Watchers

There was this lady of the birds:
White-eyes would come to her
And mouse-birds visit in her house.

Bantams crossed the drawing room.
Deprived of flight, stayed to crumbs:
Left their eggs in nest-warm chairs.

Swallows fluttered in the wide eaves,
Doves throbbed overhead: she was filled
With that life that knew the skies.

The palpitating creatures in her hands
That she nursed from blood and bone
To sharp-winged messengers of light.

They leapt from her fingers into freedom,
Came back at the signals of her need.
She would wait for them day by day.

Then she had another guest.
Her bedroom was darkened: and outside
The watchers sang violently and long.

A Poem Never Written

I have never found a poem for you
Possibly because of the excluding dedication
To brilliance sought by you untiringly
With an off-hand modesty quite absurdly

Arrogant. Then when all the obfuscations
Of your cleverness dwindled down into a simple
Muddied sweetness and we sought the streams
The slippery pools made cries like birds

Ill placed I knew I should have written it
Told the fragile little as it was
For we were then both more than what
We wanted the world to want of us.

The Grackles

The Grackles
Perturb
The boring air about me

I am grateful to them
For affirming life

Or whatever it was
We were to say
In the usual
Academic phrases.

William Branford

Colonial Experience: Four Fragments

I. The Barbarians

The evening the legion sailed, I didn't go down to the harbour.
It was excessively hot, and military ceremonial
Though I despise it in theory, makes my eyes water.
So I sat at the end of the garden and watched the transports
Edging out of the river. The westerly wind
Came up at sunset and they hoisted sail,
Heaving into the dusk, and I went indoors.

Of course, some of our closest friends are barbarians.
I remember that very evening, old Armoricus
Brought us a couple of chickens and told us not to worry:
'Now we need Roman settlers more that ever; besides
The Chief is such an exceptional man, so cultured
And quite incapable of bitter feelings.'

II. Despereert Niet

White gateway under overarching green:
Armorial bearings and the defiant words:
'Despereert Niet!'
A little the worse for weathering.
But house and garden still commemorate
Old energies, old money, that brought home
Mahratta armour, Polynesian spears
And spread the lawns and spaced the obedient trees,
Drew up the orchards and the avenues
And set their peace upon an alien earth.

For me, the possible inheritor,
Of a nominal title to diminished resources,
What is the sense of recalling *Despereert Niet;*
The Spaniard repelled, the burghers under arms,
The enlightened eye of Commissioner De Mist,
The frigate in mid-ocean overhauling,
The Liverpool slaver?

III. Fellow-travellers

Seven on a lorry,
Swing in the tail of the traffic in the rain,
Impassive faces of Dingana's spearmen
Under municipal oilskins; travellers
On the same road as I.

Starting and stopping
Behind them at the traffic lights, I take
The courtesies of the road for signals, counting
A widening eye, a flash of teeth, the shout
Ntshebe! as communication.

Thus safely separate,
Behind the windshield, in the certainty
Of a parting of our ways not far ahead,
I to the office, they to the marshalling yard—
Phatic communion has its satisfactions.

If it were otherwise?
Finally face to face unshielded, with
No alternative route:
Fraternal grasp or terrible collision,
Blood-brotherhood or blood?

Seven on a lorry,
Vanish under the bridge at the road's fork.
Hermes, master of the ways,
Protect all travellers
On the same road as I.

IV

Humpty Dumpty sits on the fence,
Thinking of his impermanence
Since he'll fall by his own volition,
We'll leave him scheduled for demolition.

Jack Cope

Patient at Stikland Neuroclinic

She said—Once over the bridge
they never come back, they are
beyond hope, lost: they are
the incurables—And she touched
me to feel in my hand the promise
of a new rising from annihilation.

—There beyond the bridge it's hell
though I don't say they know
to the bone like we do. The wildflowers
grow better that side. Have you noticed
this place is a field of crazy blossom
colours? When my head's clear
I lie deep among them and the green furred
blades of grass. They don't like us
to lie too long out there alone in the sun
under the veins of the petals, you feel
too close to the earth, too heavy, drugged.
You learn the dangerous things.

Sometimes we wave to them over
the other side, and they just stare or
wave back or do strange sorrowing things,
pull faces and cry out like something
in the night. If they sent me there
over the bridge, I don't know . . .
but of course I can walk out anytime
I like. You can come and take me away
next week-end for a drive. Will
you come if I can talk them round?
They do listen to me. And we can run
naked in the sun on the white beach again
and dive in the cold sea. It's better free—
and we'll drink cherry heering and both
smoke the same cigarette with wet fingers.

There are a hundred steep steps
up the hillside to the saint's white tomb
(we'll visit that) and a hundred pairs of shoes
outside the little mosque. We can say a prayer
together and burn sandalwood sticks

and bow ourselves to the ground. Oh
I must not see the young veiled girls
roll down the stone stairway bleeding
from cut throats!

They are coming
to tell you time's up. You will find me
in the corridors waiting for you. I wait
and wait. Let me kiss you. Sometimes
I think it's not you at all. But ah
always I know it is! there's no-one else
I have to trick myself, see.

You can come
to our dance Friday too. We dress up,
look forward to it days if we remember.
Afraid too . . . it gets bigger, it changes shape
like something real and everything happens
there also like real, love too. It's not
so sad if you see it that way. You'll be here?
Right close inside your eyes I see myself.
You unfold my sunflower petals
like a sunflower.

Patrick Cullinan

Devils

That is a country where
At midday devils
Spiral from the river
And enter good Burgers
Who doze, sweating
On cast iron beds.

Night falls. Contagion
Is complete.
The devils wind back
To the marshes.
And on the bed a thing
Sits up and scratches,
Searching for the self
It lost at noon.

I have seen a man
(The Principal, Belmotto)
Go blind with dogma,
Write theses on a blackboard
For a whining child;
Or fill by slow ammanuensis
Note-books that were logic
For his lost Empire.
And then believing he could walk
On water
He drowned one morning
With his usual fuss,
Gurgling Aramaic
In a short, last prayer.

Another one, an Alexander,
Planned to blow the State away,
Contriving bombs
He killed his brother.
Now in a Home
He plays with paper,
And slashes foolscap into shapes
You'd swear
Could almost cry.

And lately I have seen them
In this country.
They are in the air.
Yesterday one came for me
And circled my siesta.
I laughed. Reason,
Good humour, alone
Can conquer devils.

But when from the tower
At midnight,
(Or thereafter as I choose)
I leap across the town,
The devils shall acknowledge
A superior; awed
By the heights I reach.
And I'll fly high, my friends,
Higher than the steeple,
Higher than
The priest can preach.

The Garden

Perfect? Almost. The roses blow
On long green lawns; the marble steps
Are guarded by glazed, heraldic dogs.
As a guest once said: 'The eye flows.'
And so it does, past pool and pool-room,
Border, vista, park
To hills which in the distance throb
With royal shades of purple.
But somehow the guests are uneasy.
The garden is not given, cannot be
Consumed like Scotch or good cigars;
Or Cherry Duckling Flambé,
(A speciality of the house).
No, the garden can't be taken, so
Back they go indoors and, if polite,
Write long letters thanking him.
Some, the more sensitive, cannot sleep.
The night-long susurration
Of a water sprinkler
Can cause insomnia.

He came one day for the first time.
A new possession. Looking up
From a drink, dictating, he saw
That it was good, as it should be;
But for one thing:
It seemed to him
The birds screamed too much,
Were bright with 'vulgar' colour.
Luckily, then and there,
The resident Director,
Sensing a dilemma, said: 'It's quite
All right, Sir, here,
In this country,
All birds cry like that;
Experts admit the hue is "gaudy".'
The boss nodded and noted the fact.
Like God resting
On the seventh day,
He knew it was not perfect
But decided to leave it like that.

The Billiard Room

The play of his power,
the living, you can smell
it in this room: the cues glitter like weapons,
the green nap of the table
was a battleground for him where conflicts broke
in the strategy of a game.

And I remember hearing,
at night above my head,
the sound of a glass breaking, and a burst
of rich laughter; then silence,
except for the powerful tread, the pacing
from angle to angle,
and the crack of a cannon
as the white slammed into the red. It's

all snuffed out now of course, like a long
Havana cigar, a Hoyo de Monterrey perhaps,
smoked down for an inch or two, and never
much more. The act has gone, his gesture
casual on an evening thirty years ago
is obsolete; now

only a sense of ritual pervades the room and feeds
familiar on the tokens of his power:

a German ceremonial sword
he captured in South West stands rigid
in a shell case, against one wall an old
propeller rots (and somewhere stuck in a drawer
there's an album showing photographs of the crash),
so that objects of steel and brass, records
of dead encounter have made this room
a potent place, the temple of my caste
where I must pay homage, the sour pietas
of son to father, the unforgiving
love that looks for only one thing in the past:
conflict as barren as dust. I have no god
but a giant who paces above my head,
who blusters nightly that in his turn
my son shall have his saga of Fee, Fie, Fum,
to grind my bones to make his bread.

Though I stand by a half opened window
and breathe in the air
the dust still stirs about me,
raised by a step on the floor,
and the smell that comes up is the smell of old power,
unbreaking love, unfinished war.

Jennifer Davids

Poem for my Mother

That isn't everything, you said
on the afternoon I brought a poem
to you hunched over the washtub
with your hands
the shrivelled
burnt granadilla
skin of your hands
covered by foam.

And my words
slid like a ball
of hard blue soap
into the tub
to be grabbed and used by you
to rub the clothes.

A poem isn't all
there is to life, you said
with your blue-ringed gaze
scanning the page
once looking over my shoulder
and back at the immediate
dirty water

and my words
being clenched
smaller and
smaller.

For Albert Luthuli

You a fragment of the sun
go turn the world
in the long strength
of your fingers

Bounded
you gave me
knowledge of freedom

Silenced
you taught me
how to speak

Somewhere a train
has reached a destination
and tonight
the cold fist of winter
clenches around the world

But beyond it
the endless pulsations of space
grow louder
and stars breaking the dark
grow large

Walk now father
unchecked
from sun to sun

C. J. Driver

A Ballad of Hunters

My great-grandfather hunted elephants,
Shot four hundred in a year,
Till one day his death turned round
And sniggered in his ear.

The theme's the same, the method changes—
Time has planned the ending,
Has turned the hunter to the hunted
And bred the next from nothing.

My great-great-uncle farmed alone,
Made next to nothing from his land,
Till at last the cancer took him,
Eating from his living hand.

The theme's the same, the method changes—
Time has planned the ending,
Has turned the farmer to the harvest
And bred the next from nothing.

Cousins and cousins in their dozens
Were killed in their mission churches
By the tribes whose heads they broke
To teach them the Christian virtues.

The theme's the same, the method changes—
Time has planned the ending,
Has turned the clergy to the converts
And bred the next from nothing.

My father's father died at Delville Wood,
Shooting Germans for his British past—
Left his wife a private's pension
And children to make it last.

The theme's the same, the method changes—
Time has planned the ending,
Has turned the sniper to the target
And bred the next from nothing.

Both my uncles fought the war,
Like lovers died a year apart—
Left some letters and a flag or two
And silence to be their art.

The theme's the same, the method changes—
Time has planned the ending,
Has turned the fighters to the dying
And bred the next from nothing.

Now I'm my subject, a sort of hunter
Stalking the blood of my family—
But hunted too by time's revenge
For all they made of my history.

The theme's the same, the method changes—
Time will plan the ending,
Will turn the hunter to the hunted
And breed the last from nothing.

David Farrell

Vigil

Upstairs in the wide high bed
she lies, alone on the bitter edge
watching the walls start to crawl
past her gaping eyes, and far from sleep.

The night she hears, bringing sounds
from outside her: a sudden drumroll of rain
leaping against the windy window;
the private slap of the child's feet
past the room's mouth on the landing . . .
the toilet heaves and hisses
like a sleeper disturbed in the dark.
To her, now, these are sounds
of the long-gone dead.

                                        Downstairs
the snap of another page, as he licks
thumbs . . . stares in thick silence.

Her hand drags the blanket up.
The cool rain thumps like feet on the stairs
and her eyes settle to a slow soaking.
From the quiet wall of her back
the bed grows wider.

Survivor

Just after dawn, at the peach tree
the grinning Alsatian killer had him
my favourite wild cat
by the bushed foot: but still he climbed on upward
and I choked on shock at the window
at his leg stretched to tearing point from yawning socket
—then with the explosion of my scream
the whole grey leg twanged back as the dog let go
swallowed a great gulp of lust
and was somehow gone.

But in that impossible moment
when life and death pivoted on his haunch
the tufted wild cat was permanently altered
by a gross hunching limp
and the total loss of his courage.
Hunter no more, he dumbly accepted a pension
of mince and milk at the safe backdoor
having learned that the price of survival
is salvation.

Michael Fridjohn

The First Time has to be with Sun

The first time has to be with sun
Setting in clouds of glory in the west
Of course. While birds twitter in
the larky branches. There can be no sin
In waiting till the stage is best
Set for that famous old tableau
Enjoying an unprecedented run:
The Bees' great hit 'Pollen-and-Stamen Show'.

It's never difficult to find new leads
To play the old charade with quiet grace—
Uninitiates tend to confuse their needs
And compensate with feeling what they lack in pace.
Yet with this lies their coming of age:
A tacit perception that they're not on stage.

David Friedland

The Complaint

I'm tired of writing poems about God
He doesn't exist
So why can't I leave him alone
In his heaven of not being,
And he should leave me
Alone in my heaven of not believing
We all know the stars don't go out at dawn
The sun dazzles us into belief
Once I kicked a sleeping rock till my foot ached
Then we lay back to back
But nothing happened.
Any sign would have been welcome
Even a bite.

Sheila Fugard

The Voortrekkers

Trek further white man
Powerless to love
Without any illusion
Recalling no vision
The hold is of the gun
The Laager swept clean
Hamburg Gronigen Haarlem
All ports of chance
Abandoned centuries ago
Find again the absent cities
Take up the threads of an
Eighteenth century dream
Lest the black sniper's bullet
Find soft marrow of bone
The wagon wheels have left
Only ruts in the road

Stephen Gray

Mayfair

O suburb of stripped cars & highrise hollyhocks
  where the greater unemployed
swat sweat that crawls like flies down fallen legs
  where cataracted chickens gawp
from turning spits in Costa's Terminus Cafe
  where housewives vie on volume
down a one-way street flushed with soap-opera
  & their potato-fat serving girls
shine the Dandy polish on their red knees

backyard archaeology turns up a shard
  plastic rattles glass coal
& the condensed milk throat of the neighbour's
  bat-eared military son
breaks all siesta on his A minor bugle practice
  the jackpot days are over for
the Dixi Cola pensioners in the Thursday
  post-office payout queue
decay like rope around their contoured necks

the mother's clinic scrapes a formless arm with vaccine
  tetanus is in the wind
scabby wild cats track their corrugated clawy paths
  to the bins of the Limosin Hotel
& miners from Frelimo stroll in unofficial gangs
  against the menace of stick em up & defence
& trespass on the Gaza Strip where Reggie and Honey
  packing through Majestic Mansions
deny all knowledge all involvement in crime

down the plane-tree Ninth Avenue rides a blue nun
  on a cross-barred bicycle
down the brick of the Dolphin Street swimming pool
  loiter kids held up by candy floss
down the intersection bounce Clover Dairies ice cream
  sidecars & bells of appetite
down the coach-house whitewash plunge rust and creeper
  & the ritual taxi ride to church
rounds a Pentecostal Sunday curve towards heaven

O Mayfair & a Chinaman's chest flat as a slime-tray
    parades the verandas of concrete waggon wheels
how uplifting!—the pumpkin on roofs still
    the TRG car come for southern flesh
& Mr Fonseca Builder unclasps his racing pigeons
    to spiral over smallness & the dumps
the fine golden sand the cyanide lagoon the synagogue
    the alcoholic pavements & knives & curlers
into undefeated clarity of the whitest air.

Sunflower

Poor sunflower, your
neck so stretched and
drooping to your feet

can't see the mossies
can't see your own
glory reflected around

sentenced to death
dropping seed in plastic
bags, it's all over

like the hanged man
Pretoria Central
Wednesday dawn.

In Memoriam: C. Louis Leipoldt

1

The farm in the foothills
I reached in a storm so potent
it seemed the whole Atlantic
was running overhead

the kindly boerevrou
led me down mudslides
where for that night I had
one rondavel and one candle

she was very possessive
she insisted they grew the best rooibos
(I'd tasted it and boerewors and her eggs)
that I would see in the morning

as she flagged down her doek
her skull caught in that light
accusingly at my khakiness
she said you wrote Oktobermaand there.

2

So by chance as I continued at ease
touring my land also looking for
I don't know kloofs to dive down
or Bushman paintings to decode

there was your burial cave
off the road in the Cedarberg
a high sun rising now
a sign pointing towards detente

and I stumbled onto whichever stone
you are laid out beneath
read the graffiti studied the plastic
wreaths signed the visitors book

and then o bushveld doctor
o neat folk poet good for a jingle
I'm afraid I drove on found
a kloof to dive into kaal.

3

But then it was delayed reaction
I was standing beneath those cedars
on sheet-metal rock humming
so that my voice reached up

far louder than expected
water dripping off me like mud
(I was suffering from sunburn)
dazzled by sky in the stream

it was your world took me over
there was Oom Gert and the
seepkissie and even the starved
babies and hanging your patriots

and the recoil of knowing o out-
of-date Sap that it's your
people now who hang freedom and
colonise the resistant poor

threw me into the rockpool
broke up the image
in such a nosedive of history
o you'd be anti your people today.

4

And it's years later I've got
over it the blacks write now
what you wrote then *they* know
when poetry of feeling's needed
and reading through you once more
(you were strong meat for a setbook)
I envy you your sentiment
your easy righteousness

and finally I appreciate your
love of nature and curried soldiers
your desire to lie alone far from it all
where every month's October for you.

Robert Greig

The Abortion

Too late now to recriminate.
Appalled, each consulted friends.
One said she knew a doctor who might . . .
Love-making now didn't seem right.

Somehow they spoke less and less,
Knowing three months could be dangerous.
Rather the pain than marriage, she said,
But she still loved him, she confessed.

Told himself it had been worth it,
Solicitous as a husband, tense
As a murderer. 'It happens
If you're careless' was all her parents said.

They understood, took the cheque, gave consent.
That night he spent with a girl
He screwed on and off. She wouldn't get pregnant—
He'd ensured she was on the pill.

When he called with flowers,
She was loving and pale in bed.
No need for the solemn face,
She laughed. Inside he was dead.

'Yes, a bit of blood—not painful.
Feel—my breasts are all milky.'
Swollen eyes. 'Was it a boy or a girl?'
He did not expect her to cry.

The Cloud

While we slept, the cloud came:
we saw it hunched over town.
Just like a table-cloth, some said,
cameras aimed as it tested the height.
Next day it joined us: damp, white.
You couldn't open your mouth too wide—
we whispered. Then it stood on corners,
wondering where next or lost.

It got in the way of shoppers.
People offered it help, said good morning
—we're famed for hospitality—but no reply
or smile. A few protested, the way
people do about anything new.
It's a tourist attraction, the Council said,
and gave it the city's freedom. Their line changed
when it took to the streets, ate cars.
Only the few, never heard of again, could afford
special gasmasks, so we mostly stay home.
Used to speaking quietly, looking grey.
No red bleeding hearts here.
That's how we are.

Geoffrey Haresnape

Sheep

For Jack Cope

A grab at the hindquarters stopped
its bustle towards freedom:
they thonged its legs
and, wasting no time,
took the claspknife to cancel
the vein-cords tying it to life.

Its consciousness
(such as it was)
was given up without a cry:
by the wall
it lies gushing into the sand—
old Abram and his son are doing the job.

The cared-for blade finds its route
along the midriff, forking to the thighs:
knee joints are snapped like twigs:
part of skinning is like peeling
pushing down into the flanks with sideways hands,
the fell coming free from the white integuments.

They lift the rear legs
and, panting, hook them on wires:
the stomach bag
comes hurrying out
at the knife's whisper
the endless sausages of the entrails also sagging and sliding.

Patient, he takes the dirigible lungs and the heart:
severs an upside-down head:
more fluids flush:
grassmush discharges
(with gurgles) from the throathole:
he cuts off the anus—makes all neat.

They lay out the innards
on the stretched-out mat of its personal skin—
honeycomb tripes, a shining liver,
the gallbladder a black round pebble set on its own,

some sprinkles of crimson—so little blood
for so much dismemberment in the cold wind.

He touches the warm flesh gently:
how old is it then?
In jaw-depths he looks for relevant pegs
still swimming in slobber.
Later, with saw and axe, it will be squared into pieces
fit for an unperturbed eye.

This two-tooth, caught fast in the tufts it fearfully nibbled,
he takes as a gift.
His resolve: no particle will go to waste,
all must be used to strengthen the life urge.
The happening may perhaps be glossed as—
mutton, holocaust (or revolution).

Mannie Hirsch

Letter to Ben Macala

I own your woman now, Macala.
Bargained, bartered and lobola'ed for
in some swish gallery uptown
the first time she had been there.

I laid her, Ben.
Laid her on the carpet.
And let my knuckles knead
the sinking pile
beneath her rump
and called my friends to boast
I now owned Ben Macala's woman.

I wracked her, Ben,
crucified her on my wall
and tried the various tricks I know
to get her once to say
'You now own Ben Macala's woman'.

She never speaks, Ben.
Now and then I catch
the slitted eyes, the arrogant
reflected laugh
hollow through her painted thought
'Macala owns Macala's woman'.

I own your woman now, Macala,
and damn your subtle fingers
up and down my lounge
and clench my fist
and damn your woman too
and wish that I hung there upon my wall
a coloured charcoal me, Macala,
sneering through a piece of glass
watching you look in my eyes
as she so often watches me.

Peter Horn

The Poet as a Clever Invention

in purple shirt and orange tie
I the accredited clown
to this ailing society
am allowed to tell you a few truths
and similar nonsense

so listen you christened dung-heaps!
    I will lie for you
everything: I can invent: everything
    relative clauses registered clauses rehearsed clauses
    relaxed clauses reluctant clauses chopped-off clauses
the biography of a nightmare
    Sunday eats citizen its Sunday
OR (anything else for that matter)
    Uncle Dagobert invents new weapons
    for the localised war in the kindergarten
    buff. Zisch. BUMM! a comic-strip

Don't tell me
'We live in
particularly bad times'
the poet always was a pimp
providing alibis for those
that seduce:
eyes persuaded to be blind.
    (visits of exploded soldiers
    amongst
    these diving words)
Scarlet balloons cover me
    from head to toe
my face
my face creeps across sullied streets
my mouth is the laughter of many
    choked in dirt
my friends say I am crazy
    BECAUSE
my blue brain walks around
insulting people greedy for insults:

CROOKEDRIVERS! FURLOUSERS! KNOWBETTERS!
DIRTBRISTLERS! HYPOCRITEAPPRENTICES!
MURDERERS!

o how I love you all!

in purple shirt and orange tie
half-automated beauty-dispenser
I am a clever invention
of careless homicides
who wash their souls
in Ajax and Ulysses

looking at you I realise: 1 bottle of beer
is better than 1 volume of poetry
of any FORM & CONTENT poet

looking at you I realise: the only
adequate criticism
of this society
would be
TO BASH IN YOUR HEADS

I'm Getting Famous Sort Of

my first poems are published
I am getting famous
sort of

I rehearse dignity
in front of a mirror
I receive visitors
young poets
present to me
their first attempts
I
say: not too bad

no need to do a lot of thinking
from now on success
breeds success in every case
I will say
I am for peace
(naturally, who is not?)
and against the government

soon they will present me
with prizes (academies, juries, professors)
and I will smile
the prescribed smile

what I say
will be reasonable
or appropriately angry
or soothingly shocking

it is time
somebody
kicked me
in the arse

The Broth

After Po-Chui (772-840)

The mayor, whom I asked
What was necessary to help the hungry of our town,
Answered: Ten million gallons of broth
in which one could drown all of Soweto.

The Weaving Women

The net of countless threads
to catch a man
finally catches herself
Penelope.

Venus, domesticated
in a fourposter.
the final defeat
of lust.

What remains
is the eternal allegiance
to a forgotten experience.

The earth has been grazed
to the bone.
The riches of love
are stored
for the future
in dusty books
banned
by the state.

from: **The Plumstead Elegies**

The Sixth Elegy

But who are they, the ones who fled this country,
who live in exile more than we do,
who are bent by a more deliberate will to love and hate,
a will which twists and turns them, and throws them
from coast to coast, and yet draws them back more urgently.
Each morning they lean smoking against the doors
of our country, waiting in their eyes, explosives in their hands,
their shadows extending into this land lost,
as the bleeding sun is swelling
in papyrus swamps, and the wind
whips dust along deserted roads.
Rifles sing their stuttering morning
song: mechanical warblers, defending a territory: Izwe lethu!

There are many now who are driven so strongly to act
that they flower ripe and glowing in the fullness of their heart,
heroes perhaps and those destined to die early.
These storm ahead, hoping to draw others along to follow
to the place where the road drowns and water wells up
below the pacing steps measuring imaginary frontiers,
where the legions of a crumbling empire, the last dismembered fragments,
repudiated by the metropolis, hold their heads stiffly above
the swirling flood: floating debris of murderous courage.

Nor were they heroes, when they were born
in the smell of diarrhoea and unwashed diaper,
when they grew up with bloated empty bellies.
Their heroism grew out of despair, the endless defeats
in the struggle for a few pennies more to survive,
their fights to say what was needed to be said,
to awaken the masses, beaten by their masters, and resigned
to be beaten. They hardened in jails, in trials,
always prepared to give way, to avoid the fate of the fighter,
but forced by the logic of the struggle to go one step further,
so as not to be crushed. Fearing death they overcame their fear of death.
Sometimes in the early mist I hear their song
wafted across from the tent: stronger than anything,
a cold wall of knowledge, hardly a word fits into our language,
new names for new things, invented behind barbed wires,
as yet locked up in the belly of the people,
but hammering against the walls of our crumbling fortress,
filling us with hope and fright.

Fright in the hearts of those that do nothing,
see nothing, feel nothing, whose hearts are filled with
prudence and common sense: who have nothing but a touching
sense of guilt, and who wash involvement off their white hands.
Awaiting the last judgement they protest their flabby good will,
Wide-eyed, staring at the twin-headed terror, biding its time.
But they who march through unfordable dreams don't know
the experience of guilt, nor do they respect the prostrations.
Face encrusted with the salt of sweat,
they open their palms to form a jar
and pour water to quench their thirst,
before they lie down to rest.

Christopher Hope

The Flight of the White South Africans

In 1856, a young Xosa woman, named Nongquase, preached that day was approaching when Europeans in their country would be a into the sea – Encyclopaedia of Southern Africa

I

Kinshasa, we feel, is not the place to reach
At noon and leave the plane to endure inspection
By a hostile ground-hostess, observing the bleach
On her face, her cap tacked with leopard skin,
Faked, and far too tired for the erection
A good bristle requires. We make no fuss,
However, knowing why she snarls at us;
But proffer our transit cards, and march in

To stand at the urinal complaining aloud
Of filth, flies and spit, amazed that this
Is it, an Africa the white man bowed
Before, growling outside the walls of the Gents:
We fumble uncomfortably, unable to piss
Till a soldier, bursting from a booth, clodhops
Past, still buckling up, and the talking stops.
Steady yellow stains white marble in silence.

II

Perhaps, Nongquase, you have your revenge. Tell me
Why, when surf rides like skirts up a thigh, we bare
Ourselves, blind behind black glass, bellies
Up, navels gaping at the sun? We lie
Near ice-cream boys, purveyors of canvas chairs:
While they and the fishermen who stand
Off-shore, shooting seine, busily cram
Their granaries: we gasp, straining to fly:

While in the upstairs lounge, our waiting wives
Caress expensive ivory souvenirs;
By rights, white hunters' spoil; and home-made knives.
We flounder about, flying fish that fail,
Staring with the glazed eyes of seers
At our plane, hauled from the sky, lying like dead

Silver on the tarmac, feeling hooks bed
Deep in our mouths, sand heavy in our scales.

III

Our sojourn: what might dear Milne have made of it
Or Crompton, Farnol, even the later James,
Who promised homely endings, magi who lit
The lamp we wished to read by, gave us The Queen,
A Nanny we almost kissed, our English names?
We blink and are blinded by the Congo sun
Overhead, as flagrant as a raped nun.
Such light embarrasses too late. We've seen

So little in the little time spent coming
To choke on this beach of unbreathable air
Beyond the guns' safety, the good plumbing;
Prey of gulls and gaffs. We go to the wall
But Mowgli, Biggles and Alice are not there:
Nongquase, heaven unhoods its bloodshot eye
Above a displaced people; our demise
Is near, and we'll be gutted where we fall.

Morbidities

It's seldom you see an empty coffin,
but today they're loading coffins in Victoria Street;
costly, assertive, bottoms up, empty,
they go off to hug good men under:

men with frightened faces exercising after heart attacks;
or wrestlers, who move together like dough beneath the rolling pin,
landing on each other the skilful slaps of pastry cooks;
or welders, blind to the sparks at their fingertips:

even great heat has its rainbows
reflecting from sheets of toughened steel:

heaven's where grass once grey and middle-aged
is green again and lengthens unexpectedly:

frustration is in things anatomy won't allow:

everything not the end is a bonus.

Wopko Jensma

till no one

after miroslav holub

in sophiatown
can themba
climbs the steps
or what is left of them
he opens a door of a house
full onto the sky
and stands gaping over the edge

for this was the place
the world ended

then he locked up carefully
lest someone steal
and went back downstairs
and settled himself
to wait
for the house to rise again
for his people's legs and arms
to be stuck back in place

in the morning they found him
cold as a stone
sparrows pecking his eyes

the head

1

the head will march forward
over plains of desert
our souls will scream with pain
but the head will march

we will chant a song together
and sing of what we are waiting for
we will wonder why we are treated
like our own underdogs

we will wonder again
when they barge into our house
what was the sense in singing
to the marching head

2

we cut off the head
of our redeemer
his disciples run from all sides
and lick up his blood

we praise the knife
as we are on the staircase to heaven

and one by one
in the glaring light around them
we gobble up the disciples
and we file in row upon row

waiting
hungry for the flesh of tomorrow

Joburg Spiritual

1

we all sat roun a faia
a cops
squadcar holler a stop
a lump
a fool we dont run but
sit an
grin. hell. lod. i saw 'm
thump da nightwatch down
his head a ball o' blood
i a white: we dont want
to see
you here again. an what
dat ma
bitch scuttled roun da
cona. i
my pals all gone, o Lod

2

i saw her sit on a sidewalk
i saw her spit blood in a gutter
i saw her stump for a foot
i saw her clutch a stick
i saw her eyes grin toothless
i saw thorns in her burnt flesh

i see her cut her own throat
i see her corpse lie in Dark City
i see her save a multitude

3

on my way to St Peter's Gate
i see a sign looming up—
WELCOME TO SOWETO:
air-conditioned rooms with baths
we can recommend the soap—

4

he sits in glory
a red robe
a golden throne
a thorn crown
the halo
the cross
the works

on his farm
khaki shorts
chev truck
barbed wire
smoke ring
fencing pole
the works

5

today is tuesday
yesterday was monday
tomorrow will be wednesday
after that another day

time after time the sea
collapses to certain death
on its burning beaches

time after time our prime
minister proclaims lasting peace
and nails sharpeville on
another burning cross

today is dingaan's day
yesterday was republic day
tomorrow will be an ordinary day
after that a similar day

misto 3

lets
spit
lets
spill our names on blank walls
lets
spell it out: we have no future
lets
bolt
lets
howl for their waste blood, yes
lets
slit our throbbin human vein—
guts
guts
guts
(big boss, my lord, may i vomit,
i mean, my bitter, bleedin heart
flippin fool)
drum
guts
drums, hear our drippin pleadin
when will our black christ die
guts

spanner in the what? works

i was born 26 july 1939 in ventersdorp
i found myself in a situation

i was born 26 july 1939 in sophiatown
i found myself in a situation

i was born 26 july 1939 in district six
i found myself in a situation

i was born 26 july 1939 in welkom
i found myself in a situation

now, when my mind started to tick
i noticed other humans like me
shaped like me: ears eyes
hair legs arms etc . . . (i checked)
we all cast in the same shackles:
flesh mind feeling smell sight etc . . .

date today is 5 april 1975 i live
at 23 mountain drive derdepoort
phone number: 821-646, post box 26285
i still find myself in a situation

i possess a typewriter and paper
i possess tools to profess i am artist
i possess books, clothes to dress
my flesh; my fingerprint of identity
i do not possess this land, a car
much cash or other valuables
I brought three kids into this world
(as far as i know)
i prefer a private to a public life
(i feel allowed to say)
i suffer from schizophrenia
(they tell me)
i'll die, i suppose, of lung cancer
(if i read the ads correctly)

i hope to live to the age of sixty
i hope to leave some evidence
that i inhabited this world
that i sensed my situation
that i created something
out of my situation
out of my life
that i lived
as human
alive
i

i died 26 july 1999 on the costa do sol
i found myself in a situation

i died 26 july 1999 in the grasslands
i found myself in a situation

i died 26 july 1999 in the kgalagadi
i found myself in a situation

i died 26 july 1999 in an argument
i found myself in a situation

Mike Kirkwood

Henry Fynn and the Blacksmith of the Grosvenor

I

Bones sleeping in the cove — toes tight
in gullies, the sweet dreams of skulls
tucked under the sandy coverlet,
a jaw-bone braying where the swells

whiten and hiss the reef — I sing
not these first dead, the Indiaman's
quiet clerk or termagant bosun
sitting out the sea's stiff dance;

not the remaindered mythic band
who made eight hundred miles on prayer,
the flesh of oysters, limpets and
others who lost their grip, it's feared;

not those left propped up in caves,
nor the sunburned virgins with eyes
brighter than beads, whose blood still leaves
pallor on a tribesman's features;

but you, blacksmith, who chose to stay,
and by the time the last sleeve waved
or hat lifted where the long bay
turns, had hefted, hurled and heaved

pig-iron of the ship's ballast
up the beach with a realist's hands.
On that cliff-top your forge flame faced
out the tough sea, a continent's

tougher customers, the trials
by conscience, women, work
and the casual round of wars
you made your life by. And your luck

held, which was all you hoped; months, years.
Shipwrecks of kraals, extinguished tribes,
and lost scouts behind whom all ways
went thorny with spears, came to your fire.

II

Fifty years on came Fynn, starving,
living from root to root, begging
at hovels and hide-outs from skins
already too stretched and staring

to shrink from any new horror.
This was after Shaka's impis
had been that way and back. Further
north, over his morning coffee

on the beach, alone, his two guides
sweating somewhere in the undergrowth
Fynn had watched the army glide
incuriously by; in his throat

Shaka, the charm sounded over
and over, while they passed so close,
twenty thousand shield to shoulder,
he sat all morning in one place.

Light-headed from his month of hunger,
Fynn thought he'd found the Grosvenor's gold
when iron outcrops made him stumble
in long grass growing through the forge

or where the forge had been, but soon
mastered the truth: saw with calm blows
a new day's sun driven to its noon,
ship's ballast lying straight in rows.

Glanville le Sueur

Plato's Poet

Slam those brazen gates,
double-lock the iron grille;
keep out the unassuming, balding
man who knocks politely,
enquiring after suitable employment.

With golden tongue, smooth pen
and phrase of classic elegance
he wins the office chair,
the telephone, the daily tray,
the steady monthly pay.

This is the destroyer!
This is the arch-enemy
of order, foe of dividends,
protagonist of a new morality
which would stand
the building upside down,
promote the lackey to the board-room,
relegate the bosses to the poor-house
or the gutter. Slam the gates!

To a Stranger found Unconscious on Addington Beach

You must come back — back under the doctor's
enkindling slaps and hypodermic
tocsin, to face the world you would escape.
An hour more there on the ocean's shore line
and you might have fled beyond recalling.
There is no escape in this or any
other world; life is a long, lonely beach
and a long walk back from the tide mark.

Bernard Levinson

Your Small Fist

There's no need for words.
Your small fist
cupped in the palm of my hand—
I insinuate a finger
inside the curled barricade—
and read the temperature,
the amount of hurt—
the hold-tight pain of your young life.

I remember once before—
my first call to the township
between the steaming huts
on the lip of a makeshift road
where I swung my black bag
brash as a boy
safe in his Medical School.

The dark girl in labour
was younger than I.
A child bearing a child.
I fumbled in my bag
looking for words
among the shoe-horn shapes,
the trumpets and the string.
In the end she cried
and I held her hand . . .

Schizophrenia

She was naked when she danced.
A wild crow sat on her head
shrieking the rhythm.
Her young breasts nodded
while her body took the shape of music.

She was dancing for me.
When she found I had not come
she tore the papers and all the magazines,

she trailed the sheets of the wet ward-bed
and smashed a vase on the heavy door.

I found her weeping
amongst her destruction of me,
the black-raven limp and silent.
She sat on the floor
drying the hot storm of her eyes
with the back of her hand.
'We'll let it sleep
this restless angry bird.'
But it wasn't my voice that she heard.

Chaim Lewis

Kissinger: The Instant Diplomat

He is the wonder Jew of our time,
owns the branded face of History's
dispossession – the crimped hair,
the arched oval brow, the pronounced
nose, the joker's eyes, an alien
deep-throated voice of near lament,
weighing out Anglo-Saxon words
like so much foreign coin.
He brings the showman's touch
to the diplomatic art as though
the dark intent of policy were
a mere game of guileless fun.
Be not disarmed by the volatile
sensual lips curving up to the roof
of the mouth in a toothy smile;
they mask the tough persuasiveness
lodged in the thickness of the neck
and the aggressive turret of the head.
Tight discipline falters only in
the ballast of the rounding paunch
and the full-fleshed face. All in all
he is the complete exemplar of
cosmopolitan man – the prize bait
for a Streicher cartoon: the unjewed
Jew of unloved feature, the German
by schooled circumstance, the American
by adoption, a scheming Joseph
in the service of dominion, contriving
cures for the world's ills, peddling
the Pax Americana to a cross-grained
world. To his global task he brings
the high-powered gags of the pressure
salesman – a keen, 'fix-it' kit
of a brain, a will to instant success.
Like his merchant fathers before him
takes no 'no' for an answer, puts
down his carpet of compromise
for quick custom. He trades on
weakness, grabs at the heart
of your innermost fears to persuade
a commitment. Will it stick?

No matter. Deal now, pay later.
Aim for present advantage
There will be others
to ride the turbulent tomorrows.

Don Maclennan

Conversation

1

How honest can you be?
When honesty transforms
a rash of eggs on paper
into clumsy caterpillars
squirming obscenely
and evacuating chlorophyl?

II

First is to find perfection,
life or work.
I've chosen both.
Boy, am I hammered up!
I don't know what I am—
a caterpillar, moth or egg.

III

And then
that high strung woman
came and untuned herself on me
one morning in the common room.
Talk like hers is blackmail,
it's pitched in such a way
you can't ignore it—
the rhetoric of action, and all that.
And what are we, for God's sake?
A husband? a season of loving?

IV

I'm sick of holding out my heart,
vomiting epiphanies
in my private ward
my anaesthetic study room 14.
You can't go on and on!
A point I have to raise—
love and literature occur
just when you need to love or clarify or praise.

Michael Macnamara

Fare for a Needle

White-haired,
walking in dead leaves
he came.

As I waited for a bus
he sold me a needle-book
I didn't want:
Seventy
assorted nickel goldeye needles,
finest quality
with threader.
Fifteen cents.

No fare.

But, opening the book, I found
the needles were organ pipes.

For cents
I walked with Bach
in autumn.

Tale of the Cock

a poem trouvé

The earliest reported law case on obscenity was
The King v. Sir Charles Sedley, 1663.

Sedley, with Lord Buckhurst and Sir Thomas Ogle,
caroused the tavern of Oxford Kate,
'The Cock', in Bow Street, London.

Sedley was 'fined 2000 mark,
committed without bail for a week,
and bound to his good behaviour for a year,
on his confession of information against him,
for shewing himself naked in a balcony,
and throwing down bottles (pist in)
vi & armis among the people in Covent Garden,

contra pacem and to
the scandal of
the Government';
the while
preaching a quack sermon
and shouting—said Pepys—he'd for sale a power
as would make the women
flock him.

Sedley! Wist that with Pepys I had witnesst,
exalt't.

Grip of the Grease Gun

How's her chassis? Paintwork? Ride?
Her bore is 3.16 inches (80.26 mm metric);
the stroke is 3.5 (inches of course).

How's the generator? Slacken V-belt;
test the ball joints and the horn-push.

The noon, the manifold, is spinning hot, the image twists.

And hot, Forensic Foreman:
'Don't lie there
with yr thumb in yr bum
and yr brain in neutral.'

Good sir, right:
hot are the cheeks
of the disc-brake pads;
moist is the lip
of the oil-filter bowl.

'DON'T . . .'

Right. Use only the recommended lubricants.
Take out the grease gun. So.

Where are the nipples? Yes,
above the wishbone.

A clutch; a thrust; the high-speed jet.

Now
break the contact points and
CHANGE THE SETTING.

The age is reeling hot, the figments burn.

Change the engine oil:
its flow turns ancient sea.

Test the battery acid:
here, the living cells.

Retard the timing of the spark:
images fire back
to primal life.

Gone is Foreman: chuck the brain in neutral
and engage
the aeons in reverse.

According to organic theory,
oil comes from plant and animal organisms
buried in very ancient seas by mud deposits,
sealed from the air.

And
(retard it more)
lightning discharge in
a primitive atmosphere
produced the essential acids
for earliest living cells.

Foreman's back. Expediently re-engage
the auto-brain.
Belt up 6000 revs. or so;
leave off the clutch, the ancient images;
break back upon
the
motor
way.

Chris Mann

How Thomas Pringle, a Worthy Settler, was Ceremoniously Reburied

No-one reveres a dead man.
Even ridicule revives him.
Merely mention the name, and in a trice

death's circumvented as he slips
attentively into the room.
With Thom Pringle, they say resentful thunder

hit about the vaults the night before,
and gusting from baboonless crags
the raging wind was heard

to rap and rap the halyards
against their creaking poles. Crested flags
snapped and streamed from them next day.

His progeny on the stoep,
somewhat new to the business of lineage,
teeter floral china by a kitchen

full of servants. Ancestors of course,
(the worthier ones) merit remembrance
particularly a man who could farm, write,

and fight with the best, but this
seems worse than a dubious tribute.
The same bones, fleshed, fought autocracy

with their marrow, scorned in tough English
'the pusillanimous prostration
of the public mind', and left

with a bang of the door behind them
that toppled a Governor. Enough
to make the hackles of the most moderate rise

even now. Looks as if the mourners
would turn the burial into
the resurrection of the wrong man.

The Circus Train and Clown

Along these empty tracks, a circus train
its pistons gushing, once heavily gasped near.
And I, slumped against a hot boom, am now
the same confusion as that boy, his bike
forgotten, who watched inside a wet mist

the hulks of canvas, curtained carriages
and trucks that smelt of horses clacking past.
And could not grasp, how tambourines and hoops,
tumbling spangles, the brisk brass razzmatazz
could break in pieces, to sooty wreckage

that dripped, and ground without a glimmer by.
Despite the leaching glare, the sleeper-bolts
plumbagoe leaves, and signal-lamps renew
their moist intensity, a thresh of black
greens and amber, which fossil in their stress

a face—squat, wizened, grotesque, a pale gnome's
staring hungrily from behind grey glass.
The terror returns, a child's thick terror,
that trumpets and cartwheels are adult tricks,
their sleights of mind, to keep him from a dreary truth.

Zastron

Jupiter blooms in the flowerbed night
above the small flowerbeds of Zastron.

And Zastron yawns in its doilied rooms
and lowers the wick of its paraffin lamps.

Nine o'clock tings from the single steeple,
and in silence the tall night absorbs it.

The siren howls the nine o'clock curfew,
and the river quietly rubs its stones.

Even the mongrels have pattered homewards,
past the co-op and funeral parlour,

under the windows of the chinkless bank,
and a traveller in the darkened hotel.

Michael Morris

Of the Genitals

Of the genitals I
shall not
speak. But
on my left
a hand, not so neatly
severed.
And near to it
the head. The hair
was gone and the eyelids
brows
and lashes
simply
missing
although somewhere I saw an eye . . .
The rest adorned
a bush
and the lower limbs
of a tree. Strange
how the head
the hands and
legs
detach in predictable
patterns
at neck, wrist, and knee. Of
the genitals
I shall not speak. They
are neither
strong
nor protected,
and the blast
is always
from below.

Mike Nicol

Livingstone

Having arced in
A long year from the coast,
North of the Zambezi and the Falls,

The fever and heat
Laid him out. A short job
They made of it, his worthy few,

Who left heart
And guts to find new life
In Africa. The corpse they

Tramped back
To Westminster and a cramped lot.
It's a hundred years since he died.

But he's still here
Within the exhibition stands. A piece
Of cloth, a sweat-rimmed helmet:

The awed hush
Of bent tourists straining to hear
A dim heart-beat.

After Cavafy

For years I have been preparing to leave.
That way it will be easier when the time comes:
The change will not be so absolute and
I shall have familiar comforts in my new life.
Yet, after all these years, it is worth waiting.

There may be a chance that things won't change.
But I have watched people on the streets
And listened to conversations on the bus.
The people are a good indication, never still:
In their talk I have sensed a troubled mood.

There is great excitement on the mines. Strikes.
Fights and occasionally deaths. Nothing too

Serious but a new insolence has vocalised.
There are always small signs that mean nothing
At first, but gain authority with time.

It was not always like this: when the great
City was quieter and only the trams worried us,
A man could do with less and still enjoy
The weather. Then there was no threat.
Each year now I pack more things in readiness.

I have read the papers and heard the stories
Of those who returned older and greyer
From the north. They have sent the danger
Beyond the river. Have caught some walking
With packs and guns through our mielie fields.

Yet here we sit waiting for them on stone
Verandahs in the long evenings, with nothing
To interrupt the dark but the voices
Of neighbours and others we do not know:
All waiting for the inevitable over cold beers.

It has been months since our border
Countries last sent word. For many years
There was no hint of unrest, just the isolated
Murder on a farm somewhere in the bush.
Those were small signs, not often repeated.

After the wars that lasted no longer than
A few weeks, there has been only the silence:
Not even rumours of what has happened since.
What are we to read into that?
If not that the barbarians are coming.

It is night again and perhaps they have come.
Tomorrow in the rose-beds there will be
Strange footprints. But the dogs do not bark
And if they have come it will be weeks
Before we know. The signs will be small.

Whatever has happened we carry on building.
Each year we have better roads and business
Prospers: it is a way of ignoring defeat.
Without work, waiting would be impossible:
Defeat would be always before our minds.

Walter Saunders

Later Confessions of Mr Prufrock

What you must understand is that
I could no more have proposed to Mrs Cople-Thea
than to my own mother. The identification was as complete
as the attraction, though, of course, I did not know it
at the time.
                    The point I should like to make
is this: those references to John the Baptist,
Lazarus and Hamlet can only be seen in true
significance if, like nettles, you grasp them boldly.
The fact that I did my best to play them down is something
that increases rather than diminishes their importance.
Hamlet, as you know, had an unenviable task which
he could not bring himself to perform until (you might say)
it was too late.
                    Why the delay?
                                        His
failure to act (I mean the hidden shadow that fell
between him and his action) was the same as mine:
we could neither of us, in all sickening conscience,
become father-supplanters; instead it was our bitter
destiny to feel the misery of unsuccess and the torments of
a spiteful guilt we could not understand.
                                        Hamlet (in a sense)
was lucky. The death of his mother released him (unlike
unhappy Oedipus) from his worst of fears. In his dying
moments he was at last a free man, giving the King
the *coup de grâce* without a second's hesitation.
The end was a bloody show but good (if I may
give a new turn to that rather vulgar expression).

I had no such luck, and I use the word with caution for
I do appreciate how ironic luck can be.
                                        Throughout the poem
I kept giving way to depression. You note frequent
digressions, the repeated desire to sleep, to be hidden,
or to drown (idyllically in the embrace of mermaids);
I kept giving myself reasons (reasons preposterously
prophetic) why I wasn't interested in her; I even told
myself (and tried to tell you) that what I most deeply
wanted (marriage, what else?) would not have worked after all.

The truth stares through the lines: at heart I felt
dreadfully unmanned (perhaps you, too, have experienced
the humiliation of inhibition and impotence?)
But what
of Lazarus? and John the Baptist?
Ah, that precipitate dread!

'I've seen his head
Brought in upon a platter . . .'

Castration, sir, terror of castration, that awful
penalty for the most illicit of desires:

'Off with his head
Off with his head . . .'

As for Lazarus: death and rebirth,
those unappeasable womb-cravings, the ultimate
in escapism and possession. To escape with security,
who does not crave this? Who could possibly crave more?

Pot-Pourri

I slept last night in a room with rose petals on the floor
and rose petals on the bed next to mine
(shiny brass bedstead that tinkled at the slightest jar),
'You can absorb their power while you sleep,' she had said.
Deed, deep, I slept but woke with a start at three
in dark, utter dark, not remembering where I was.
Did I sleep again or did those dreams blast me?

In early daylight I got up to swim,
taking a mauve towel, mauve like the petals on the floor,
walking out under the white gables of the house asleep.
An olive thrush called from the pool.
The water was covered with mulberry catkins
that jostled as I swam.

I carried her basket to a feast of roses.
We clambered over a stone wall, treading thyme and marjoram,
'And what's that? Is it fennel?' 'No, Queen Anne's Lace' –
chevelure of lifted white.
She cut the blooms,
letting the burnt ones drop and throwing the bright ones in,

'I want to beat the sun'—it promised hot.
'That's the famous Peace, and that is Charles Mallerin,
and that's Dust Cloud, a lovely fragrance. Smell!'
I stooped, all nose.
'I only planted it this year but look, how generous!'
She counted the blooms, cut some, others reprieved.
In the soft air between us no hunger or fear of loss,
I cannot say how unlike love it was.

Peter Strauss

Bishop Bernward's Door

This vehemence,
The shouts, the tears, the pointing
Puzzles, mostly

Till you recognise the playground situation:
Something's been spoilt,
And now there must be apportioning of blame.

And then you see it's Adam and Eve
And not children at all
(But all the misery of childhood is with them)

It's the sculptor's incompetence that makes them children
(Short, stocky bodies, bitten-off heads
Thumbed from the clay)

And not one of them is in balance
(Toppling either forward or back)
And so their terrible vehemence—

God himself is a child, the censorious one you always get,
Falling off his feet to wag two fingers
At offending Adam

(He's invested too much in this
And *it's all gone wrong)*
Adam

Points anxiously the quickest way
(Under his arm) at Eve
His accusation cannot spend or contain his guilt

Eve says *it's the serpent, the serpent—*
Who curls, like a puzzled dog
At her feet. And she gestures, a forefinger.

(All the accusations are figs
And all the fig-leaves
Accusations . . .)

It is endless, it is a child's quarrel, it couldn't end
If the serpent weren't there to be pointed to
and end it

He
Smiles, puzzled, lolling his tongue,
Household pet,
Absorbing the family miseries.

Mark Swift

History Speaks Volumes

The cumbersome history of the dead
is easily luggaged in the living head—
    in the buttressed nave
        that comprises the skull
Christ is flayed and dies into life
in a single hour of reading.
        The wombs we plumb
    with hand-line and instinct
        were peopled before,
the armies march out from the cradle.
Sharpeville sprawls on the sands
of Dunkirk, the inmates of Belsen
    suffer from the bathroom mirror.
        Victims straddle
their victims, old men haunt
        the graves of their sons
    as wisdom comes too late.
        In the legends
of the part, the execution place, killers
ride to victory; tracer streams
    from a child's hand and a clumsy
        home-carved gun.

Peter Wilhelm

With my Father in the Bar at Naboomspruit

From dead bone in Naboomspruit
the I-Am-All speaks out of Africa:
trophied in a bar with glass and eyes,
indivisible in unction,
dead Calvin's dead God articulates this ambience.

'The thing came out of the dark
and stood there in my headlights:
I had time to get my gun.'

My father orders brandy and water
and I order brandy and water:
the afternoon turns to brandy and water.
My drinking grows
though it lacks the stature of the horned thing
in my headlights.
I am also a trophy.

'We made biltong
and gave the skin to the kaffirs.'

(Calvin burned the children in Geneva.
Here too:
put on the skin and look out.)

Brandy and water is a skin
over
the church the hotel the bakery the location.

'You go on to Potgietersrust
and then to Pietersburg
and then to Duiwelskloof
and then to Tzaneen
and then to Klonkieskraal.'

A journey with my father
has no end.

A journey with Our Father
has an end:
bone nailed on a wall
speaking the unutterable.

Colin Style

Rhodes's Bed

In my grandfather's house
is a bed Rhodes slept in—
one of the many sweating catafalques
scattered on his last journey.
It is covered by a plain quilt,
in an unoccupied room floored by black planks.
There are no windows
to report on the sodden, swart air.
Its twin doors, opening to the verandah,
have swollen to seal tightly without pliers and leaden nails;
its brass handles tarnished and just faintly elaborate.
The adjacent dining-room, with porous bricks,
wizened clock on mantelshelf, is his ante-room,
for on his bed lies the heap of flesh;
waistcoat, damp, screwed-up shirts
drape the bedposts and marble wash-stand.
His watch-chain dangles from the table.
(the hands are hard points of assegai
ticking like splinters crushed by Cape-carts).
A receptacle full of smoking yellow fluid is half-under the bed
and the man himself, blue cheeks,
breathing like thunder as he watches the ceiling,
Empires slowly drying at the bottom of his eyes.

Paul Chidyausiku

Grandpa

They say they are healthier than me
though they can't walk to the end of a mile;
At their age I walked forty at night
To wage a battle at dawn.

They think they are healthier than me:
If their socks get wet they catch a cold;
When my sockless feet got wet, I never sneezed—
But they still think they are healthier than me.

On a soft mattress over a spring bed,
They still have to take a sleeping-pill:
But I, with reeds cutting into my ribs,
My head resting on a piece of wood,
I sleep like a babe and snore.

They blow their noses and pocket the stuff—
That's hygienic so they tell me:
I blow my nose into the fire,
But they say that is barbaric.

If a dear one dies I weep without shame;
If someone jokes I laugh with all my heart.
They stifle a tear as if to cry was something wrong,
But they also stifle a laugh,
As if to laugh was something wrong, too.
No wonder they need psychiatrists!

They think they have more power of will than me.
Our women were scarcely covered in days of yore,
But adultery was a thing unknown:
Today they go wild on seeing a slip on a hanger!

When I have more than one wife
They tell me that hell is my destination,
But when they have one and countless mistresses,
They pride themselves on cheating the world!

No, let them learn to be honest with themselves first
Before they persuade me to change my ways,
Says my grandfather, the proud old man.

Charles Mungoshi

Important Matters

There are important matters on the agenda—
matters of life and death.
The gravity and importance of these matters
showed in our deeply furrowed faces
as we sat watching the empty throne
waiting for the chairman who was already hours late
to come and open the meeting
although each of us secretly felt and wished
    he would come in and just say:
Call it a day, boys!

Hours later, a messenger came in to say
the chairman had taken his girl
for a boatride on Lake McIlwaine.

We sat hunched round the empty chair—
the day suddenly pulled from right under us.
There and then we began to plan an air-tight plot
that would without fail bring about the downfall
of the chairman.
We looked at the plan from all angles
under all kinds of light
and when we were satisfied with it
we stepped out into the evening world
clutching our bags with faces that said
It's been a trying day.

D.E. Borrell

Nativity

A black Christ with parch'd lips and empty hand
—Arthur Shearly Cripps

We sought for him
until we found him in the dumba;
it was as the spirits had said:
we travelled behind the mine-vehicle
until we reached the protected village.

At the gate, armed men
passed their hands over our garments
and an official inquired
if our tax were paid.

We came as the spirits said
and we knew his totem—

but there were many people and many babies
and the people were afraid to speak:
afraid of atrocities in the fields,
of violence on the dirt roads,
the muroyi among the neighbours.

In their village rutted with feet,
one elbowed us drunkenly,
smelling of urine; in doorways,
people answered us coarsely,
without the right ceremony,
poking porridge in their mouths.

This could not be the place.

Yet in each doorway I cried: 'Musiki!'

At last, they gestured us to the headman
sitting under the special tree
with those who killed a black cock.

They cried: 'Did you see the bateleur?
No? Well, it sees us walking:
those eagles see everything—
they are our grandfathers!'

This could not be the place.

Even at the last we were too early:

the crones had cleared away the newspaper
with the after-birth but the washing-dish
still stood red; they were angry.
jealous; they swept the ox-dung floor
hissing like geese.

Their muti-bag was already on his chest;
when we had performed our ceremonies
to the mother, we gazed solely at it,
for we were afraid.

Farira mwana wedangwe! In all tongues:
rejoice about the first-born child!

But when we raised our eyes
the great one looked wrinkled, old—
old, like a chief of many years.

He lay—and we whisked the flies from him
and did not know our part.

It was not as we expected.

dumba—temporary hut; muroyi —witch; Musiki—Creator.

Musa B. Zimunya

The Reason

to Joy Lowe

In my letter
I feared the loss of love
inside my frame.
Apologies that it shocked you
I was only being frank.
Every day you see all these men—
prisoners—
misery playing a dead show
in their countenances
laughing unconscious of
the negativeness their voices betray;
some of them too innocent to kill a louse
others too old to know whether they are dead
    or alive
the backs of these old men bled
perhaps they gave food to guerilla fighters
I was shown one back: an incomprehensible
tattoo of sjambok tracks showing pink
and this man will be here for five years
a grandad from the backwoods,
he knows not what Rhodesia is,
what Zimbabwe is or what this war is all about!

conscience lambasts you
like a gust of the August wind
disappears like a wisp of cigar smoke
questions unanswered block your thinking
frustration fumes and fumes

Now where is the room
for love?

Rooster

What now, Rooster, Rooster,
now that there is no chicken-mother
to throw your wing-spread laughter around
and blow up dust in the run in the sun?

Rooster, Rooster,
you and I confront the acid side of life and things,
so, what, now, what indeed
now that the umbrella roof-top is no more—
fire once teased snarled all the way to ash—
where once your neck-stretched seizure of time
gave yellow dawn the form of sound?

In the village curfews have usurped your task
like plunder, and woe! the shadows astray.
Hunger and gangrene and disease and the smell
of burnt corpses and things
attest to the latest human appetite.

But nature has always provided us with abandon
as caves are home once again—
a century after Mzilikazi.

So stand on one leg on the mountain of Chitungwiza,
erect and cloud-high on the boulder's fontanelle
suspicious even of the sun with your eagle-searching eye
as true as the Zimbabwe bird,
herald at the edge of time, Rooster, Rooster,
awaken thunder with your wings
throw your eyes to the sky
and seizing the anguished moment in a throat
echo the overdue Hope
until Vhumba and Matopo answer:
else what dawn would you let us hear you announce?

Chirwa P. Chipeya

Today

Today
the war
has ended
the people sing
freedom has arrived
the people are singing
songs
of joy or
songs for the dead.

Casey Motsisi

The Efficacy of Prayer

They called him Dan the Drunk.
The old people refuse to say how old he was,
Nobody knows where he came from — but they all
Called him Dan the Drunk.
He was a drunk, but perhaps his name was not really Dan.
Who knows, he might have been Sam.
But why bother, he's dead, poor Dan.
Gave him a pauper's funeral, they did.
Just dumped him into a hole to rest in eternal drunkenness.
Somehow the old people are glad that Dan the Drunk is dead.
Ghastly!
They say he was a bad influence on the children.
But the kids are sad that Dan the Drunk is no more.
No more will the kids frolic on the music that used to flow out
of his battered concertina. Or listen to the tales he used to tell.
All followed him into that pauper's hole.
How the kids used to worship Dan the Drunk!
He was just one of them grown older too soon.
'I'm going to be just like Dan the Drunk,' a little girl said to her parents
of a night cold while they crowded around a sleepy brazier.
The parents looked at each other and their eyes prayed.
'God Almighty, save our little Sally.'
God heard their prayer.
He saved their Sally.
Prayer. It can work miracles.
Sally grew up to become a nanny . . .

Oswald Mtshali

Boy on a Swing

Slowly he moves
to and fro, to and fro,
then faster and faster
he swishes up and down.

His blue shirt
billows in the breeze
like a tattered kite.

The world whirls by:
east becomes west,
north turns to south;
the four cardinal points
meet in his head.

Mother!
Where did I come from?
When will I wear long trousers?
Why was my father jailed?

The Moulting Country Bird

I wish
I was not a bird
red and tender of body
with the mark of the tribe
branded on me as a fledgling
hatched in the Zulu grass hut.

Pierced in the lobe of the ear
by the burning spike of the elderman;
he drew my blood like a butcher bird
that impales the grasshopper on the thorn.

As a full fledged starling
hopping in the city street,
scratching the building corridor,
I want to moult
from the dung-smeared down
tattered like a fieldworker's shirt,

tighter than the skin of a snake
that sleeps as the plough turns the sod.

Boots caked with mud,
wooden stoppers flapping from earlobes
and a beaded little gourd dangling on a hirsute chest,
all to stoke the incinerator.

I want to be adorned
by a silken suit so scintillating in sheen,
it pales even the peacock's plumage,
and catches the enchanted eye
of a harlot hiding in an alley:
'Come! my moulten bird,
I will not charge you a price!'

An Abandoned Bundle

The morning mist
and chimney smoke
of White City Jabavu
flowed thick yellow
as pus oozing
from a gigantic sore.

It smothered our little houses
like fish caught in a net.

Scavenging dogs
draped in red bandanas of blood
fought fiercely
for a squirming bundle.

I threw a brick;
they bared fangs
flicked velvet tongues of scarlet
and scurried away,
leaving a mutilated corpse—
an infant dumped on a rubbish head—
'Oh! Baby in the Manger
sleep well
on human dung.'

Its mother
had melted into the rays of the rising sun,
her face glittering with innocence
her heart as pure as untrampled dew.

Weep not for a Warrior

A warrior drinks the goat's blood for bravery
as a willow in a swamp sucks water
to grow stalwart and stay evergreen.

A warrior never perishes;
he is sustained by the glorious deeds of the departed;
he eats the raw meat of fearlessness
and awaits his canonisation in the realm of heroes,
where all the freedom fighters dwell;
their numerous names are inscribed for posterity
in the massive girth of the baobab tree.

Fear has no roots
strong enough to pierce
the armoured heart of a man in bondage,
whose unbridled anger tears the tiger from its lair,
grabs the lion by its tail,
spears the elephant on its trunk.

Tears were not made
to fall like rain on the grave of the warrior,
to drown the indomitable spirit,
and wash away his halo of martyrdom.

As the clouds of war gather,
and the southern sky frowns with rage,
and the mountains quiver like broth,
and the lightning swords the firmament,
and the clouds melt into cascades of water,
and the gushing torrents collect the corpses
and flush them like logs into a raging sea,
the death knell will echo to every corner.

The warrior will lie there, solemn
in his impregnable casket.
His proud widow and children will say,
'Weep not for him,
He was a brave warrior;
Let him rest on the buffalo-hide bed,
where his forefathers repose.'

Bicca Maseko

Mate

Dedicated to the Family Planning Clinic

Don't smile at me staff nurse
I gate-crashed into this life
You did not want me to be born
I beat the barricades of your birth control scheme
I swallowed the pill
In her womb
I diluted the solution you distribute
I was a tiny spermatozoon
Wagging my tail
Invisible invincible
I glided past your loop
Dashed straight to the ovule
To mate you
Check!

King Mzilikazi Revisited

In the beginning
I was a ghost in your night
An assegai flash in a Mosega night

Later
I was a ballet dancer
In your dreams
Dancing, laughing and laughed at
A cabaret artist in your night clubs
Singing and clowning

I am
Once again
A Limpopo nightmare
A stray bullet . . .

Mandlenkosi Langa

The Pension Jiveass

I lead her in,
A sepia figure 100 years old.
Blue ice chips gaze
And a red slash gapes:
'What does she want?'
I translate: 'Pension, sir.'
'Useless kaffir crone,
Lazy as the black devil.
She'll get fuck-all.'
I translate.
'My man toiled
And rendered himself impotent
With hard labour.
He paid tax like you.
I am old enough to get pension.
I was born before the great wars
And saw my father slit your likes' throats!'
I don't translate, but
She loses her pension anyhow.

Mafika P. Mbuli

Mother

Weep not child,
Your father is gone
Cry not child,
The men have gone
To the wood
To tame a predator-lion
That you little child
Be safe from its evil,
And I your mother
Will remain to weep
If he should not return.

Do not weep child,
I hold your life
In my hands
While your father
Tames his life
To make your life longer:
But if I should ask:
Will they bring it home?

Give me strength child,
To answer your question:
Will it be tame?

I know a man
Who killed a stone,
I have seen a man
kill a river,
I knew a man
Who killed fire
Will that fire die?
Did that stone die?
Who killed the river?
When did the river die?
Who killed that man?

Stanley Mogoba

Cement

An unprecedented abundance of cement
Below, above and all round
A notorious capacity to retain cold
Without an equal facility for warmth

Inside is captured a column of air
And a solid mass of human substance
A pertinent question poses itself:
Which loses heat to which?

As complete an enclosure as possible
Throwing its presence all around
Until recognised by all five senses
Achieving the results of refrigeration

Hovering relentlessly is the stubborn stillness
Permeating both solid and gas
A free play of winged imagination
And the inevitable introspection
Stretch themselves painfully over
The reluctant minutes of the marathon day.

Stanley Motjuwadi

White Lies

Humming Maggie.
Hit by a virus,
the Caucasian Craze,
sees horror in the mirror
Frantic and dutifully
she corrodes a sooty face,
braves a hot iron comb
on a shrubby scalp;
I look on.

I know pure white,
a white heart,
white, peace, ultimate virtue.
Angels are white
angels are good.
Me I'm black,
black as sin stuffed in a snuff-tin.
Lord, I've been brainwhitewashed.

But for Heaven's sake God,
just let me be.
Under cover of my darkness
let me crusade.
On a canvas stretching from here
to Dallas, Memphis, Belsen, Golgotha,
I'll daub a white devil.
Let me teach black truth.
That dark clouds aren't a sign of doom,
but hope. Rain. Life.
Let me unleash a volty bolt of black,
so all around may know black right.

Njabulo S. Ndebele

Portrait of Love

There is my wife. There she is.
She's old now, my wife;
She is old under those
Four gallons of water,
(It was said taps in the streets
Would be our new rivers.)
But my wife fetches the water
(Down Second Avenue)
We drink and we eat.
I watch my wife: she is old.

Sitting outside on the pavement,
I watch my old wife;
Our fond noses brush
Above the black clouds.

Nana brought her brood of five last year:
'Mkhulu' they had shouted.
Dudu brought his also:
'Gogo' they had shouted,
And we laughed in our hearts. O!
Khulu married this year,
A week before Christ's birth.

My wife and I . . .?
We met long ago
When the bird's love songs were green,
When they were green,
And the virgin lay under me
Red sobs forming into a flower
As reeds sprouted out of the black soil.
In the mist of our love,
We rolled over seedlings
Leaving them crushed
In the forms of our bodysteps.

Who killed the plants?
Who killed the plants?

And like the dog's frightened tail,
We hid

And the voices of our beads
Yelled with guilt
And we ran and we ran
And hid in our nothingness in the city.

Our children . . .?
Dudu is a poet.
Nana paints—the one Black woman!
Khulu, bless them, my child,
With the sign of the cross.

Those who kick love in the face
And when it bleeds, laugh at it.
Yes, it's true, we just lived together.
It is true:
But we love each other, my child,
We do we do!

Here am I now, an old man
With an old wife,
Sitting outside on the pavement
With our old furniture:
Tomorrow, out of the womb of time,
Shall be born a new year.

Men, men are milling about us:
Cameras and police uniforms,
Men, men, women and children—
'My children? Have they got it? The telegram?'
Men, men women and children
My children have white friends;
They will help us, Ha! Ha!
They will shout in the papers.
And now those who have just moved in
Say they want to sweep their pavement,
Tomorrow is New Year.
Men, men women and children
Men, men are milling about us.

Anyway, here am I on the pavement,
Jealous neighbours smiling in their cheeks.
My wife puts down the tin—she is old.
We drink and we eat not,
Thinking of an old sin—the sin—
(How now we look for leaves
To cover our bareness)

Thinking of the void of our union in the Law,
Thinking of love—just love.

Now let us begin . . .

Little Dudu

I

Dudu slid off a cheek of God,
And was born into the world.

II

Little Dudu was the beggar's wish-bone;
Men, demented, would moan,
Turning upon him for redemption:
(O newly born coffin!)
Withered hands, mourning their own deaths,
Would grope for the feel of his body
Until a thorn of conscience burst . . .
Until a thorn of conscience burst the bubble

III

Little Dudu lay on his belly
On the dome of a hippo's mouth;
A small speck on the dome,
He lay and wept:
'Where am I?'
On the dome of a hippo's mouth.
'Where am I?,
On the dome of a hippo's mouth.

IV

When the roots of his mind
Began to bore through his head
Into the sunshine,
Into the winds,
He began to stir,
Little Dudu began to stir,
And, disturbed, the brittle hippo began to move.

V

Dudu plays . . .
Dudu chases butterflies . . .
Dudu traps birds . . .
Dudu traps moles . . .
He spies his body during hide-and-seek . . .
Dudu throws dice . . .
Dudu sees his own blood in town . . .
Now Dudu is at school.

VI

Who lost the shade of the breast
    Under the breast,
When the breast sidled away
To seek for gloomier pastures:
For rustier waters to suck? For Pastures?
Who lost the breast?
Who lost the shade of the breast
    Under the breast,
When the breast flirted away
To seek for another Dudu?
It was he, Dudu:
And the hippo began to feel his weight
And opened his mouth;
Dudu slid off the dome of the hippo,
And fell into the mire.
The hippo turned on him.

VII

Now, exposed to the grin of heat,
Big Dudu falls in love,
And lo, in the grin of heat,
An embryo swells gradually like a wicked smile
'No!' he cries;
'No, no!' she cries.
He makes her drink ink;
But 'Yes, yes!' in its first wails,
The embryo unfurls its newness.

VIII

But in the child is the beginning,
In the child
Is the beginning of an awareness of a cycle,
A cycle that has no mouth
Opening with laughter:
(O play; O butterflies; O moles; O birds . . .
O my own blood!
O my own blood flowing over the roots of my desires.)
A cycle of mouths that only moan and groan,
That only grin by force of cruelty,
Cruelty that shuts the mind
To the discernment of all goodness.

IX

O!
(And Dudu throws the child into the dust-bin.
It dies in the fumes of its own bright soul)
The child . . .

X

And the hippo's mouth snapped
Dudu is behind bars of teeth.
Dudu will never be Dudu again.
He will never again play with the whisk of God
No: Not youth rotten in
The dankness of wicked minds:
No. Not helpless youth . . .
His soul, occasionally,
Would leap out of the bars,
And fly with the birds,
Then it would come back,
To wait for another 'occasionally',
But the birds wait—always.

Mongane Wally Serote

City Johannesburg

This way I salute you:
My hand pulses to my back trousers pocket
Or into my inner jacket pocket
For my pass, my life,
Jo'burg City.
My hand like a starved snake rears my pockets
For my thin, ever lean wallet,
While my stomach groans a friendly smile to hunger,
Jo'burg City.
My stomach also devours coppers and papers
Don't you know?
Jo'burg City, I salute you;
When I run out, or roar in a bus to you,
I leave behind me, my love,
My comic houses and people, my dongas and my ever whirling dust,
My death,
That's so related to me as a wink to the eye.
Jo'burg City
I travel on your black and white and robotted roads,
Through your thick iron breath that you inhale,
At six in the morning and exhale from five noon.
Jo'burg City
That is the time when I come to you,
When your neon flowers flaunt from your electrical wind,
That is the time when I leave you,
When your neon flowers flaunt their way through the falling darkness
On your cement trees.
And as I go back, to my love,
My dongas, my dust, my people, my death,
Where death lurks in the dark like a blade in the flesh,
I can feel your roots, anchoring your might, my feebleness
In my flesh, in my mind, in my blood,
And everything about you says it,
That, that is all you need of me.
Jo'burg City, Johannesburg,
Listen when I tell you,
There is no fun, nothing, in it.
When you leave the women and men with such frozen expressions,
Expressions that have tears like furrows of soil erosion,
Jo'burg City, you are like death,
Jo'burg City, Johannesburg, Jo'burg City.

Alexandra

Were it possible to say,
Mother, I have seen more beautiful mothers,
A most loving mother,
And tell her there I will go,
Alexandra, I would have long gone from you.

But we have only one mother, none can replace,
Just as we have no choice to be born,
We can't choose mothers;
We fall out of them like we fall out of life to death.

And Alexandra,
My beginning was knotted to you,
Just like you knot my destiny.
You throb in my inside silences
You are silent in my heart-beat that's loud to me.
Alexandra often I've cried.
When I was thirsty my tongue tasted dust,
Dust burdening your nipples.
I cry Alexandra when I am thirsty.
Your breasts ooze the dirty waters of your dongas,
Waters diluted with the blood of my brothers, your children,
Who once chose dongas for death-beds.
Do you love me Alexandra, or what are you doing to me?

You frighten me, Mama,
You wear expressions like you would be nasty to me,
You frighten me, Mama,
When I lie on your breast to rest, something tells me,
You are bloody cruel.
Alexandra, hell
What have you done to me?
I have seen people but I feel like I'm not one,
Alexandra what are you doing to me?
I feel I have sunk to such meekness!
I lie flat while others walk on me to far places.
I have gone from you, many times,
I come back.
Alexandra, I love you;
I know
When all these worlds became funny to me,
I silently waded back to you
And amid the rubble I lay,
Simple and black.

Christmas

Like flames of fuel you catch on,
So silent,
Like the rising sun.
The pages of time now lie heaped on the left,
And the legs of men have become wings,
Their hearts freeze as they fly to you.

This day when death frowns,
For it will know defeat,
This day when the horizon embraces a woman's stomach
For out of there he fell and went to exile.
This day that we catch on
As flames lick fuel.

We shall race to lick,
And behind us, like footsteps dried in mud,
Memories in the minds of others—
Death.

For Don M. – Banned

it is a dry white season
dark leaves don't last, their brief lives dry out
and with a broken heart they dive down gently headed for the earth,
not even bleeding.
it is a dry white season brother,
only the trees know the pain as they still stand erect
dry like steel, their breaches dry like wire,
indeed, it is a dry white season
but seasons come to pass.

A Poem on Black and White

if i pour petrol on a white child's face
and give flames the taste of his flesh
it won't be a new thing
i wonder how i will feel when his eyes pop
and when my nostrils sip the smell of his flesh
and his scream touches my heart
i wonder if i will be able to sleep;
i understand alas i do understand
the rage of a whiteman pouring petrol on a black child's face

setting it alight and shooting him in a pretoria street,
pretoria has never been my home
i have crawled its streets with pain
i have ripped my scrotal sack at every door i intended entering in that city
and jo'burg city has never seen me, has never heard me
the pain of my heart has been the issue of my heart
sung by me
freezing in the air
but who has not been witness to my smile?
yet, alexandra's night shadow is soaked and drips with my tears.

Introit

I have lain on my back
flat like a long dead reptile
I lie here while my load clutches my heart like a frightened child
And the horrors of my stomach throb to my eyes
I am a black manchild
I am he who has defeated defeat
I am a surprise which surprises me
The load of the day leaves my shoulders red and bruised
But alas
the Chest of the night heaves into my eyes
The whore's scream and the barking dogs are my companions
The snap of life and the making of death have woven my strides
My thick footsteps pulsate on black shadows
They rumble, rumble like a journey with a destination
Aaahw the blackmanchild

I have lain on my back dead just like pulled out weeds
while blood flowed in me like a river
My pores have been holes pouring out sweat which flooded lies
I have built the day like every man has
I have broken the day to shadows which came and lay gently over my house
I am no big blackman
I am a blackmanchild

I have tamed the stallion-woman beneath me
I have held children's hands in mine and led them
Alas the children
They have looked up at me as if my eyes were ripe fruit dangling from a tree
the children have seen the sun shine into my eyes
they have seen my face glow silver with the light of the moon
maybe they have heard me weep too

for I have wept
Lord I wept
my heart bleeds through my eyes
for indeed my eyes are a bloody memory

What's in this Black 'Shit'

It is not the steaming little rot
In the toilet bucket,
It is the upheaval of the bowels
Bleeding and coming out through the mouth
And swallowed back,
Rolling in the mouth,
Feeling its taste and wondering what's next like it.

Now I'm talking about this;
'Shit' you hear an old woman say,
Right there, squeezed in her little match-box
With her fatness and gigantic life experience,
Which makes her a child,
'Cause the next day she's right there,
Right there serving tea to the woman
Who's lying in bed at 10 a.m. sick with wealth,
Which she's prepared to give her life for
'Rather than you marry my son or daughter.'

This 'Shit' can take the form of action;
My younger sister under the full weight of my father,
And her face colliding with his steel hand,
''Cause she spilled sugar that I work so hard for'
He says, not feeling satisfied with the damage his hands
Do to my yelling little sister.

I'm learning to pronounce this 'Shit' well,
Since the other day,
At the pass office,
When I went to get employment,
The officer there endorsed me to Middelburg,
So I said, hard and with all my might, 'Shit!'
I felt a little better;
But what's good, is, I said it in his face,
A thing my father wouldn't dare do.
That's what's in this black 'Shit'.

Sipho Sepamla

To Whom it may Concern

Bearer
Bare of everything but particulars
Is a Bantu
The language of a people in southern Africa
He seeks to proceed from here to there
Please pass him on
Subject to these particulars
He lives
Subject to the provisions
Of the Urban Natives Act of 1925
Amended often
To update it to his sophistication
Subject to the provisions of the said Act
He may roam freely within a prescribed area
Free only from the anxiety of conscription
In terms of the Abolition of Passes Act
A latter-day amendment
In keeping with moon-age naming
Bearer's designation is Reference number 417181
And (he) acquires a niche in the said area
As a temporary sojourner
To which he must betake himself
At all times
When his services are dispensed with for the day
As a permanent measure of law and order
Please note
The remains of R/N 417181
Will be laid to rest in peace
On a plot
Set aside for Methodist Xhosas
A measure also adopted
At the express request of the Bantu
In anticipation of any faction fight
Before the Day of Judgement.

Three-Legged No More

He would sit gazing at the east and beyond
He would stand wobbling on his three legs
Then to walk he tottered past regrets

Tall
Gaunt
Ever haunted by a coming never arriving
Pale
Grey
Today was like yesterday
Tomorrow dragged its yesterdays along
Aged
Wasted
Lips muttered whispers crowded by a loneliness
Angular
Wrinkled
He was one of those withered by hope
Today
This past moment
A bleak sunless winter has fanned him away
Windows are daubed white with tears
Voices hoarse
Mouths muffled
His dismembered bed lies in the pale sun
Traces of a strength that once was
The
Unbending
His walking stick a dumb unlikely companion
Cleanshaven
Knotted
Will wear a smoothed crown in a house-nook
I too
Shall
Bury him
The only gift I offer.

Zoom the Kwela-Kwela

In these days of unsaid commentaries
thoughts moulding under our armpits
of hands kept in the pockets
people holding to their lives tight
or simply shaking heads in distress
of babies babbling the ills of bedroom existence
or father and son hating over one girlfriend
I never know a man when I meet one
my head spins on a tilted fulcrum
resting on one illusion after another
such that the expressive character

of a youth on crutches
never seems anything more than
the epitome of the age
like that one I saw the other day
hobble on a pair of crutches
the length of a Reef road
lean them on massive pillars
of a 'native' shop
that has often heard pitched cries
of hustled customers
and began to play football
on sound agile legs
the very moment after
the kwela-kwela had zoomed by

Darkness

yes sir i have arrived
walk the night if you dare
there i reign over death
'swonder you legislate the night
i walk erect in the night
you crouch in retreat
crowding each nook in fear
of the stench of my blackness
agitated by a darkness

Motshile wa Nthodi

South African Dialogue

Morning Baas,
Baas,
Baas Kleinbaas says,
I must come and tell
Baas that,
Baas Ben's Baasboy says,
Baas Ben want to see
Baas Kleinbaas if
Baas don't use
Baas Kleinbaas,
Baas.

Tell
Baas Kleinbaas that,
Baas says,
Baas Kleinbaas must tell
Baas Ben's Baasboy that,
Baas Ben's Baasboy must tell
Baas Ben that,
Baas says,
If Baas Ben want to see
Baas Kleinbaas,
Baas Ben must come and see
Baas Kleinbaas here.

Thank you
Baas.
I'll tell
Baas Kleinbaas that,
Baas says,
Baas Kleinbaas must tell
Baas Ben's Baasboy that,
Baas Ben's Baasboy must tell
Baas Ben that,
Baas says,
If Baas Ben want to see
Baas Kleinbaas,
Baas Ben must come and see
Baas Kleinbaas here,
Baas.
Goodbye Baas.

Baas Kleinbaas,
Baas says,
I must come and tell
Baas Kleinbaas that,
Baas Kleinbaas must tell
Baas Ben's Baasboy that,
Baas Ben's Baasboy must tell
Baas Ben that,
Baas says,
If Baas Ben want to see
Baas Kleinbaas,
Baas Ben must come and see
Baas Kleinbaas here,
Baas Kleinbaas.

Baasboy,
Tell Baas Ben that,
Baas Kleinbaas says,
Baas says,
If Baas Ben want to see me
(Kleinbaas)
Baas Ben must come and
See me (Kleinbaas) here.

Thank you
Baas Kleinbaas,
I'll tell
Baas Ben that,
Baas Kleinbaas says,
Baas says,
If Baas Ben want to see
Baas Kleinbaas,
Baas Ben must come and see
Baas Kleinbaas here,
Baas Kleinbaas.
Goodbye
Baas Kleinbaas.

Baas Ben,
Baas Kleinbaas says,
I must come and tell
Baas Ben that,
Baas says,
If Baas Ben want to see
Baas Kleinbaas,
Baas Ben must come and see

Baas Kleinbaas there,
Baas Ben.
Baas Ben,
Baas Be-ne . . .
Baas Ben
Goodbye
Baas Ben.

Magoleng wa Selepe

My Name
Nomgqibelo Ncamisile Mnqhibisa

Look what they have done to my name . . .
the wonderful name of my great-great-grandmothers
Nomgqibelo Ncamisile Mnqhibisa

The burly bureaucrat was surprised.
What he heard was music to his ears
'Wat is daai, sê nou weer?'
'I am from Chief Daluxolo Velayigodle of emaMpodweni
And my name is *Nomgqibelo Ncamisile Mnqhibisa.'*

Messia, help me!
My name is so simple
and yet so meaningful,
but to this man it is trash . . .

He gives me a name
Convenient enough to answer his whim:
I end up being
Maria . . .
I . . .
Nomgqibelo Ncamisile Mnqhibisa.

Mafika Gwala

Kwela-Ride

Dompas!
I looked back
Dompas!
I went through my pockets
Not there.

They bit into my flesh (handcuffs).

Came the kwela-kwela
We crawled in.
The young men sang.
In that dark moment

It all became familiar.

From the Outside

We buried Madaza
on a Sunday;
big crowd:
hangarounds, churchgoers,
drunks and goofs;
even the fuzz
was there
as the priest
hurried
the burial sermon—
and we filled the grave
with red soil,
the mourning song
pitched fistedly high;
—what got my brow itching though
is that none
of the cops present
dared to stand out
and say
Madaza was a 'Wanted'.

from: **Getting off the Ride**

I know this ride bloody well.
I'm from those squatted mothers
Those squatted mothers in the draughty air;
Those mothers selling handouts,
Those mothers selling fruits,
Those mothers selling vegetables,
Those mothers selling till dusk
in the dusty street of Clermont, Thembisa,
Alex, Galeshewe, Dimbaza, Pietersburg.
Those mothers in dusty and tearful streets
that are found in Stanger, Mandeni, Empangeni
Hammarsdale, Mabopane, Machibisa, Soweto.
I'm one of the sons of those black mamas,
Was brought up in those dust streets;
I'm the black mama's son who vomits
on the doorstep of his shack home, pissed with
concoction. Because his world and the world
in town are as separate as the mountain ranges
and the deep sea.
I'm the naked boy
running down a muddy road,
the rain pouring bleatingly
in Verulam's Mission Station;
With the removal trucks brawling for starts
Starts leading to some stifling redbricked
ghetto of four-roomed houses at Ntuzuma.
I'm the pipeskyf pulling cat
standing in the passage behind Ndlovu's barbershop
Making dreams and dreams
Dreaming makes and makes;
Dreaming, making and making, dreaming
with poetry and drama scripts
rotting under mats
or being eaten by the rats.
I'm the staggering cat on Saturday morning's
West Street. The cat whose shattered hopes
were bottled up in beers, cane, vodka;
Hopes shattered by a system that once offered
liquor to 'Exempted Natives' only.
I'm the bitter son leaning against the lamp post
Not wishing to go to school
where his elder brother spent years, wasted years
at school wanting to be white; only to end as
messenger boy.

I'm the skolly who's thrown himself
out of a fast moving train
Just to avoid blows, kicks and the hole.
I'm one of the surviving children of Sharpeville
Whose black mothers spelled it out in blood.
I'm the skhotheni who confronts devileyed cops
down Durban's May Street . . .
Since he's got no way to go out.
I'm the young tsotsi found murdered in a donga
in the unlit streets of Edendale, Mdantsane.

. . .
I'm the puzzled student
burning to make head and tail of Aristotle
because he hasn't heard of the buried
Kingdom of Benin or the Zimbabwe Empire,
The student who is swotting himself to madness
striving for universal truths made untrue.
I'm the black South African exile who has come
across a coughing drunk nursing his tuberculosis
on a New York pavement and remembered
he's not free.
I'm the black newspaper vendor
standing on the street corner 2 o'clock
in the morning of Sunday,
Distributing news to those night life crazy
nice-timers who will oneday come into knocks
with the real news
I'm the youthful Black with hopes of life
standing on file queue for a job
at the local chief's kraal,
This chief who has let himself and his people
into some confused Bantustan kaak
Where there's bare soil, rocks and cracking cakes
of rondavel mudbricks.
I'm the lonely poet
who trudges the township's ghetto passages
pursuing the light,
The light that can only come through a totality
of change:
Change in minds, change
Change in social standings, change
Change in means of living, change
Change in dreams and hopes, change

Dreams and hopes that are Black
Dreams and hopes where games end
Dreams where there's end to man's
creation of gas chambers and concentration camps.
I'm the Africa Kwela instrumentalist whose notes
profess change.

Ingoapele Madingoane

from: **africa my beginning**

black trial

peace in africa will be restored
not because man in africa is black but
because he's suffered under the common enemy
for we in africa will not bring colour
between man and reality

so when I say that don't think
politics will be brought into art
for art is in its own
right above politics   bear in mind
brother whatever you do which is not harmful
to the community
has an artistic message of use to the society
and yourself
remember
africa's pride can be expressed in many ways
your face and music
    your pain with music
        your joy with music
and of course your artistic gift
is as important as your presence
wherever the clan gathers so
stick to them brother because
even man is no man without
the structure of his culture
    so beautifully created
    that black natural gift
    from the mould of the african womb
    pity the day it rots
    in the traditional african tomb

. . .
in the heart of africa africans shall meet as one
and africa *uta swema kiswabili* to seal the african bond
before i die

    how i long to be there
    in that part of you africa
    and drink from the calabash

umuthi we inkululeko
before i die
how i long to be loved africa
by that african woman in africa
as lonely as the river nile in the blazing
desert of sahara waiting
for the man of her heart to slip on
that canemade ring on the finger that points out
the path to our future
before i die
how i long africa *o swema kiswahili*
to appear african as africa
have with me a family to love
be glad i am black
before i die

. . .
say how beautiful
run the rows
of your plaited hair
mosadi   hee mosadi

mosadi   say how smart
is *sefaga seo* around your neck
how womanly is the fold
of your doek   mosadi

mosadi   hee mosadi   say what a counsellor
is that african emblem
on your dress   mosadi

mosadi   say mosadi   how bright your face looks
with those wooden earrings
and how warm your breast is
for that man in africa who so much
loves you   mosadi

mosadi   hee mosadi   what is it that you want
when love   man   beauty
and home as well as your roots
are in the soil
you are now standing on
mosadi

. . .
it has been my wish and still is my wish
that whatever happens between me and africa when we part ways
it will not be through cowardice or should i say
betrayal of my beloved fatherland

i would be glad if i could be buried like a true african
of african definition
when i take my soul
to its destination
when the gong of departure
reaches my eardrum
and the cloud of death dominates my eye
wrap me safely
with the hide of an african ox
i will be glad
deliver me to the ancestral village
cast no flowers on my soil
i am an african as for beauty
i never had a chance to admire it 'cause
africa was not free
i will join the masses that went before me
and as one we shall fight
the ancestral war until justice
is done.

Jiggs

Doornfontein

Doornfontein
ek sê
is not like it was.

Rollicking full of life
you met all the manne
everywhere.

Those ous from Corrie
or the Ville musn't
come make shit here.
we Doorie owens
won't take their cac.

Throbbing and bursting
shebeens and brothels,
Ou Cecil Rhodes and
Barney Barnato must
shit
in their graves
to check what
is happening in their
old koesters.

Nay there's no shit here,
the lanies we get on with
they are just like us.

And now they are
bulldozing the place down
there's hardly anyone left,
except the whores and oere
and of course all
the Mac Fuggers
looking for meat

Sometime we going to
Bulldoze down their
Homes ek sê
And send them to a
Township and see
How they like it.

Hey man, all the
High Bucks come
from Doorie

What High Bucks ek sê

No Umfo Doorie
Was the place
There were playwhites
And there will are
But just like Sophiatown,
And Jepps and so on,
They moving us all out
of town
Making scars on our
Lives and in Josie
But Doorie will
Always be Doorie
Ek sê.

Mothobi Mutloatse

Ngwana wa Azania

a proemdra for oral delivery

- The future of the black child, the recalcitrant Azanian child in South Africa, is as bright as night and this child, forever uprooted, shall grow into a big sitting duck for the uniformed gunslinger.
- From ages two to four he shall ponder over whiteness and its intrigue. From ages five to eight he shall prise open his jacket-like ears and eyes to the stark realisation of his proud skin of ebony. From ages nine to fifteen he shall harden into an aggressive victim of brainbashing and yet prevail. From ages sixteen to twenty-one he shall eventually graduate from a wavering township candle into a flickering life-prisoner of hate and revenge and hate in endless fury. This motherchild shall be crippled mentally and physically for experimental purposes by concerned quack statesmen parading as philanthropists.
- This motherchild shall be protected and educated free of state subsidy in an enterprising private business asylum by Mr Nobody. This motherchild shall mother the fatherless thousands and father boldly the motherless million pariahs. This nkgonochild shall recall seasons of greed and injustice to her war-triumphant and liberated Azachilds. This mkhuluchild shall pipesmoke in the peace and tranquillity of liberation, and this landchild of the earth shall never be carved up ravenously again and the free and the wild and the proud shall but live together in their original own unrestricted domain without fear of one another, and this waterchild shall gaily bear its load without a fuss like any other happy mother after many suns and moons of fruitlessness in diabolical inhumanity.
- This gamble-child of zwêpe shall spin coins with his own delicate life to win the spoils of struggle that is life itself. This child of despair shall shit in the kitchen; shit in the lounge, shit in the bedroom-cum-lounge-cum-kitchen; he shall shit himself dead; and shall shit everybody as well in solidarity and in his old-age shall dump his shit legacy for the benefit of his granny-childs: this very ngwana of redemptive suffering; this umtwana shall but revel in revealing off-beat, creative, original graffiti sugar-coated with sweet nothings like:

re tlaa ba etsa power/re-lease Mandela/azikhwelwa at all costs/we shall not kneel down to white power/release Sisulu/jo' ma se moer/black power will be back tonight/release or charge all detainees/msunuwakho/down with booze/ Mashinini is going to be back with a bang/to bloody hell with bantu education/ don't shoot – we are not fighting/Azania eyethu/masende akho/majority is coming soon/freedom does not walk it sprints/inkululeko ngoku!

- This child born in a never-ending war situation shall play marbles seasonably with TNTs and knife nearly everyone in sight in the neighbourhood for touch and feel with reality, this child of an insane and degenerated society shall know love of hatred and the eager teeth of specially-trained biting dogs and he will speak animatedly of love and rage under the influence of glue and resistance.

- This marathon child shall trudge barefooted, thousands of kilometres through icy and windy and stormy and rainy days and nights to and from rickety church-cum-stable-cum-classrooms with bloated tummy to strengthen him for urban work and toil in the goldmines, the diamond mines, the coal mines, the platinum mines, the uranium mines so that he should survive countless weekly rockfalls, pipe bursts, and traditional faction fights over a meal of maiza that has been recommended for family planning.
- This child of raw indecision and experimentation shall sell newspapers from street corners and between fast moving cars for a dear living breadwinning instead of learning about life in free and compulsory school, and shall provide the capitalistic country with the cheapest form of slavery the labourglobe has ever known and the governor of the reserve bank shall reward him with a thanks-for-nothing-thanks-for-enriching-the-rich kick in the arse for having flattened inflation alone hands-down.
- This child of the tunnels shall occasionally sleep malunde for an on-the-spot research into the effects of legalised separation of families and he shall find his migrant long-lost father during a knife-duel in a men's hostel and his domestic mother shall he ultimately embrace passionately in a cul de sac in the kitchen in a gang-bang.
- This child of concrete shall record and computerise how the boss shouts and swears publicly at his heroically shy father-boy and how the madam arrogantly sends his mother-girl from pillar to bust. He shall photograph how the superior doctor addresses his enkempt mother in untailored talk as if mother-stupid had conceived a baboon-child.
- This observant child shall taste its first balanced meal in an i.c.u., and in the very intensive care unit shall he be revived to further life and misery and mal-nutrition in this immensely-wealthy land to loosen up the bones down to their perforated marrow.
- This child of the donga shall watch in jubilation and ecstasy and ire as its godforsaken, godgiven home called squatter camp is razed through its permission down to the ground by demolishing bulldozers lately referred to as front-enders.
- This child of nowhere shall of his own free will join the bandwagon and ravaza its own Botshabelo to lighten the merciless soil conservationists' burden for a place in the sun of uncertainty, he shall show absolute respect for his elders with a hard kierie blow across the grey head and shall be unanimously nominat-ed for a nobel peace prize for his untold, numerous contributions to human science at a local mortuary.
- This child born into a callous and too individualistically-selfish society shall be considered sane until further notice by psychopaths masquerading as men of law. He shall be an unmatched hero with an undecided following, having para-lysed parents and preachers alike with his frankness and willingness not only to whisper nor speak about wanting to be free but to bloody well move moun-tains to be free!
- This child of evictions shall sleep in toilets while its off-spring cross the borders for possible m.t.
- This child of rags to rags and more rags to riches school uniform tatters shall

quench his thirst with dishwater in the suburbs and also with methylated spirits in the deadendstreet camps to communicate with the gods.

- This child shall breastfeed her first baby before her seventeenth birthday and be highly pleased with motherhood lacking essential fatherhood. This child of uneasiness shall trust nobody, believe in no one, even himself, except perhaps when he's sober. This ghettochild shall excel in the pipi-olympics with gold and bronze medals in raping grannies with every wayward erection and eviction from home resulting from ntate's chronic unemployment and inability to pay the hovel rent.

- This growing child of the kindergarten shall psychologically avoid a school uniform admired telegraphically by uniformed gunfighters of maintenance of chaos and supremacy. He shall smother moderation good bye and throttle reason in one hell of a fell swoop, and the whole scheming world shall cheer him up to the winning post with its courage in the mud and its heart in its pink arse. This child of dissipation shall loiter in the shebeen in earnest search for its parents and shall be battered and abused to hell and gone by its roving parents when reunited in frustration in an alleyway.

- This child of bastardised society and bastard people-in-high-office and colour-obsession and paranoid of communism and humanism, shall break through and snap the chain of repression with its bare hands, and this child, with its rotten background and slightly bleak future shall however liberate this nuclear crazy world with Nkulunkulu's greatest gift to man: ubuntu.

- This lambschild shall remind the nation of the oft-remembered but never used ISINTU:

Mangwana o tshwara thipa ka fa bogaleng.

Christopher van Wyk

In Detention

He fell from the ninth floor
He hanged himself
He slipped on a piece of soap while washing
He hanged himself
He slipped on a piece of soap while washing
He fell from the ninth floor
He hanged himself while washing
He slipped from the ninth floor
He hung from the ninth floor
He slipped on the ninth floor while washing
He fell from a piece of soap while slipping
He hung from the ninth floor
He washed from the ninth floor while slipping
He hung from a piece of soap while washing

About Graffiti

Graffiti is the writing on the wall
the writing on the wall as at Western
Heroes die young

In Noordgesig you'll see graffiti
Why Lord can't we live together?

Smeared on a wall in Eldorado Park
Love is?

In an alley somewhere
Sex in unlimited

Graffiti is painted on a wall
in District Six
Welcome to Fairyland

Graffiti can move too
Graffiti worms out of noses
of slum kids

Graffiti scrawls in piss
calls itself V.D.
clogs in priapic places-hurts

Bob Marley shouts reggae
from township cafés
'A hungry stomach
is a hungry man
Graffiti'

Graffiti is a dirty child
who scratches for sweets
and himself
in rubbish dumps

Graffiti is the gang
the gang who burnt a nice-time cherrie
and left her behind the shops
for dogs to eat off her left leg

Graffiti is children playing
around broken live wires from lampposts
and the Electricity Department fixing it
after somebody has burnt to death
has been shocked through the conduits
of his slum ignorance

When one black child tells another
'Ek sal jou klap
dan cross ek die border'
it's graffiti

and

When another child says
'I don't like Vorstra and Kruga
because they want us
to speak Afrikaans'

Graffiti screams from a sonorous woman
as the hymens of her sanity rupture
suddenly
in a night

Graffiti shouts from the lips of a township
Kyk voor jou die Welfare sal agter jou kyk

Graffiti calls Soweto Sovieto

Graffiti is a scar on a face

The mine dump is graffiti

A cockroach is graffiti

Candle grease is graffiti

A rabid dog is graffiti

Adrenalin and blood in the township,
that's graffiti

Soon graffiti will break loose
into an ugly plethora
drift into Jo'burg
soil share certificates
deface billboards
dishonour cheques
drown managers, clerks, executives

Soon graffiti will wade into Jo'burg
unhampered by the tourniquet of influx control

The Chosen Ones

Some people
it seems
have to carry
their crosses
for the rest
of their lives.

Others think
they can get away
with it
simply by
throwing theirs
into ballot boxes.

Fhazel Johennesse

the african pot

it is round and fat and squat
it has no handle and the rim has no spout
at first it seems as if the colours have
no coordination and no rhythm
the yellow and brown stripes circle
the pot in quick diagonals

i puzzle over the absence of the handle
and then suddenly i think of a young woman
wearing beads walking to a river with
the pot gracefully balanced on her head

and then the colours begin to rhyme
yellow zigzagging around the top
makes me think of harvest time   of golden corn
of dancers around an autumn fire   of ripe fruit
and of men drinking homebrewed beer

and as i stroke the brown
i can almost feel the full earth between
my fingers   earth that echoes the thunderous
stamp of warriors going to war   earth that
offers base accompaniment to dancing feet
i can almost see an ox pulling a plough
steered by a man of infinite patience
making ordered rows of upturned loam

the maker made this pot
with a song in his heart
and a vision in his eyes
lifting it up i can almost hear
him say

    i am man
    life is but clay in my hands
    creation is at my fingertips

my township sunset

when the sun begins to melt just above the
horizon and the clouds disappear to undress
the stars i'll squat against a corroded
washline pole and take a deep breath
sigh and breathe again

i always enjoy these dusk solitudes
these languid cigarettes and floating smoke
rings and i'll note with surprise how content
the overflowing dustbin looks
but the zenith of my township sunset is when
the swallows begin to chase the retreating light
the sudden dip smooth bank and frenzied darting
is a ballet at high speed

but just as the last drop of sunlight
dribbles below the skyline my sunset will
reach it's nadir and i'll flick my
cigarette butt angrily because it is then
that my graceful ballerinas become
sneering devils flitting to a
tune with words by langenhoven

Essop Patel

They Came at Dawn

for Omar

Beyond
    the Carlton Centre
the sunbeams
    projecting
like warheads,
    they came
in uniform trucks,
    they came
rapping thunder
    on the door,
asking
    questions,
demanding
    answers.

They came at dawn
    they left at dusk
taking a poem
    written
on a bronze autumn leaf,
    written
in the shadow of bars,
    as evidence
for a banning order.

Achmed Dangor

The Voices that are Dead

I

There is a silence
upon the river tonight.
No great floods of song
flow out into the darkness,
our voices are dead.

And the midnight moon
White and cold
over the ashen streets
reveals nothing but shadows
fleeing from one darkness
to the next.

Mattera, Mohapi, Mathe,
Nortje, Nakasa
and you Brutus,
names and voices
that few remember.

II

Oh, my brothers,
poets of the earth
who ripped handfuls
of flesh from the land
as salt for the tears
in your songs
And today,
like black madrigals
sing with gilded voices
in the great white halls,
at the soirées
of a people whose souls
are famished

And you are their final,
sad repast,
whom they sit down to sup
with the now uncertain air
of imperial ceremony

Oh, my brothers—
you too are dead,
your voices rage barrenly
within the august halls
of the doomed,

but are not heard
by the cowherd who treads
his unknowing peace,
nor is it heard
in the ashen townships
where soon your memory
will fit unlovingly
from one darkness to the next

III

Yet, I can write of hope,
though the voice I hear
in the icy dawn
is still frail and tremulous,
and the mists are a portend
of a familiar and savage storm

I can sing a hymn
to the glory of my land,
from the ashes something stirs,
new voices are being heard.

I can look with love
at the harsh landscape
pockmarked by ghettoes,
in the dust and the dirt
new voices sing new songs.

Yet still the morning rises
as if drenched in blood.
Oh Lord, save them
from the gunfire
and the jackboot.

Biographies

Although every effort has been made by the staff of The National English Literary Museum and Documentation Centre, it has not always been possible to trace birth dates or other biographical data for a number of poets included in this volume. As information becomes available, the publishers will be pleased to include it in future reprints or new editions. Where certain contemporary poets did not want specific biographical details to be printed their wishes have been respected.

Abrahams, Lionel (1928–) Born and lives in Johannesburg. Founded the literary magazine *The Purple Renoster,* and Renoster Books; is on the editorial board of Bateleur Press. Novelist and short-story writer; co-editor of *South African Writing Today* (1967) and of *Quarry* '76, '77, '78 and '79. Published a collection of poetry *Thresholds of Tolerance* (1975). Joint recipient with Sipho Sepamla of the 1976 Pringle Award.

Abrahams, Peter Henry (1919–) Born in Vrededorp. Left South Africa for England in 1939. Journalist for the *Observer* and the BBC. Moved to Jamaica 1955, edited *The West Indian Economist.* Published novels, an autobiography and a collection of poetry *A Blackman Speaks of Freedom!* (1940).

Adams, Perseus, pen-name for Peter Robert Charles Adams (1933–) Born in Cape Town, has lived in the Far East and the Greek Islands, now teaching in London. Short-story writer; has won several poetry prizes, including the 1963 South African Poetry Prize. Poetry publications: *The Land at my Door* (1965) and *Grass for the Unicorn* (1975).

A.G.E. Poem published in *Cape Monthly Magazine,* XII, 68, February 1876.

Alder, Alice Mabel (1879/89–?) Born in Australia, came to South Africa in 1903. Married poet F.E. Walrond, lived in Natal, Chairman of Veldsingers Club, poetry published in *Veldsingers' Verse* (1910).

Anon. 'Shantytown' published in *Inkululeko,* July 1946.

Bain, Andrew Geddes (1797–1864) Born in Scotland, came to South Africa in 1816. Pioneer explorer, road-builder, geologist, as well as artist; correspondent of the *South African Commercial Advertiser.* Wrote poetry and contributed factual articles to numerous periodicals. *Kaatje Kekkelbek or Life Among the Hottentots* performed in Grahamstown in 1838.

Banoobhai, Shabbir (1949–) Born in Durban. Currently lecturer in Department of Accountancy and Auditing, University of Durban–Westville. Has published one poetry collection: *Echoes of my Other Self* (1980).

Beaumont, John Howland (1911–1979) Born in the Karoo, deaf from early childhood. Proof-reader on the *Cape Times,* lived in England for a few years, returning to South Africa in 1965. Editor of *Panorama* till 1968. Contributed poems to the *Cape Times,* the *London Times* and the *Christian Science Monitor.* Published a collection of short stories, and *Poems* (1957).

Beeton, Douglas Ridley (1929–) Born in Zeerust. Professor of English at the University of South Africa. Author of *Olive Schreiner: a Short Guide to her Writings* (1974); editor; compiled, with Helen Dorner, *A Dictionary of English Usage in Southern Africa* (1975). Poetry published in South African anthologies and one collection: *The Landscape of Requirement* (1981).

Black, Stephen William (1880–1931) Born in Cape Town, Crime reporter for the *Cape Argus,* later prospector in Rhodesia (Zimbabwe), farmer in France 1919–1927, journalist for the *London Daily Mail.* Novelist and playwright. After his return to South Africa, editor of the sensational paper *Sjambok* where occasional poems of his appeared.

Blackburn, Douglas (1857–1929) Born in South London. Arrived in Johannesburg to write for *The Star;* edited the satirical paper *The Moon,* and from 1894 *The Transvaal Sentinel* in Krugersdorp. Wrote seven novels. Returned to England in 1908 and worked for *The Tonbridge Free Press* till his death. Poems appeared in *The New Age* (London).

Borrell (Finn), Dorothy Elizabeth (1928–)Born in England. Immigrated to Rhodesia (Zimbabwe) in 1956. Lecturer, teacher, free-lance writer, on editorial board of *Rhodesian Poetry,* elected to Pen Rhodesia, edited *Poetry in Rhodesia 75 Years* (1968). Published one poetry collection: *A Patch of Sky* (1979).

Bosman, Herman Charles, sometimes used the pen-name Herman Malan (1905–1951) Born near Cape Town. Taught in the Groot Marico district, then travelled as a journalist in Europe 1934 – 1940. Returning to South Africa, he co-edited *Touleier, The New Sjambok* and *The New LSD.* Wrote short stories, novels, plays, a prison chronicle and three pamphlets of poetry: *The Blue Princess*

(1932), *Rust* (1932) and *Jesus* (1933). A posthumous collection, *The Earth is Waiting* (1974).

Brand, Dollar (Abdullah Ibrahim) Born in Cape Town. Travelled in Europe and USA 1960 – 1968. Jazz musician; poetry published in *The Journal of the New South African Literature and Arts* and in Cosmo Pieterse's *Seven South African Poets* (1970).

Branford, William Richard Grenville (1927–) Born in Southampton. Came to South Africa as a boy. Professor of Linguistics at Rhodes University. Playwright, translator, published linguistic manuals and contributed to *A Book of South African Verse* (1959) and the new revised edition (1979).

Brettell, Noel Harry (1908–) Born in England. Arrived in Rhodesia (Zimbabwe) in early 1930s. Retired school-headmaster. President of Pen Zimbabwe. Literary awards include the 1972 Pen Literary Award. Poetry publications: *A Rhodesian Leave* (privately published), *Bronze Frieze* (1950) and *Season and Pretext* (1977).

Brodrick, Albert (1830–1908) Born in Hampshire. Came to South Africa in 1859, settling in Pretoria as a merchant. Gold prospector; contributed poetry to *De Volksstem* and wrote this paper's weekly supplement, *The Tse Tse Fly.* Published two poetry collections, *Fifty Fugitive Fancies in Verse* (1875) and *A Wanderer's Rhymes* (1893).

Brooks, Frederic (Birth and death dates unknown.) Though not an 1820 Settler arrived at the Cape in that year, and returned to England in 1826. Published as periodical literature a satirical description of life in Cape Town at the time, entitled *South African Grins: or The Quizzical Depot of General Humbug* (1825).

Brutus, Dennis Vincent (1924–) Born in Salisbury. Teacher, President of the SA Non Racial Olympic Committee, left South Africa in 1966 after political imprisonment. Has travelled and lectured extensively, now Professor of English at Northwestern University, Illinois. Received a prize in the Mbari Literary Competition in 1962. Poetry publications include *Sirens, Knuckles, Boots* (1963), *Thoughts Abroad* (1970 under the pen-name John Bruin), *Stubborn Hope* (1979).

Butler, Frederick Guy (1918–) Born in Cradock. Since 1952 Professor of English at Rhodes University. He was English editor of *Standpunte* and co-founded *New Coin;* has edited collections of poetry and Settler writing, and written plays and an autobiography. Awarded several poetry prizes including the CNA Literary Award for *Selected Poems* (1975). Other poetry publications include *Stranger to Europe* (1952 and 1960), *South of the Zambesi* (1966) and *Songs and Ballads* (1978).

Campbell, Ignatius Royston Dunnachie (Roy) (1901–1957) Born in Durban. During 1926, together with Laurens Van der Post and William Plomer, edited *Voorslag.* Lived in England, France, Spain and Portugal. In 1951 he received the Foyle Prize for Poetry for a translation from Spanish, and in 1954 an honorary doctorate from Natal University. Novelist, wrote two volumes of autobiography. Poetry publications include *The Flaming Terrapin* (1924), *Adamastor* (1930), *Talking Bronco* (1946) and *Selected Poems* (1981).

Chidyausiku, Paul (1927–) Born in Salisbury. Taught agriculture; joined Mambo Press in Gwelo in 1960. Has published five books in Shona and edits the Shona newspaper *Moto.*

Chipeya, Chirwa. Contemporary Zimbabwean poet who has published poetry in the Johannesburg literary magazine, *Staffrider.*

Cloete, Edward Fairley Stuart Graham (1897–1976) Born in Paris. Farmed in the Transvaal before travelling to London and the USA. Returned to South Africa after World War II and lived from 1947 at Hermanus. Wrote short stories, numerous novels translated into twenty-three languages, two volumes of autobiography and a volume of poetry, *The Young Men and the Old* (1941).

Clouts, Sydney David (1926–) Born in Cape Town. Contributed to the foundation of *Contrast.* Moved to London in 1961, returned to South Africa as Research Fellow at Rhodes University in 1969; has lived since the early 1970s in London, working as a librarian. Contributed widely to South African and British periodicals and anthologies. Poetry collection *One Life* (1966) won the 1967 Ingrid Jonker Prize and the Olive Schreiner Prize in 1968.

Clothier, Norman Moser (1915–) Born in England. Retired company director, National President of the South African Legion for last seven years. Poetry published in anthologies and in one collection: *Libyan Winter: Poems by a Corporal in the First Division* (1943).

Colvin, Ian Duncan, sometimes used pen-name 'Rip van Winkle' (1877–1938) Born in Inverness. He was assistant editor of the *Cape Times* 1903 – 1907, returned to England in about 1909 and wrote for the *Morning Post.* Publications include factual books on South Africa, biographies and collections of satirical poetry including *The Parliament of Beasts* (1905) and *Party Whips* (1912).

Cope, Robert Knox (Jack) (1913–) Born in Natal. Worked as journalist in South Africa and London. Novelist, short-story writer; joint founder in 1960 and editor for nineteen years of *Contrast;* co-editor with Uys Krige of the *Penguin Book of South African Verse* (1968). Literary prizes include the CNA Literary Award and The Argus Prize for his novel *The Rain-Maker* (1971). Poetry publications are *Marie: A South African Satire* (1948), *Lyrics and Diatribes* (1948), and *Recorded in the Sun* (1979). Currently living in England.

Received an honorary doctorate from Rhodes University in 1981.

Craig, Thomas (Birth and death dates unknown) Worked for the then Rhodesian Railways. Poetry publications include *Beira Ballads and ·Rhodesian Rhymes* (1907).

Cripps, Arthur Shearly (1869–1952) Born at Tunbridge Wells. Arrived in South Africa in 1901. Chaplain in the East African Campaign 1915 – 1916, worked as a missionary in Mashonaland till his death. Novelist, short-story writer, won The Oxford University Sacred Poem Prize in 1902 and 1926. Poetry publications include *Titania and Other Poems* (1900), *The Black Christ* (1902), *Jonathan* (1902), *Lyra Evangelista* (1909) and *African Verses* (1939).

Cullinan, Patrick Roland, has also used the pen-name Patrick Roland (1932–) Born in Pretoria. Novelist; in 1974 co-founder with Lionel Abrahams, of Bateleur Press; since 1980 editor of *The Bloody Horse.* His poetry publications are *The Horizon Forty Miles Away* (1973) and *Today is not Different* (1978). He was awarded, with Christopher van Wyk, the 1980 Olive Schreiner Prize.

Currey, Ralph Nixon (1907–) Born in Mafikeng. English teacher, broadcaster, editor and translator. He travelled widely and contributed poems, short stories and critical articles to South African periodicals. Awarded the Viceroy's Poetry Prize in 1945 and, with Anthony Delius, the South African Poetry Prize in 1959. Poetry publications include *Tiresias and Other Poems* (1940), *This Other Planet* (1945) and *The Africa We Knew* (1973). Now living in England.

Dangor, Achmed (1948–) Born in Johannesburg. Materials manager for a cosmetics factory. Novelist, playwright; received the 1979 Mfolo-Plomer Prize for a short-story collection. Banned in 1973 – 1978. Poetry published in South African periodicals like *Wietie* and *Staffrider.*

Davids, Jennifer (1945–) Born in Cape Town. School teacher in England from 1969, she returned to Cape Town in 1972. Since 1966 her poems have appeared in South African periodicals like *Contrast, New Coin* and *New Nation.* Published a collection of poetry, *Searching for Words* (1974).

Dederick, Robert (1919–) Born in England. Settled in South Africa in 1951. Retired solicitor and legal adviser; freelance broadcaster and sports journalist on the *Cape Argus.* Won the 1967 State Poetry Prize, and the 1971 Pringle Award. His poetry collections are *The Quest and Other Poems* (1968) and *Bi-focal* (1974).

Delius, Anthony Roland St. Martin (1916–) Born in Simonstown. Journalist since 1947, Parliamentary correspondent and leader writer on the *Cape Times.* English editor of *Standpunte* till 1956; broadcaster on the BBC, now lives in London. Satirist, playwright, travel-writer; in 1959 he received, with R.N. Currey, the South African Poetry Prize, and in 1976 the CNA Literary Award for his novel *Border* (1976). Poetry publications include *An Unknown Border* (1954), *The Last Division* (1959) and *Black South Easter* (1966).

Dhlomo, Herbert Isaac Ernest, sometimes used the pen-names 'Busy B' amd 'X' (1903–1956). Born in Natal, teacher in Johannesburg, journalist on *The Bantu World,* Librarian-Organiser for the Carnegie Library in Germiston. Returning to Durban in the early 1940s, he was assistant editor to his brother R.R.R. Dhlomo on the Zulu-English newspaper *Ilanga Lase Natal.* Wrote plays, short stories, essays on African Literature and many poems, the only independently published poem being the long *Valley of a Thousand Hills* (1941).

Driver, Charles Jonathan (Jonty) (1939–) Born in Cape Town. President of NUSAS in 1963 and 1964, he left South Africa for England after political detention and is currently school headmaster in Hong Kong. Novelist; poetry published in a number of British and South African periodicals. One independent collection *Occasional Light* (1979).

Dugmore, Henry Hare (1810–1897) Born in Birmingham. Came to South Africa with the 1820 Settlers. Ordained in 1839, became a missionary in the Eastern Cape. Translated the Psalms and numerous New Testament books into Xhosa, wrote reminiscences and published a pamphlet of poetry entitled *Octogenerian Musings: A Legacy for my Children* (1896). A posthumous collection, *Verse* (1920) was edited by E.H. Crouch.

Eglington, Charles Beaumont (1918–1971) Born in Johannesburg. Linguist, broadcaster, biographer, translator, journalist and from 1962 editor for Anglo-American Corporation's journal *Optima.* Poems included in various South African journals and anthologies, a series appearing in Uys Krige's magazine *Vandag,* and posthumously collected in *Under the Horizon* (1977).

Eybers, Elizabeth Françoise (1915–) Born in Klerksdorp. Lived in Amsterdam since 1961. Received numerous literary awards including the Hertzog Prize for *Belydenis in die Skemering* (1936) and the CNA Literary Award for *Einder* (1977); also received an honorary doctorate from the University of the Witwatersrand in 1971. Published a selection of poems with English translations, *The Quiet Adventure* (1948); included in *Afrikaans Poets with English Translations* (1962). Other poetry publications include *Tussengang* (1950) and *Onderdak* (1968).

Fairbridge, Kingsley Ogilvie (1885–1924) Born in Grahamstown. Went to Mashonaland in 1896, then to England where *Veld Verse* (1909) was published. Immigrated to Australia in 1912 and established the Fairbridge Farm School for child immigrants. Autobiography posthumously published in 1927.

Farrell, David (1941–) Born in England. Came to South Africa as a child;

worked on the *Weekend World,* currently sub-editor on the *Rand Daily Mail.* One independent collection: *The Charlie Manson False Bay Talking Rock Blues* (1974).

Fridjohn, Michael (1952–) Born in Johannesburg, where he works as a wine consultant. Poetry included in a number of periodicals including *Contrast,* the University of the Witwatersrand publication *Critique,* and *New Nation;* also in translation in a Portuguese anthology.

Friedland, David (1936–) Born in Johannesburg, where he teaches English and Latin.

Fugard, Sheila Mary (1932–) Born in Birmingham. Arrived in South Africa in 1937. Received the 1972 CNA Literary Award and the 1973 Olive Schreiner Prize for her first novel *The Castaways* (1972). Published two poetry collections: *Threshold* (1975) and *Mythic Things* (1981).

Gibbon, Perceval (1879–1926) Born in Wales. Journalist on the *Natal Witness* towards the end of the Anglo-Boer War, joined the *Rand Daily Mail* on its inception in 1902. Novelist and short-story writer; published one volume of poetry, *African Items* (1903).

Goodwin, Harold (1893–1969) Born in Grahamstown. Travelled in Europe and Africa, working as an accountant in Malawi from 1919 – 1953. Returned to Grahamstown, where he regularly contributed satirical poems to *Grocott's Mail;* a selection of this poetry was published as *Songs from the Settler City* (1963).

Gouldsbury, Henry Cullen (1881–1916). Joined the British South African Company in 1902; became District Officer in Northern Rhodesia (Zambia) in 1908. Wrote novels, historical accounts; several of his volumes of poetry including *Rhodesian Rhymes* (1909) and *From the Outposts* (1914) were collected as *Rhodesian Rhymes* (1932).

Gray, Stephen (1941–) Born in Cape Town. Associate-Professor of English at the Rand Afrikaans University. Novelist; literary researcher and author of *Southern African Literature: An Introduction* (1979); editor of anthologies of South African stories, poetry and drama and past editor of *Izwi;* has collaborated with artist Cecil Skotnes on five publications. Poetry collections are *It's About Time* (1974) and *Hottentot Venus and Other Poems* (1979).

Greig, Robert (1948–) Born in Johannesburg. Feature-writer and reviewer on the *Cape Times,* theatre critic on *The Star* in Johannesburg, currently special writer on the Port Elizabeth *Evening Post.* In 1976 he received a Pringle Award for reviews published during the previous year, and in 1977 the Olive Schreiner Prize for his collection of poetry, *Talking Bull* (1975).

Grover, M. Australian.

Gwala, Mafika Pascal (1946–) Born in Natal. Has worked as a legal clerk, teacher, factory hand and publications researcher. Edited *Black Review* (1973) and published a poetry collection, *Jol 'iinkomo* (1977).

Haresnape, Geoffrey Laurence (1939–) Born in Durban. Critic, broadcaster, short-story writer; editor of collections of short stories and poetry and of *Contrast.* Professor of English at the University of Cape Town. One poetry collection: *Drive of the Tide* (1976).

Hastings, Lewis Macdonald (1882–1966) Born in London. Rhodesian Parliamentarian. Began Tobacco Growers Association in London, BBC commentator on military matters. Poetry publications include *Ballads of Botha's Army* (1915) and *The Painted Snipe* (1937).

Hirsch, Mannie (1938–) Born in Oudtshoorn. Since 1960 has travelled between South Africa and Israel. Advertising Consultant; sometime editor on the *Jerusalem Post.* Poetry published in South African periodicals like *Ophir* and *Quarry.*

Hope, Christopher David Tuliy (1944–) Born in Pretoria. Left South Africa for England in 1974. Playwright, novelist, scriptwriter. Received the 1973 Pringle Award and the 1979 Cholmondeley Prize for Poetry. His poetry collections are: *Whitewashes* (1971) and *Cape Drives* (1974).

Horn, Peter Rudolph Gisela (1934–) Born in Czechoslovakia. Immigrated to South Africa in 1955. Professor of German at the University of Cape Town, has been writing in English since 1964. Received a 1974 Pringle Award for literary articles. Critic; compiled South African poetry anthology in German translation (1980). Founder and co-editor with Walter Saunders of *Ophir.* Poetry publications: *Walking Through our Sleep* (1974) and *Silence in Jail* (1979).

Jensma, Wopko Pieter (1939–) Born in the Transvaal. Returned to South Africa in 1971 from Botswana where he had taught art and worked as a graphic artist for that country's Department of Information. Sculptor, painter; poetry publications are *Sing for our Execution* (1973), *Where White is the Colour, Black is the Number* (1974: banned) and *I must show you my clippings* (1977).

Jiggs, pen-name of Colin Smuts (1944–) Born in Johannesburg. Directs the creative arts programme for the Open School in Doornfontein. Poetry published in *Douche, New Traffic,* and other periodicals.

Johennesse, Fhazel (1956–) Born in Johannesburg. Co-director with Christopher van Wyk of Sable Books. Published one poetry collection, *The Rainmaker* (1979).

Jolobe, James James Ranisi (1902–1976) Born in the Cape Province. School teacher, minister of religion, essayist, novelist, playwright, translator. Helped compose the Xhosa-English-Afrikaans dictionary. Received several literary awards including the 1952 Vilakazi Memorial Prize for Literature, and an honorary doctorate from the University of Fort Hare in 1974. Poetry publications include *Umyeso* (1936) and *Ilitha* (1959) in Xhosa and *Poems of an African* (1946), translations from *Umyeso.*

Juvenalis Secundus, the pen-name of an anonymous early Cape writer.

Kgositsile, Keorapetse (1938–) Born in Johannesburg. Journalist. Since 1962 living in USA. Recently attached to the Columbia University Writing Programme and on the staff of *Black Dialogue Magazine* in New York. Poetry publications are *Spirits Unchained* (1969), *For Melba* (1969) *My Name is Afrika* (1971) and *The Present is a Dangerous Place to Live* (1974).

Kipling, Joseph Rudyard (1865–1936) Born in Bombay. Visited and worked periodically in South Africa between 1896 and 1908. Associate editor of *The Friend* in Bloemfontein during the Anglo-Boer War. Novelist and short-story writer; received several honorary doctorates from British and European universities. Awarded the Nobel Prize for Literature in 1907, and in 1928 the gold medal of the Royal Society of Literature. Poetry publications include *Barrack Room Ballads* (1892), *The Five Nations* (1903) and *Twenty Poems* (1918).

Kirkwood, Robert Michael (1943–) Born in West Indies. Lecturer, editor. Currently co-director of Ravan Press. His poetry publications are *Whitewashes* (1971).

Kolbe, Friedrich Charl (1854–1936) Born in George. Lawyer, became a Roman Catholic priest and edited the *Catholic Magazine.* Theologian, botanist, novelist and short-story writer; he received an honorary doctorate from the University of South Africa in 1919. Poetry publication: *Thoughts and Fancies* (1907).

Krige, Mattheus Uys (1910–) Born near Swellendam. Journalist, war-correspondent, short-story writer, playwright. On the editorial board of *Vandag* and, later, of *Contrast.* Received several prizes from the Akademie vir Wetenskap en Kuns for translated work, and honorary doctorates from three South African universities. Awarded the Hertzog Prize in 1974 for the collection *Uys Krige: 'n Keur uit sy Gedigte.* Other poetry publications include *Oorlogsgedigte* (1942) and *Ballade van die Groot Begeer en ander Gedigte* (1960).

Kunene, Raymond Mazisi (1930–) Born in Durban. Won the Bantu Literary Competition Award in 1956. Left South Africa in 1959. Has been Associate-Professor of African Literature and Language at the University of California in Los Angeles. Poetry collected in *Zulu Poems* (1970); he translated the Zulu oral epic *Emperor Chaka the Great* (1979).

L.R. On the staff of *Umteteleni wa Bantu.* '"Civilised" Labour Policy' appeared in this paper 29 October 1932. Identity unknown.

Langa, Mandlenkosi, now living in Botswana. Co-founder with Mongane Wally Serote of the Medu Art Ensemble (Gaborone). Poetry has appeared in an anthology of black South African poetry, *To Whom it May Concern* (1973).

Lefebvre, Denys, pen-name 'Syned' (1879–) Born in Jersey, came to South Africa as a journalist in 1901, on the staff of *The Star* in Johannesburg for many years. Poetry publications include *War and Other Poems* (1918) and *The Land of Wavering* (1907).

Leipoldt, Christian Frederick Louis (1880–1947) Born in Worcester. Pediatrician in Cape Town; Balkan War correspondent and medical correspondent on the *Cape Argus,* editor of *The South African Medical Journal* and for two years editor of *De Volksstem.* Wrote stories, medical articles, plays, books on wine and cookery; received in 1934 the Hertzog Prize for Poetry and an honorary doctorate from the University of the Witwatersrand. Poetry publications include *Geseënde Skaduwees* (1949) and *The Ballad of Dick King and Other Poems* (1949), his only volume of English poems.

Le Sueur, Rijk Andrew Glanville (1914–) Born in Pretoria. Joined the then Rhodesian Civil Service. Returned to South Africa, worked in commerce before becoming a full-time artist in Durban. Privately published one collection of poems, *Encounter.*

Levinson, Bernard (1926–) Born in Johannesburg. Spent his childhood in Chicago; qualified as a doctor at the University of the Witwatersrand in 1951. Specialised in psychiatry and practises in Johannesburg. Published a poetry collection *From Breakfast to Madness* (1974).

Lewis, Chaim, Born in London. In 1964 arrived in South Africa. Editor, published his memoirs (1965). Past Director of the Cultural Department of the South African Jewish Board of Deputies and editor of *Jewish Affairs;* now living in England. Published a collection of poetry: *Shadow in the Sun* (1972).

Livingstone, Douglas James (1932–) Born in Malaya and arrived in South Africa at the age of ten. Trained as a bacteriologist in Rhodesia (Zimbabwe) and returned to South Africa in 1964; in charge of marine bacteriological research in Durban. In 1965 he received the Guinness Poetry Award, in 1970 the Cholmondeley Prize for Poetry for *Eyes Closed Against the Sun* and in 1975 the Olive Schreiner Prize for a play, *A Rhino for the Boardroom.* Other poetry publications are *The Skull in the Mud* (1960), *Sjambok, and other poems from Africa* (1964), *Rosary of Bone* (1975) and *The Anvil's Undertone* (1978).

Lyster, Lynn, the pen-name of Major Thomas Leander Millar (1856–1925).

Officer in the army; served in the office of the paymaster in Pretoria and Natal; lived in Pietermaritzburg. Contributed to newspapers, published *The Song of Indongeni or Dick King's Ride* (no date), *Voortrekker's Liederen* (no date) and *Ballads of the Veld-land* (1913).

Maclennan, Donald Alasdair Calum (1929–) Born in London. Came to South Africa in 1938. Short-story writer, playwright; Senior Lecturer in English at Rhodes University. Poetry published in various South African periodicals. One volume of poems: *Life Songs* (1977).

Macnab, Roy Martin (1923–) Born in Durban. Journalist, biographer, editor of several poetry anthologies. Since 1968, director of the South African Foundation in London. Poetry publications: *Testament of a South African* (1947), *The Man of Grass and Other Poems* (1960) and *Winged Quagga* (1981).

Macnamara, Michael Raymond Harley (1925–) Born in Bloemfontein. Professor of Philosophy at the University of South Africa. Founder chairman of the Pasquino (anti-censorship) society. Poetry in South African and overseas literary journals and collected in *The Falls Run Back* (1976) and in *Joggo and Jezz* (1981).

Madingoane, Ingoapele. His epic *africa my beginning*/'black trial' (1979) has played a part in reviving a post-Soweto-1976 'tradition' of oral poetry in the black townships.

Mann, Christopher Michael Zithulele (1948–) Born in Port Elizabeth. School master, English lecturer at Rhodes University, now working with Valley Trust in Natal. Poetry in *New Nation, Contrast, New Coin* and one collection, *First Poems* (1977).

Maquarie, Arthur (birth and death dates unknown). Published *The Voice in the Sun* (1909).

Maseko, Bicca. Works in Swaziland. Poems have been published in South African periodicals like *New Classic.*

Mbuli, Mafika. His poetry has appeared in South African periodicals like *Staffrider* and in an anthology of black South African poetry *To Whom it May Concern* (1973).

Miller, Ruth (1919–1969) Born in Uitenhage. School teacher and office worker. Awarded the Ingrid Jonker Prize for Poetry for *Floating Island* (1965). Also published *Selected Poems* (1968).

Moodie, Duncan Campbell Francis (1838–1891) Born in Cape Town. Left South Africa in 1858. Newspaper editor in Australia. Returned to South Africa during 1880s. Historian, biographer. Poetry publication: *Southern Songs* (1887).

Mogoba, Stanley. His poetry has appeared in an anthology of black South African poetry *To Whom it May Concern* (1973).

Morris, Michael Spence Lowdell (1940–) Former member of South African Police Force. Founder and editor of *Poetry South.* Poetry publications include *Dreams of War* (1967), *Requiem* (1971) and *The Only Peace is Death* (1972).

Motjuwadi, Stanley. Editor f *Drum,* his poetry has appeared in an anthology of black South African poetry *To Whom it May Concern* (1973).

Motsisi, Moses Karabo (Casey) (1932–1977) Short-story writer, journalist on *Drum,* known as 'The Kid'. Published poetry in *The Classic;* articles collected in *Casey & Co.* (1978) edited by Mothobi Mutloatse.

Mtshali, Oswald Mbuyiseni (1940–) Born in Vryheid. Awarded the 1974 Olive Schreiner Prize for Poetry for *Sounds of a Cowhide Drum* (1971). On his return from Columbia University in 1980 *Fireflames* was published. Currently vice-principal of a Soweto College.

Mungoshi, Charles (1947–) Born Manyene TTL. On the editorial staff of the Zimbabwe Literature Bureau. His novel *Waiting for the Rain* won the 1976 Rhodesian Pen Award. Poetry published in an anthology *Zimbabwe Poetry in English* (1978).

Murray Johnstone, G., pen-name 'Mome' (1882–?) Born in Southampton. Came to South Africa in 1901 as a captain in the British army, later farmed near Bethal. Poetry publications are *The Off-wheeler: Ballads and Other Verses* (1910), *The Avengers and Other Poems from South Africa* (1918) and *One Smith* (1913).

Mutloatse, Mothobi. (1950–) Born in Johannesburg. Chief sub-editor of *The Voice.* Edited Casey Motsisi's *Casey & Co* (1978) and *Forced Landing* (1980). Poetry published in periodicals like *Staffrider.*

Naudé, Adèle (1910–) Born in Pretoria. Free-lance journalist, radio script-writer and broadcaster, has edited various English and Afrikaans women's journals. Poetry publications are *Pity the Spring* (1953), *No Longer at Ease* (1956), *Only a Setting Forth* (1965) and *Time and Memory* (1974).

Ndebele, Njabulo. Lecturer at the University of Lesotho, his poetry has been published in South African periodicals like *The Purple Renoster* and *Staffrider* as well as in the anthology *To Whom it May Concern* (1973).

Nicol, Mike (1951–) Born in Cape Town. Editor of *African Wildlife.* Poems contributed to *Contrast, Izwi, New Coin, London Magazine,* and published in one volume, *Among the Souvenirs* (1978), which won the Ingrid Jonker Poetry

Prize in 1980.

Nortje, Arthur Kenneth (1942–1970) Born in Oudtshoorn. Studied in Oxford where he returned in 1965 after teaching in Canada. Won a prize in the Mbari Poetry Competition in 1962. Poems included in various anthologies; collected in New Coin's volume, *Lonely Against the Light* (1973), and in *Dead Roots* (1973).

Nthodi, Motshile wa (1948–) Born near Pretoria. Has exhibited graphic art widely in South Africa. Poems included in *Quarry '76*. Published *From the Calabash: Poems and Woodcuts* (1978).

Ould, Charles Woodrooffe (1898–?) Born and educated in Grahamstown. Journalist, he wrote *William Stapleton Royce: A Memoir* (1925). Moved to England. Poetry published in South African anthologies.

Patel, Essop. Trained as an attorney. Edited *The World of Nat Nakasa* (1975). Poetry published in periodicals like *Ophir* and in a collection *They Came at Dawn* (1980).

Pater, Elias, pen-name for Jacob Horace Friedman (1916–) Born in Cape Town. Medical doctor; left South Africa in 1940 to study for the priesthood in England. Since 1954, Carmelite monk at Stella Maris monastery in Israel. Awarded the 1971 Olive Schreiner Prize for Poetry. Poetry publications include *In Praise of Night* (1969) and *Selected Poems of Rachel* (1974 – translated from Hebrew).

Paton, Alan Stewart (1903–) Born in Pietermaritzburg. School teacher, Principal of Diepkloof Reformatory. National President of the South African Liberal Party for its duration. Playwright, novelist, has written religious meditations and articles on contemporary South Africa, received CNA Literary Award (1964; 1973) for two biographies; published first volume of autobiography. Awarded honorary doctorates from many universities and in 1960 the Freedom Award of the USA. Poetry included in a collection of his shorter works, *Knocking on the Door* (1975).

Plomer, William Charles Franklyn (1903–1973) Born in Pietersburg. Collaborated with Roy Campbell and Laurens Van der Post to produce *Voorslag*. Left South Africa in 1926. Eventually settled in England, literary adviser to a London publisher. Novelist; short-story writer, editor; several volumes of autobiography. Received an honorary doctorate, in 1963 the Queen's Gold Medal for Poetry, in 1968 the CBE and, posthumously, in 1973, the Whitbread Literary Award. Poetry publications include *Selected Poems* (1940), *Taste and Remember* (1966), *Celebrations* (1972) and *Collected Poems* (1960; 1973).

Pringle, Thomas (1789–1834) Born in Scotland. Journalist, editor. Arrived in South Africa with 1820 Settlers; with Fairbairn, established *The South African Journal* (1824) and through opposition to governor Somerset achieved freedom of the Press in South Africa. Returned to England in 1826, working as Secretary to the Anti-Slavery Society. His complete poetry can be found in *Thomas Pringle: His Life, Times, and Poems* (1912).

Reitz, Francis William (1844–1934) Born in Swellendam. Journalist with the *Cape Argus;* advocate; from 1874 President of the Orange Free State Appeal Court; became President of the Orange Free State in 1889. Wrote topical and satirical poems in English, Dutch and early Afrikaans. Publications include *Klaas Gezwint en Zyn Paert: and Other Songs and Rijmpies of South Africa* (1884) and *Oorlogs en Ander Gedichten* (1910, 1911).

Runcie, John. (Birth date unknown, died 1939) Born in Scotland. Worked on the staff of the *Cape Times* for many years. Published a poetry collection, *Songs by the Stoep* (1905), and a poetry and prose collection *Idylls by Two Oceans* (1910).

Sampson, Harold Fehrsen (1890–1973) Born and educacted in Grahamstown. Advocate and later Professor of Law at Rhodes University. Published political writing, literary criticism and collections of poetry including *Animals in Amber* (1937) and *Selected Poems* (1972).

Saunders, Walter (1930–) Born in Durban. Editor of *Quarry*. Joint founder and editor, with Peter Horn, of *Ophir,* and of the collection of *Ophir* poems, *It's Getting Late* (1974). Senior Lecturer in English at the University of South Africa. Poems included in *New Coin, New Nation,* a collection entitled *Faces, Masks, Animae* (1975).

Schreiner, Olive Emilie Albertina (1855–1920) Born in the Cape. Governess on Cape farms; in 1881 went to England where her novel *The Story of an African Farm* (1882) was published under the pen-name Ralph Iron. Lived in South Africa from 1889, in England again from 1913, finally returning to South Africa in 1920. Short-story writer; wrote widely on feminism. Occasional poetry.

Scully, William Charles (1855–1943) Born in Dublin. Came to the Cape in 1967. Diamond and gold prospector; joined the Civil Service in 1876 and became a magistrate. Lived in England (1898) and Canada (1914/15) then returned to South Africa. Received an honorary doctorate from Stellenbosch University in 1938. Published novels, short stories, reminiscences and two volumes of poetry, *The Wreck of the Grosvenor and Other South African Poems* (1886) and *Poems* (1892).

Selepe, Magoleng wa. Poems have been published in the South African periodical *Staffrider.*

Selwyn, William (1834(?)–1892) Born in England. Came to Grahamstown as a young boy; taught in Bathurst and later lived in Port Elizabeth where he served on numerous committees and institutional boards. Published *Cape Carols and Miscellaneous Verse* (1891).

Sepamla, Sipho (1932–) Born in Krugersdorp. Trained teacher; was editor of *New Classic* and *S'ketch.* Director of Fuba (Federated Union of Black Artists). Shared with Lionel Abrahams a 1976 Pringle Award. Has written short stories, plays and novels. Poetry publications include *Hurry up to it!* (1975), *The Blues is You in Me* (1976) and *The Soweto I Love* (1977: banned).

Serote, Mongane Wally (1944–) Born in Sophiatown, Johannesburg. In political detention for nine months in 1969. Received the Ingrid Jonker Prize in 1973; now living in Gaborone, attached to the Medu Art Ensemble. Poetry publications are *Yakhal 'inkomo* (1972), *Tsetlo* (1974), *No Baby Must Weep* (1975) and *Behold Mama, Flowers* (1978).

Sinclair, Francis Duncan (1921–1961) Born in Scotland. Visited South Africa with the RAF and returned to settle here. Lectured English at the University of South Africa; poetry publications include *April to March* (1942), *The Island: A Metamorphosis* (1951), and *Lovers and Hermits* (1956).

Slater, Francis Carey (1876–1958) Born in Alice, worked in banks in Eastern Province towns. Editor of the anthology *A Centenary Book of South African Verse* (1925 and 1945). President of the South African Pen Club (1950 – 1958), awarded an honorary degree by the University of South Africa. Published novels, short stories, autobiographies and volumes of poetry including *Drought* (1929) under the pen-name Jan van Avond, *Veld Patriarch and Other Poems* (1949) and *Collected Poems* (1957).

Sowden, Lewis (?–1974) Born in Manchester. Worked for eighteen years as a journalist in South Africa, becoming assistant editor of the *Rand Daily Mail;* settled in Israel in 1966 and worked as staff editor of *Encyclopaedia Judaica* until 1971. Published novels, short stories, plays and poetry including *Poems with Flute* (1955) and *Poems on Themes Drawn from the Bible* (1960).

Soga, Allan Kirkland. Journalist, magistrate and son of the famous Tiyo Soga. Poem published in *Imvo Zabantsundu* 3.2.1898.

Spranger Harrison, J. No details known; wrote poems about the diamond fields.

Strauss, Peter Erik (1941–) Born in Pietermaritzburg. Spent several years in England and Germany. Senior Lecturer in English at the University of Natal; critic and co-editor of the literary journal *Donga;* recipient in 1971 of a Pringle Award. One poetry publication: *Photographs of Bushmen* (1974).

Style, Colin Thomas Elliot (1937–) Born in Salisbury. Broadcaster on SABC, and then RBC and Rhodesian T.V. Co-editor of *Chirimo*, co-producer of the L.P. record *Rhodesian Poets.* Poetry included in anthologies, won the Rhodesian Poetry Prize in 1956; published *Baobab Tree* (1977) for which he was awarded the Ingrid Jonker Prize. Currently living in England.

Swart, Edward Vincent (1911–1961) Born in the Transvaal. Lectured in English at the University of the Witwatersrand; poetry first published in the university's magazine, subsequently included in anthologies like *The Year's Poetry* (1937) and *Poets of Tomorrow* (1940) and in *Collected Poems* (1981).

Swift, Mark (1946–) Born in Queenstown. Librarian, publisher's editor. Currently sub-editor and reviewer on the *Cape Argus.* Has exhibited graphics, published prose, children's verse and written the text for Sigurd Olivier's banned collection of photography, *Gentlewoman* (1976). Received the 1975 Ingrid Jonker Poetry Prize. Poetry publications: *Treading Water* (1974) and *Seconds Out* (1981).

van Wyk, Christopher (1957–) Born in Johannesburg. Co-director with Fhazel Johennesse of Sable Books, edits *Wietie.* Poetry published in *The Voice.* He was joint recipient, with Patrick Cullinan, of the 1980 Olive Schreiner Prize for *It is Time to go Home* (1979).

van Zyl, Tania (1908–) Born in Cape Town. Artist, sculptor. Has lived in Paris and Vienna. Poetry publications include *Window and Other Poems* (1947) and *Rock, Leaf and Grass* (1968).

Walrond, Francis Ernley (1875–?) Born in Edinburgh. Arrived in South Africa in 1904. Bank manager. Retired to Isipingo, Natal in 1935. Poetry publications include *Silence Absolute and Other Poems* (1900), *The Lady Beautiful and Other Poems* (1906) and *The Gods of Africa and Other Poems* (1912).

Webster, Mary Morison (1894–1980). Born in Edinburgh. Arrived in South Africa in 1920. Novelist, artist, book reviewer for the *Rand Daily Mail* and the *Sunday Times;* received a Pringle Award for book reviewing. Poetry publications include *Tomorrow* (1922), *Flowers from Four Gardens* (1951) and *A Litter of Leaves* (1977).

Welsh, Anne (1922–) Born in Johannesburg. Economics lecturer at Witwatersrand University. Currently working in the Registry of Oxford University. Poetry publications: *Uneven World* (1958) and *Set in Brightness* (1968).

Wilhelm, Peter (1943 –) Born in Johannesburg. Novelist, short-story writer, Senior Political Editor on the *Financial Mail.* Joint recipient with Mbulelo Mzamane of the 1977 Mofolo–Plomer Prize for *An Island Full of Grass* (novel). Edited *Poetry South Africa* (1976). Poetry collection *White Flowers* (1977).

Wilmot, John Alexander (1836–1923) Born in Edinburgh. Arrived in South Africa in 1853. Historian, biographer. Postmaster in Port Elizabeth from 1859 until retirement. From 1889 – 1910 member of Cape Legislative Council. Edited *The Poetry of South Africa* (1887). Poetry publications: *In the Droughtlands of South Africa* (1880) and *South African Verses and Others* (1906).

Wilson-Moore, C. & A.P. Brothers who worked on the mines in Kimberley and Barberton. Poems collected in *Diggers' Doggerel* (1890).

Wore, G.W.M. Served with the Worcestershire Regiment in the Anglo-Boer War. Manuscript of single poem found in leather satchel on farm Rockdale in Kestell district by Mr Zan Swartzberg; farm belongs to Mousley family who during the war gave information and provisions to the British. (Johannesburg *Star* 19.1.1980).

Wright, David John Murray (1920–) Born in Johannesburg. Left South Africa in 1934, now living in England. Deaf from childhood. Translator, edited numerous anthologies, co-edited *X* and *Nimbus.* Received several literary awards including 1950 Atlantic Award for Literature. Poetry publications include *Poems* (1949), *Nerve Ends* (1962) and *Selected Poems* (1980).

Zimunya, Musaemura (Bonus). Born in Umtali. Left Rhodesia in 1975 following imprisonment after a demonstration. Currently research fellow University of Zimbabwe. Poems published in *Chirimo, New Coin,* etc., one collection: *Zimbabwe Ruins* (1979).

Acknowledgements

Although every effort has been made to trace the copyright holders this has not always been possible. Should any infringement have occurred the publisher apologises and undertakes to amend the omission in the event of a reprint.

The editor and publisher gratefully acknowledge the following copyright holders:

Lionel Abrahams and Bateleur Press ('Professional Secret'; 'For Charles Eglington', from *Thresholds of Tolerance)* **Peter Abrahams** ('For Laughter', from *A Blackman Speaks of Freedom!)* **Perseus Adams** and Juta ('The Leviathans'; 'The Cafe Bioscope', from *Grass for the Unicorn)* **Shabbir Banoobhai** and Ravan Press ('echoes of my other self'; 'by your own definition'; 'the border'; 'for my father', from *Echoes of my Other Self)* **John Howland Beaumont** (estate) and A.A. Balkema ('Address Unspeakable', from *Poems)* **Ridley Beeton** and Ad. Donker ('The Watchers'; 'A Poem Never Written'; 'The Grackles', from *The Landscape of Requirement)* **Stephen Black** (estate) ('The Soldier's Prayer) **D.E. Borrell** and The Poetry Society of Rhodesia ('Nativity', from *A Patch of Sky)* **Herman Charles Bosman** (estate – Helena Lake) and Human & Rousseau ('Seed'; 'The Poet', from *The Earth is Waiting)* **Dollar Brand (Abdullah Ibrahim)** ('Africa, Music and Show Business', from *The Classic)* **William Branford** ('Colonial Experience: Four Fragments') **N.H. Brettell** and OUP ('Giraffes', from *Bronze Frieze);* Poetry Society of Rhodesia ('African Student', from *Season & Pretext)* **Guy Butler** and Ad. Donker ('Karoo Town, 1939'; 'Myths'; 'Ayliff and the Lepers'; 'Tourist Insight into Things', from *Selected Poems)* **Roy Campbell** (estate) ('The Flaming Terrapin'; 'The Zebras'; 'The Serf'; 'The Zulu Girl'; 'On Some South African Novelists'; 'To a Pet Cobra'; 'The Sisters'; 'Rounding the Cape'; 'Overtime'; 'To the Sun'; 'On the Martyrdom of F. Garcia Lorca'; 'Song of the Horseman'; 'Luis de Camoes'; 'The Volunteer's Reply to the Poet'; 'Dreaming Spires') **Paul Chidyausiku** ('Grandpa', from *African Voices)* **Chirwa P. Chipeya** ('Today', from *Staffrider)* **Stuart Cloete** (estate) ('La Femme de Quarante Ans', from *The Young Men and the Old)* **Norman Clothier** and CNA ('Libyan Winter'; 'Confession'; 'Latrine Thoughts', from *Libyan Winter)* **Sydney Clouts** and Purnell ('Epic'; 'Dawn Hippo'; 'Of Thomas Traherne and the Pebble Outside'; 'Within'; 'After the Poem'; 'Intimate Lightning'; 'The Discovery'; 'The Sleeper'; 'Idiot Child'; 'For the Thunder', from *One Life)* **Jack Cope** and David Philip ('Patient at Stikland Neuroclinic', from *Recorded in the Sun)* **Arthur Shearly Cripps** (estate) and OUP ('Resurgat'; 'The Black Christ's Crusade', from *African Verses)* **Patrick Cullinan** ('Devils', from *The Horizon Forty Miles Away);* David Philip ('The Garden'; 'The Billiard Room', from *Today is not Different)* **R.N. Currey** and Routledge ('Unseen Fire', from *This Other Planet);* David Philip ('Lost World', from *The Africa We Knew)* **Achmed Dangor** ('The Voices that are Dead', from *Wietie)* **Jennifer Davids** and David Philip ('Poem for My Mother'; 'For Albert Luthuli', from *Searching for Words)* **Robert Dederick** and Purnell ('On a Theme of Tennyson's – Mariana Farther South', from *The Quest and Other Poems);* David Philip ('Whilst Walking in a Dry River-Bed', from *Bi-Focal)* **Anthony Delius** and Human & Rousseau (from *The Last Division;* 'Lady Anne Bathing', from *A Corner of the World)* **H.I.E. Dhlomo** (estate) ('Not for Me'); Knox *(Valley of a Thousand Hills)* **C.J. Driver** and David Philip ('A Ballad of Hunters', from *Occasional Light)* **Charles Eglington** (estate) and Purnell ('The Vanquished'; 'A Sword for the Group Captain'; 'Lourenço Marques', from *Under the Horizon)* **Elisabeth Eybers** and Dalro ('Hagar', from *The Quiet Adventure)* **David Farrell** and Bateleur Press ('Vigil'; 'Survivor', from *The Charlie Manson False Bay Talking Rock Blues)* **Michael Fridjohn** ('The First Time has to be with Sun') **David Friedland** ('The Complaint') **Sheila Fugard** ('The Voortrekkers', from *Staffrider)* **Stephen Gray** and David Philip ('Mayfair'; 'Sunflower', from *It's About Time;* 'In Memoriam: C. Louis Leipoldt', from *Hottentot Venus)* **Robert Greig** and Bateleur Press ('The Cloud';'The Abortion', from *Talking Bull)* **Harold Goodwin** (estate) ('Glorious?', from *Songs from the Settler City)* **Mafika Gwala** and Ad. Donker ('Kwela-ride'; 'From the Outside'; 'Getting off the Ride', from *Jol'iinkomo)* **Geoffrey Haresnape** and Maskew Miller ('Sheep', from *Drive of the Tide)* **L.M. Hastings** (estate) ('Snapshot of Menelaus', from *The Painted Snipe)* **Mannie Hirsch** ('Letter to Ben Macala') **Christopher Hope** and London Magazine ('Flight of the White South Africans'; 'Morbidities', from *Cape Drives)* **Peter Horn** and Ravan Press; ('The Poet as a Clever Invention'; 'I'm Getting Famous Sort Of'; 'The Broth'; 'The Weaving Women', from *Walking Through Our Sleep);* Scribe Press ('The Plumstead Elegies', from *Silence in Jail)* **Wopko Jensma** and Ravan Press ('Jo'burg Spiritual'; 'till no one'; 'the head'; 'misto 3', from *Sing for our Execution;* 'spanner in the what? works', from *I must show you my clippings)* **Jiggs** ('Doornfontein', from *Douche)* **Fhazel Johennesse** and Ravan Press ('the african pot'; 'my township sunset', from *The Rainmaker)* **J.J.R. Jolobe** and Lovedale Press ('Thuthula', from *Poems of an African)* **Keorapetse Kgositsile** and Third World Press ('Notes from No Sanctuary', from *The Present is a Dangerous Place to Live)* **Rudyard Kipling** (The National Trust) and Eyre Methuen Ltd. ('Bridge-guard in the Karroo'; 'Recessional', from *The Five Nations)* **Uys Krige** ('The Taking of the Koppie') **Mazisi Kunene** and Holmes & Meier ('The Civilisation of Iron'; 'The Gold-miners', from *Zulu Poems)* **Mandlenkosi Langa** and Ad. Donker ('The Pension Jiveass'), from *To Whom it*

May Concern) **C. Louis Leipoldt** and the Jagger Library ('Recordatio', from *The Ballad of Dick King & Other Poems;* 'Grandmother's Workbox') **Glanville Le Sueur** ('To a Stranger Found Unconscious on Addington Beach'; 'Plato's Poet', from *Encounter)* **Bernard Levinson** and Ravan Press ('Your Small Fist'; 'Schizophrenia', from *From Breakfast to Madness)* **Chaim Lewis** ('Kissinger: the Instant Diplomat', from *Quarry)* **Douglas Livingstone** and OUP ('Sjambok, An Essay'; 'Stormshelter'; 'Lake Morning in Autumn'; 'Johnny Twenty-Three'; 'Gentling a Wildcat'; 'Steel Giraffes', from *Sjambok and other poems from Africa* and *Eyes Closed Against the Sun);* David Philip ('Locus'; 'Giovanni Jacopo Meditates: on Aspects of Art & Love'; 'Giovanni Jacopo Meditates: on his Weighting in the Last Great Scorer's Book'; 'Map Reference', from *A Rosary of Bone);* Ad. Donker ('A Natural History of the Negatio Bacillus'; 'Under Capricorn'; 'Sonatina of Peter Govender, Beached'; 'The Zoo Affair'; 'Dust', from *The Anvil's Undertone)* **Don Maclennan** and Bateleur Press ('Conversation', from *Life Songs)* **Roy Macnab** and St Catherine Press ('The Hippopotamus'; 'Rhodes', from *The Man of Grass)* **Michael Macnamara** and Ravan Press ('Fare for a Needle'; 'Tale of the Cock'; 'Grip of the Grease Gun', from *The Falls Run Back)* **Ingoapele Madingoane** and Ravan Press (from *africa my beginning)* **Chris Mann** ('The Circus Train and Clown'); Bateleur Press ('How Thomas Pringle, A Worthy Settler, was Ceremoniously Reburied'; 'Zastron', from *First Poems)* **Bicca Maseko** ('Mate'; 'King Mzilikazi Revisited', from *The Classic)* **Mafika P. Mbuli** ('Mother', from *Staffrider)* **Ruth Miller** (estate) and Lionel Abrahams ('Across'; 'Submarine'; 'Spider'; 'Aspects of Love'; 'Long Journey'; 'Trees'; 'Birds'; 'Voicebox'; 'The Stranger'; 'Pebble', from *Selected Poems)* **Stanley Mogoba** and Ad. Donker ('Cement', from *To Whom it May Concern)* **Michael Morris** ('Of the Genitals', from *The Only Peace is Death)* **Stanley Motjuwadi** and Ad. Donker ('White Lies', from *To Whom it May Concern)* **Casey Motsisi** and Ad. Donker ('The Efficacy of Prayer', from *To Whom it May Concern)* **Oswald Mtshali** and Renoster Books ('Boy on a Swing'; 'An Abandoned Bundle'; 'The Moulting Country Bird', from *Sounds of a Cowhide Drum)* Shuter & Shooter ('Weep not for a Warrior', from *Fireflames)* **Charles Mungoshi** and Mambo Press ('Important Matters', from *Zimbabwe Poetry in English)* **Mothobi Mutloatse** ('Ngwana wa Azania', from *Staffrider)* **Adèle Naudé** and A.A. Balkema ('Memling's Virgin with Apple', from *No Longer at Ease)* **Njabulo S. Ndebele** and Ad. Donker ('Little Dudu', from *To Whom it May Concern;* 'Portrait of Love', from *The Purple Renoster)* **Mike Nicol** and Ravan Press ('Livingstone'; 'After Cavafy', from *Among the Souvenirs)* **Arthur Nortje** (estate) ('Apology from London'); Heinemann ('Waiting', from *Dead Roots)* **Motshile wa Nthodi** ('South African Dialogue', from *Quarry)* **Essop Patel** and Blac ('They Came at Dawn', from *They Came at Dawn)* **Elias Pater** and Purnell ('The Madman whom Jesus Cured', from *In Praise of Night)* **Alan Paton** and David Philip ('Dancing Boy'; 'To a Small Boy who Died at Diepkloof Reformatory', from *Knocking on the Door)* **William Plomer** (estate) and Jonathan Cape ('Conquistadors'; 'The Big Game Hunter'; 'The Boer War'; 'The Scorpion'; 'The Death of a Zulu'; 'A Transvaal Morning', from *Collected Poems;* 'Not Where We Came In', from *Taste and Remember)* **Harold Fehrsen Sampson** (estate) ('Murder in a Hut'; 'To "Miracle", a Cat', from *Songs from Another Valley)* **John Runcie** (estate) and Cape Times ('The Bells of Allah', from *Idylls by Two Oceans;* 'Three Phases', from *Songs by the Stoep)* **Walter Saunders** ('Pot-Pourri'; 'Later Confessions of Mr Prufrock') **Sipho Sepamla** and Ad. Donker ('To Whom it May Concern'; 'Three-Legged No More'; 'Darkness', from *Hurry up to It!;* 'Zoom the Kwela–Kwela', from *The Blues is You in Me)* **W.C. Scully** (estate) (''Nkongane'; 'The White Commonwealths', from *Poems)* **Magoleng wa Selepe** ('My Name', from *Staffrider)* **Mongane W. Serote** and Ad. Donker ('For Don M. – Banned'; 'A Poem on Black and White'; 'Introit', from *Tsetlo);* Renoster Books ('City Johannesburg'; 'Christmas'; 'Alexandra'; 'What's in this Black "Shit"', from *Yakhal 'Inkomo)* **F.D. Sinclair** (estate) and Rustica Press ('Free State', from *The Cold Veld)* **Francis Carey Slater** (estate) and Blackwoods/CNA ('Lament for a Dead Cow'; 'Captive'; 'Drought', from *Collected Poems)* **Lewis Sowden** (estate) ('Hosea') **Peter Strauss** ('Bishop Bernward's Door', from *The Bloody Horse)* **Colin Style** and Bateleur Press ('Rhodes's Bed', from *Baobab Tree)* **E. Vincent Swart** (estate) and Ad. Donker ('Casey Jones'; 'Walk onto Headland Height', from *Collected Poems)* **Mark Swift** and Ad. Donker ('History Speaks Volumes', from *A World of their Own* **Christopher van Wyk** and Ad. Donker ('About Graffiti'; 'In Detention'; 'The Chosen Ones', from *It is Time To Go Home)* **Tania van Zyl** ('The Ballad of the White Camelia', from *Contrast)* **Mary Morison Webster** (estate) ('Rain After Drought'; 'The Quiet of the Dead'; 'The Ox', from *Flowers from Four Gardens* **Anne Welsh** and Purnell ('That Way', from *Set In Brightness)* **Peter Wilhelm** and Bateleur Press ('With My Father in the Bar at Naboomspruit', from *White Flowers)* **David Wright** and Ad. Donker ('Monologue of a Deaf Man'; 'Notes on a Visit', from *Selected Poems)* **Musa B. Zimunya** and The Poetry Society of Rhodesia ('The Reason'; 'Rooster', from *Zimbabwe Ruins)*

Index of poets

Index of titles